Merthyr Historian

MERTHYR HISTORIAN

— *Volume Eight* —

MERTHYR TYDFIL HISTORICAL SOCIETY
SOUTH WALES
1996

ISBN 0 9504845 9 8
1996
Printed and Bound in the UK by WBC
Book Manufacturers Bridgend
Mid Glamorgan
Typeset by Photosetting, Yeovil (01935) 23684

Introduction

The Merthyr Tydfil Historical Society presents Volume Eight in the *Merthyr Historian* series.

The first essay, written by Dowlais-born Professor Sir Glanmor Williams, gives an account of the author's time at Cyfarthfa Castle School from 1931. Sir Glanmor previously contributed autobiographical essays to *Merthyr Historian*, Volumes Six and Seven. He has supported Merthyr institutions, including the Historical Society, the Standing Conference, the Museum and the Library, over many years, and his lectures invariably draw capacity crowds of old and new friends and admirers.

The Merthyr Tydfil Historical Society congratulates Sir Glanmor and Lady Williams on the well-deserved recognition they have recently received.

The second contribution, by Dr. Joseph Gross, gives an account of the early days of the Cyfarthfa Iron Works, from Charles Wood's Diaries, 1766-67, when the Works were under construction.

Dr. Gross, veteran President of the Historical Society, with many publications to his name, contributed a history of "The Standing Conference of the History of the South Wales Valleys" to Volume Seven, *Merthyr Historian*. On the demise of the Standing Conference in 1994, this history was reproduced in booklet form, with the addition of biographical accounts of Dr. and Mrs. Gross. This booklet was circulated to supporters of the Standing Conference.

The third item is an account of The Winter Art Exhibition, staged at Cyfarthfa Castle in 1909-10, the momentum generated by this Exhibition led to the formation of a permanent Museum and Art Gallery at Cyfarthfa Castle.

Next, a contribution from Canon Roger Lee Brown, formerly based at Tongwynlais, now at Welshpool. Canon Brown is the author of many books on local history and Church history, and devoted profits from his ventures to charities. His present essay, some notes on the history of the parish of Merthyr Tydfil before Disestablishment, is derived from the files of Queen Anne's Bounty and the Ecclesiastical Commission.

The fifth paper discusses the Literary Associations of Merthyr Tydfil and examines the works of local poets, the Eisteddfod, Thomas Stephens, Lady Charlotte Guest, George Thomas Clark, Taliesin Williams, Charles Wilkins and others.

The next study is an account of the Gilchrist Scientific Lectures, delivered locally by scientists of international repute.

Item Seven gives an account of Early Libraries at Dowlais, and was first published in 1907.

The eighth contribution, by D. W. R. Whicker, tells the story of The Assyrian Bas-Relief, discovered at Canford School, former home of Lady Charlotte Guest. This item is reproduced from the Canford School Magazine by the kind permission of Mr. D. Lever, Headmaster, and the author.

Item Nine, written in 1975, "Memories of my Childhood in Dowlais", by Elizabeth M. Doggett, recalls life in Dowlais in the early twentieth century. The Historical Society is grateful to Mr. Douglas Williams, stalwart of the Cynon Valley History Society, for access to this material.

Then comes J. Barry Davies' review of Professor T. V. Davies' monumental work on *The Farms and Farmers of Senghenydd Lordship*. This work was privately printed and only twenty copies were produced. We aim to publicise its existence.

Leo Davies, Merthyr expert on local bridges, has contributed an account of the Dowlais Railway or Incline, including hair-raising stories of rides to school at Twynrodyn.

Many men who subsequently "made their mark" in Merthyr, first "cut their teeth" or "made their mistakes" at Aberdare. One such was the Rector of Merthyr, John Griffith, discussed in Canon R. L. Brown's article. Another, Thomas Williams, J.P. (1823-1903), scaled the heights in Aberdare, then made an indelible mark in Merthyr religious and business circles. Our twelfth essay gives a biographical account of the early life of Thomas Williams. Some account of Thomas Williams' contribution to chapel building was given in an essay "Foundations, 1893-1902", which appeared in *Merthyr Historian*, Volume Seven, 1994.

Merthyr learned societies have been well-served by academics from the University of Wales, Swansea. Names which readily come to mind include Glanmor Williams, Hywel Teifi Edwards, Peter Stead, Huw Williams and T. R. (Dick) Owen. New contributor, Swansea post-graduate student Claire Louise Thomas, has written about the public life and image of Lady Charlotte Guest, and the society in which she lived, 1833-1852. We wish Claire every success in her career as a historian.

A letter was received and is reproduced from Walter W. Rees, Aberdare, re. Nathan Dyfed's father. Huw Williams contributed an essay on Nathan Dyfed to *Merthyr Historian*, Volume Six.

"Merthyr Tydfil During The War Years" is the subject of long-serving Society Secretary Hugh Watkins' contribution. Hugh Watkins wrote an essay "From Chaos to Calm" for *Merthyr Historian*, Volume Seven; this discussed the educational aftermath of the Aberfan Disaster. Hugh was responsible for a history of the first 25 years of Afon Taf High School, which appeared in *Merthyr Historian*, Volume Five. He has many other publications to his credit.

Anecdotes about an old Merthyr theatre are the substance of item sixteen.

Next, an account of the life and work of Mrs. Clark, wife of G. T. Clark, Dowlais Works Trustee, written by Merthyr family historian Mrs. Eira M. Smith.

Item Eighteen records the fascinating life and travels of Abercanaid-born Edward Rhys-Price, in New York and elsewhere in America. The Society is grateful to Mrs. I. Stevens, Miss C. Gibbon and Mrs. M. Hopson for access to this material.

There follows an account of an Ynysfach murder, told by Mrs. Eira M. Smith. This essay derives from a talk given at Ynysfach Engine House to the Friends of Merthyr Tydfil Heritage Trust.

Item Twenty is a well-illustrated history of the Merthyr close harmony group *The Lifeguards*, compiled by teacher David Lewis Jones, husband of Marilyn and father of Helen and Andrew. The Lewis Jones family is well-known in the world of BOWLS and has obtained international recognition in the sport.

The next essay is an account, compiled by Huw Williams, of the life and work of the Merthyr Stipendiary Magistrate and scholar, Sir Thomas Marchant Williams. Huw Williams showed the way to a generation of local history writers when, in the 1980s, he edited and published three books on aspects of the history of Merthyr and one on aspects of Pontypridd history. All four books were based on essays submitted by members of University extra-mural classes conducted by Huw Williams; their publication was a source of satisfaction and encouragement to the numerous students involved.

The final essay, "Ladies of Letters", was submitted by Exmouth resident Ray Jones, who was born and brought up in Aberfan.

The Editor thanks the authors for placing their essays at the disposal of the Historical Society, for publication. Thanks are also due to the Committee for advice and encouragement to the Editor and to members of the Society, the general public and Institutions, who have purchased the Society's publications.

The staff of Merthyr and Dowlais Libraries, including Mr. James, Mrs. Carolyn Jacob, Mr. J. Downey and Mrs. Cynthia Roberts are thanked for their help, willingly given.

Finally, thanks are due to Colin Mawer, Commercial Director, W. B. C. Book Manufacturers Limited, Bridgend, for his invaluable help with Volume Eight and the three previous Volumes.

Copies of *Merthyr Historian*, Volume Eight, may be purchased from
Merthyr Tydfil Central Library,
Ynysfach Engine House, Merthyr,
W. H. Smith, Merthyr,
H.M.S.O. Oriel, Cardiff and
Lockyer's Bookshop, Abergavenny.

The Historical Society at present holds stocks of *Merthyr Historian*, Volumes Seven and Eight. Volumes One to Six are out of print.

Copies of Volumes Five and Six may be held by some of the above stockists.

T. F. HOLLEY, Ph.D.
Chairman and Editor.
52, Chester Close, Heolgerrig,
Merthyr Tydfil. CF 48. 1SW.

CONTENTS

Merthyr Historian

Life in "The Castle"

by GLANMOR WILLIAMS

That intense sense of excitement and anticipation that I experienced during those summer months before starting in Cyfarthfa Castle School – "the Castle", as we all knew it – in September 1931 is as fresh now as it was then. It's well over 60 years ago, but I vividly recall how keyed up I was about proceeding to a new school, about which I'd heard so much from older friends who were already pupils there. I very much wanted to acquire the regalia that would signal me, too, as a member of that distinguished academy of learning: the navy-blue cap, with its distinctive yellow stripes and the "Martyr" Tydfil badge; the blazer with its comparable insignia blazoned on the upper breast-pocket; and the blue-and-yellow tie. Having had them bought for me, I was just a little apprehensive about how soon it was "proper" for me to wear them. To sport this finery too soon was to run the risk of being regarded as an intolerable "show-off". However, the problem was neatly solved for me because I was going to stay with my grandparents, who now lived in Cardiff, for a week or two. There, in the relative anonymity of a big city, I could appear like Solomon in all my glory. Not that anyone paid the slightest attention to me! Then, there was the school satchel. I'd never previously had anything to carry to Pant School except a "copy-book", in which I'd done my homework; but now, I should have textbooks and a variety of exercise books to transport. It's strange how evocative some smells can be – I can never scent new leather without instantly recalling that school-bag and the early days at Cyfarthfa. There was also the little tin case of mathematical instruments and the box of coloured pencils which we'd been instructed to obtain. My father, bless him, had been very bright at mathematics at school, and he patiently initiated me into the mysteries of using the compass, the dividers, the set-squares, and the like. Kindly and helpful as he was, he didn't quite succeed in removing the sense of trepidation I felt about whether or not I should be up to making effective use of these formidable-looking instruments. My misgivings were to prove to be all too well-founded.

Going to the "Castle" was a big step forward for an eleven-year-old. For one thing, it was a long way to walk to school; it must have been three to four miles each way, with no convenient transport other than "shanks's pony". Cyfarthfa, on the outskirts of Merthyr, was really in a very awkwardly-placed spot for boys and girls from Dowlais and the upper end of the borough. It wasn't so bad going to school in the mornings; downhill all the way out, coming back uphill between 4.15 and 5.15 in the afternoon, after a tiring day with lessons, was another story. We did, though, have a lot of fun *en route*; there were quite a crowd of us going down and coming home together, including a very lively contingent from Penywern, with whom we used to link up. One of the strange ironies that comes back to me clearly now is that there were a number of boys who'd been in Pant School with us who had chosen to go to the other secondary school, the "County", i.e., the Merthyr Intermediate School. We remained on excellent terms with them personally, in spite of the intense rivalry that prevailed between the two schools. The annual rugby matches between the schools were tense encounters; not because there was any violence between the teams or the spectators, but on account of the furious, and totally biased, partisanship on both sides. However, I do remember one very distressing occasion when the two sides played. A member of the "County" team, a youth called Jimmy Doherty, who was an especially good player and had already been "capped" for the Welsh Secondary Schools, collapsed and later died. The news cast a desolating sense of sadness over us all, and we slunk away from the ground, glum and dispirited, in almost total and unbelieving silence.

Cyfarthfa Castle, I need hardly mention, is an impressive pile. It was built on the basis of the vast fortunes made by the Crawshay family of ironmasters and was intended to emulate those medieval fortresses built by the landed aristocrats so as to give the *nouveaux riches* industrialists the style and status they so ardently coveted. Its huge size, tall towers and massive walls made it one of the most impressive buildings I'd ever seen – it looked more like a palace than a school to my ingenuous eyes. The high, large rooms and long, rambling corridors made me feel thoroughly insignificant, even after I'd got more familiar with them. But the feature which made the most lasting impression on me was the surrounding park. I still count it a piece of remarkable good fortune that I spent many of my most impressionable years in such an exquisitely attractive setting. All the more so, because its barbered lawns and luxuriant flowerbeds were in such stark contrast to the wild, bare, empty hill and moorland around my home. Both landscapes, startlingly different from one another as they were, held their deep-seated fascination for me. I'm not sure that I realized at the time just how profoundly they were leaving their mark on me, but the emotion has often been remembered in tranquillity since then. Oddly enough, this past summer, I revisited Cyfarthfa for the first time for many years. We drove out of the park as it was getting dusk on a warm, idyllic summer evening. As we went slowly down the slope towards the gate at the Cefn end of the park, the sight of the gentle, grassy incline down in the direction of the lake, absolutely still and flat, brought back a flood of nostalgic memories of the hours that I'd spent around there in days gone by. Especially I recalled the times when we'd been out in the rowing boats on the lake, sitting as still as we could, and watching as the fish swam close, hungrily eager, to snap up the bits of bread – saved for the purpose from school dinners – that we threw to them. On one all-too-memorable occasion, I became too eager and fell overboard in my enthusiasm. Dampened in more senses than one, I was dispatched to the caretaker's house and wrapped in a blanket as my clothes dried out.

Behind the castle were the woods, that changed their garb and their colours with the passing seasons and where, when autumn came round, we, like needy peasants, garnered nuts, especially the sweet chestnuts, which grew in abundance, to stuff ourselves with. There were small pools, too, that often froze solid in winter and so could safely be slid upon. In another part of the park was a charming old bandstand, where I always longed to hear a brass band playing but never achieved my ambition. Birds nested in profusion in the surrounding bushes; and we searched for their nests, often unintentionally scaring the unfortunate inmates away by our over-solicitous curiosity. Mention of curiosity reminds me of that unforgettable morning when, as we walked along the drive to the castle, looking down over the grassy slope, we saw, to our utter astonishment two elephants and a giraffe grazing contentedly. We found it difficult to believe our eyes. Only later did we learn that a circus had arrived in town overnight and had temporarily taken up residence in the park. These delights of the park were secrets best known to those of us who were "dinner boys", boys who couldn't get home and had to stay in school for lunch.

When I first arrived in Cyfarthfa, one of the things that struck me most forcibly was how grown-up the prefects and sixth-formers seemed to be. They appeared to be – indeed were – young men. Of course, they were seventeen or eighteen years of age, but they seemed unbelievably mature to a little boy of eleven. When I saw them turn out at rugby, or cricket, or swimming, their size, strength and physical prowess seemed to be almost more than human. To me, there didn't seem to be any appreciable difference between them and some of the younger members of staff. When I first went to Assembly in the Hall in the morning, I actually thought that two or three of the younger masters, who stood on the outer fringes of the serried ranks of the teaching staff, were senior pupils co-opted to help in keeping order until, a little later, some of those same "pupils" appeared in the classroom to teach us. The masters were a varied and wide-ranging group, going from senior figures in their sixties, like the senior master, Mr. Sam Adams or Mr. Harry Evans ("Sheepy"), down the ranks to the newest recruits, like Mr. Havard Walters or Mr. Dan Jones, both of whom, I'm glad to say, are still alive and well. They all had their nicknames, some of which showed very little imagination, and others of which left me somewhat baffled by their relevance to the individual concerned. Mr. Adams, or "Sammy", was a short man but a figure of great natural dignity who could command order in the mornings by a single clap of the hands and a quelling glance over the bridge of his Roman nose. His favourite phrase was "there will be a weeping and a wailing and a gnashing of teeth", a threat more honoured in the utterance than the fulfilment thereof.

There were, I remember, three Davieses among the masters, which could at times cause a measure of confusion. There was the headmaster, Mr. D. J. Davies, known to us all as "the Boss", Mr. E. L. Davies ("Dai Bump") and Mr. J. E. Davies ("Johnny Stinks"), who lived on a farm and used to appear on wet mornings, of which there were many, resplendent in shiny brown-leather farmer's leggings. Early on in my career I was sent to the staffroom with a message for "Dai Bump". I had enough sense to know that I should ask for Mr. Davies, but when I had knocked the door and was asked, "Which Mr. Davies do you want?" I was stumped. I thought that if we called him "Dai Bump" his Christian name must be "David" and, politely, as I supposed, I asked for "Mr. David Davies". Luckily for me, it was one of the younger and more good-humoured members of the staff who'd asked me the question, and he rather charmingly corrected me, saying, "I think it must be Mr. *E. L.* Davies you want". To my shame, Mr. E. L. Davies's mother and sister were members of the same chapel which my parents attended, so in all conscience I ought to have known what his initials were. E. L. Davies was in many respects an idiosyncratic character and was famous, among other things, for being the owner of a motor-car – a very rare possession in those days. It rejoiced in being a "Bean" by make and, not surprisingly, was known to us irreverent boys as the "Has Been".

Not only were we now being brought into contact with a much larger and more diversified range of teachers but also with a wider spectrum of subjects. I liked most of the new subjects we now encountered, though I still found some difficulty with mathematical topics. What I did tend to note, however, was that it wasn't so much subjects that appealed to me as the individuals who taught them. I still recall that there were one or two masters with whom I was never at cross-purposes myself, but who nevertheless used to make me feel extremely nervous. One of them had a distinctly uncertain temper and, when roused, would go white with anger and tremble with rage. It didn't happen very often, but I was always scared that one day I would do something that might upset him and he would vent his wrath on me. I know that I didn't do very well in the subject he taught, largely because of the uncertainty that he roused in me. I wasn't all that good at Art, either, but I always enjoyed the Art lessons with Mr. Charlie Holder who, in addition to being our Art master, was also Curator of the Cyfarthfa Museum and frequently took us into the Museum for our Art lessons. Being so much more relaxed and informal affairs, I think we always rather revelled in being let loose in the Museum.

At the end of the second year we had to make a choice of subjects, which virtually entailed choosing between Arts and Science for the rest of one's school career. In spite of what I said earlier about not being very good at mathematical studies, I had taken well to Physics and Chemistry and would have liked to pursue them further. But in order to do so I should have been obliged to give up Arts' subjects, which I liked even better, so I opted for Arts. In the sixth form I remember feeling distinctly peeved that I couldn't study more science. What accounted for this hankering after science was that we, as Arts' students, were very sensibly required to pursue for two hours a week what was called "General Science". Oddly enough, it was J. E. Davies who was deputed to guide our uncertain footsteps. In the first two years at school he had taught us Physics and, it must be said, not very well. But when it came to General Science in the sixth form, he seemed to be an entirely different person. He was not only genuinely interested in the subject but he succeeded in infusing the same interest into us. We talked about Rutherford and the splitting of the atom and its possible implications, about the Curies and the discovery of radium and X-rays, and, most fascinating for me, about Darwin and evolution. It left me, thereafter, with a lively, if undisciplined, interest in science and scientific discovery, which still persists.

However, for good or ill, I had opted for Arts' subjects, at which I seemed to perform pretty well. What I appeared to be more than averagely good at was essay-writing and, rather against my will, was encouraged (I won't say dragooned) into entering essay competitions. I hadn't much fancied the idea of entering the competitions, but a number of prizes came my way. I must confess to feeling rather chuffed when, having won the *Western Mail*'s St. David's Day essay competition, I found myself being photographed, by the newspaper's photographer, receiving the prize from the headmaster in morning assembly. Talking of competitions and performances, I was also considered to be a competent reciter and actor in those days. We not only used to have a school eisteddfod every St. David's Day but we also had a lively and active branch of the Urdd at school. Mr. Havard Walters, who taught Welsh, was extremely enthusiastic about the Urdd and, because he was young and good-humoured, we responded readily to his urgings. He was keen that we should avail ourselves of the opportunity of going to the eisteddfodau and the summer camps organised by the Urdd. A memorable occasion was the eisteddfod held at Colwyn Bay, which we attended as a group shepherded by Mr. Walters. We left Merthyr in the small hours and arrived at Colwyn Bay about breakfast time. We were all starving by that time and were taken off to the first available café. About twenty of us, I suppose, were sitting around the table, and a gargantuan enamel teapot was dumped in front of Mr. Walters. He picked it up, his arms trembling under the sheer strain, and aimed in the direction of the nearest teacup. So heavy was the pot, and so full, that a stream of tea poured out in a long, graceful arc and landed in one of the cups furthest away from him. So the process continued, the most distant cups being filled first, in descending order until he could manage the nearest ones. The Urdd camps, too, were very popular. We'd gone to the one at Llangrannog, and one of our number who enjoyed a whiff on the sly had gone into an empty hut for a quick drag. A suspicious *swyddog* ("officer") came nosing around the hut. The errant one promptly ducked down under the bed out of sight; but when the *swyddog* threw open the door and called out, "Pwy sy mewn 'ma?" (Who's in here?), the sinner was unthinking enough to reply, "Neb" (No one)!

I probably enjoyed my two years in the sixth form best of all. Not that I found it at all easy to choose what subjects I should study. The die was already cast in favour of its being an Arts' course. The difficulty was which of the Arts' subjects should I choose? The result of the Senior Certificate level examinations gave me some useful guidance. I had done pretty well in all the subjects I'd sat, but had scored the highest marks in English, History, Welsh and Geography, so it seemed that I ought to think seriously about "perming" three out of these four. The most difficult choice lay between Welsh and Geography, because in practice it was impossible to study both simultaneously. I liked Geography very much and had found the master who taught it particularly stimulating. At this stage in my life, however, I was seriously considering entering the Christian ministry, and I thought that perhaps Welsh would be a more appropriate subject for me. In the end, I settled for English, Welsh and History.

One of the appealing things about the sixth form was that you'd reduced your range of subjects to three, which you liked and at which you were reasonably good. Another advantage was that the classes were quite small, and were more like tutorial or discussion groups than the large classes of 30 to 35 to which one had been accustomed. Another attractive feature was that you were now allowed a number of "free periods" in the course of the week which could be used for private reading. It was at this time that I came to realize what a relatively good library the school had, and to make good use of it. That, in turn, stimulated me to make much more intensive use of the municipal libraries in Merthyr and in Dowlais. It was about the same time that Penguin books began to appear on the market, and I recall with enormous pleasure the thrill of being able to acquire great works like Élie Halèvy's *History* for sixpence a volume. I became, and have remained, a confirmed Penguin buyer, though they come at rather more than sixpence a time these days. I shouldn't want to try to give the impression that we were always model students, at all times making the best possible academic use of our free periods. We were often given to discussing and arguing fiercely about politics, religion, or social problems, as well as many less weighty issues. This, after all, was the mid-1930s, the years when unemployment, depression, Abyssinia, Spain, and Manchuria, and demonic individuals like Hither and Mussolini loomed large in all our imaginations. Nor were all our conversations confined to the bounds of the school; we often took the opportunity on warm spring and summer afternoons to continue them – and our lazing – out in the park.

It was the headmaster who taught us European History in the sixth. If the truth be told, he wasn't an especially good teacher, but he had a tremendous delight in the subject, which he successfully conveyed to us. Theoretically, we were studying the period from 1763 to 1914, but "the Boss" had such an absorption, almost amounting to an obsession, in the French Revolution and Napoleon, that we never got much further than 1815. Even so, it was he who introduced me to great historians like H. A. L. Fisher and Albert Mathiez, and also opened my eyes to what superb literary writers like Thomas Carlyle and Charles Dickens had to contribute to our understanding of history. He was also very good at encouraging us to go to the Merthyr Settlement to listen to talks by eminent figures like R. H. S. Crossman, who came there. I owe him a great debt in that respect as, indeed, I do to Mr. Gwilym Williams, who taught us British History. He was always known to the boys as "Nero", though I've never known quite why, because a less dictatorial or imperialistic type it would be difficult to imagine. Mr. Sam Adams was responsible for English. Though he was a rather dry, serious man, without much obvious sense of humour, he was an excellent teacher of the old school. It was he who initiated us into the world of literary criticism, and for the first time in my life I really began to grasp what the poet's art was all about. It was he, too, who opened up to me what a towering genius Shakespeare was and something of the nature of the perennial human problems which he had so searchingly unveiled. I hardly needed any encouraging from him to plunge into the works of the great literary critics he brought to our notice. What I derived enormous stimulation from was the contribution being made to our discussion by a tiny, élite group of third-year sixth-formers, who were back in school preparing to sit university scholarships.

One of the privileges of being in the sixth form was that you were allowed to venture upstairs to the sacred precincts of the girls' school to study certain subjects. Welsh was one of those more favoured ones. The boys' school on the ground floor, and the girls' school on the floor above, were kept strictly apart and never the twain were allowed to meet, except for some interchanges of subject at sixth-form level. I mentioned earlier on how evocative some smells can be, and the smell of beeswax polish immediately brings back that pungent scent that greeted you as you opened the door that led up to the girls' school. The floors there were highly polished, and the girls were obliged to wear gym. shoes and strictly forbidden to wear outdoor shoes while in school. The Welsh mistress, Miss Hettie Morris, was in sharp contrast to the Welsh master I had hitherto known. Whereas he was young, humorous, and unusually affable, she was middle-aged, stern, and severe. But she was a remarkably thorough and effective teacher, who gave her pupils a penetrating appreciation of the merits of modern and ancient Welsh literature, even if she was a bit too serious-minded for our admittedly frivolous temperaments. I do remember her melting on at least one noteworthy occasion. It was the last lesson in the afternoon, and although it had turned 4.15, when we were supposed to be released, and I could hear the rest of the boys' school making their way home, Miss Morris was insistent on completing the discussion of the subject on which she was engaged, *viz.*, the literary merits of the greatest Welsh hymn writers. Perhaps because she could see that my gaze and my attention were wandering, she asked me if I had a favourite hymn. I replied, in what I've since realized was a world-weary tone, "Yes I have, Miss Morris. It's

"Mae 'nghyfeillion adre'n myned
O fy mlaen o un i un."

(My friends are homeward bound;
going before me, one by one.")

I'm surprised I took the risk of giving such a flippant reply; but in fairness to Miss Morris, she saw the funny side of it and burst into laughter.

Another extraordinary episode which befell us as a Welsh class occurred one day when we were late arriving for a lesson. There were only three of us in the group, and one of us was inclined to be something of a harum-scarum. He was late on this occasion – as indeed he very frequently was – and we were waiting for him to join us before going into the classroom. As he dashed helter-skelter round the corner, Miss A. C. Davenport, the headmistress of the girls' school, was arriving on the scene. I should explain that Miss Davenport was a tall, handsome lady, with an impeccable carriage, beautiful white hair, and singularly piercing blue eyes. She was a stickler for dignity and discipline, and was very strict about those boys who were allowed to encroach upon her hallowed domain behaving with due decorum – and perhaps a bit more. On this ill-fated occasion, however, neither she nor our colleague could see each other as they approached the corner of destiny. Crash! The late-comer went full tilt into her and both ended up on the floor, undignifiedly sitting on their posteriors and gazing helplessly at one another. I doubt whether Miss Davenport had ever before suffered such *lèse-majesté*; but she was too taken aback to say anything. We hastily stepped forward to help her to her feet, apologizing profusely for the mishap. I think she just couldn't recover her poise sufficiently to do more than say, in breathless tones, "See that never happens again." As if we would!

I left Cyfarthfa a year sooner than I'd expected to do. After two years in the sixth form I sat the Higher Certificate examination when I was only seventeen and one month. I'd always cherished the hope that I might be able to go on to university, all being well; but I'd always known that I should have to win a scholarship to be sure of doing so. I'd seen many bright boys having to leave school after passing Senior Certificate because their parents weren't able to face the costs of maintaining them in higher education. I'd imagined that I stood a reasonable chance of passing the Higher Certificate first time, but that if I wanted to win a scholarship I should have to go back to school to improve on my record. So I'd made no inquiries about going to university that year. The results of the examination, when they were announced, surpassed my wildest expectations, however. I'd been awarded a distinction in History and in Welsh, and a near-distinction in English. Shortly afterwards, I was also told that I'd been awarded a State Studentship, the Sir Owen Edwards Scholarship. I was walking around in a mixture of ecstasy and bewilderment, but I still thought I should stick to my original intention of returning to school for another year. I thought then – for that matter I think now – that I really was too young to go to university and wasn't sufficiently prepared, intellectually or emotionally, for the transition.

I hadn't, however, counted on the attitude of "the Boss". When I went to see him, he was naturally very pleased and warmly congratulated me on doing so well. Then he said, "Now I think you must change course for the future. I want you to go to the London School of Economics like Aubrey Jones did." (Aubrey Jones was an outstandingly gifted pupil, who later became an M.P. and a member of the government as Minister of Supply.) "When you come back to school, I want you to drop English and Welsh, and take Economics and German instead." I was quite flabbergasted by this suggestion; I'd never studied Economics or German, and I didn't think I wanted to either, particularly as I should have had to pursue them very largely on my own. I had no idea at that stage whether or not I should be any good at them. I demurred and said that I'd hoped to come back to school and extend my reading; that I didn't think I was ready to go to university. I don't think that "the Boss" had expected me to go counter to his wishes, and I'd obviously flicked him on an exposed nerve. From then on, the interview deteriorated in tone, and it ended up with him saying, a bit brusquely, "I don't want you coming back and repeating the subjects you've already done; you'll be far too likely simply to waste your time." I felt disappointed and a bit aggrieved and said, somewhat sulkily, I thought I'd rather go to university and undertake something I wanted to study than come back to school to do something I had no interest in. I think we ought both to have exercised rather more patience and restraint.

Anyway, the upshot was that I took myself to the University College of Wales, Aberystwyth. I've more than once asked myself whether or not that was the right thing to have done. Certainly, I was very happy in Aberystwyth, and it worked out uncommonly well in the end. In any event, it's impossible to tell what would have happened if I'd taken the other path at that cross-roads. Life isn't an experiment you can re-run in different circumstances. Dwelling on the might-have-beens serves no useful purpose; I shall never know how things would have turned out. I should just be grateful that my life proved to be as happy and fulfilling as it did.

The Early Days of the Cyfarthfa Iron Works From Charles Wood's Diaries 1766-67

by JOSEPH GROSS

Introduction

Records of iron making in the Merthyr Tydfil area go back to the late 16th century, when Anthony Morley, a member of a wealthy Sussex family, owned a furnace in Pontygwaith. He died in 1586. He was succeeded in the occupation of the works by Thomas Menyfee, a man from Kent. We next learn that the works in Pontygwaith were owned by Thomas Erbury, early in the 17th century. Thomas Erbury was probably a Quaker, the father of William Erbury, one time Vicar at St. Mary's, Cardiff. Thomas Erbury also owned a furnace in Pontyrhun (Troedyrhiw), near the present Furnace Row. Remains of another old blast furnace are to be found near Blaencanaid Farm.[1]

The method of producing iron remained essentially the same until the middle of the 18th century. The first stage in producing iron is to convert ore into cast iron. This was done in a blast furnace, a stone structure where the iron ore was mixed with lime stone and charcoal and melted into a liquid state. A blast of air had to be supplied to the interior of the furnace, originally produced by bellows driven by a water wheel, later by metal cylinders. The iron when molten was then tapped from the blast furnace into a mould in a casting floor of sand and formed into blocks or "pigs" of cast iron, thus cast iron is also known as pig iron. Cast iron can be made into vessels, parts of machinery and other products. It is brittle, as it contains 2-4% of carbon and breaks if hit by a hammer or dropped. Where a tougher metal is needed, the carbon content must be reduced. The cast iron has to be refined. For this purpose, it has to be reheated in a chafery fire and finally forged under a forge hammer. The resultant metal is called bar iron and has a carbon content of some 1%. The forge hammers are huge, driven by water wheels.[2] The bars then had to be sent to a slitting mill, to be cut into rods to make nails, wire, bolts, etc., or were sent to blacksmiths, who could make horseshoes, gates, fencing, etc. Some bar iron was used to make steel, which stands between bar iron and pig iron in carbon content.

A great deal of fuel was required in the smelting and fining of iron, which up to the middle of the 18th century was almost exclusively charcoal. Sixteen hundredweight of charcoal were needed to produce a ton of pig iron. To produce one ton of bar iron one needed one-and-a-half ton of pig iron and 24 cwt of charcoal.[3] This high consumption of charcoal, which was increasingly more difficult to obtain, led ironmasters to experiment with other fuels, particularly coal. Raw coal, however, is not suitable to produce pig iron, as the sulphur fumes released in burning coal contaminate the iron and make it brittle. The Darbys of Coalbrookdale eventually succeeded in about 1718, by using coke instead of charcoal as fuel. No other ironmasters used coke until the 1750s. The reason was probably that charcoal smelting retained a cost advantage until then. The reason why the Darbys could operate profitably was probably that they could use coke to produce thin walled castings, which was not possible with charcoal smelting.[4] Thus they could produce iron pots and other vessels which were lighter than those of their competitors. It was not until the 1750s that the other ironmasters adopted coke smelting. By then the cost of charcoal had risen dramatically, mainly due to a much higher output of cast iron and greater demand for charcoal, which could not easily be met, and thus the price of charcoal increased.[5] It was now that new iron works were started in Merthyr. The first works were the Dowlais Iron Works, built after Alice, Lady Windsor, granted a lease in 1759 to a partnership of merchants and capitalists from Bristol and Cardiff. The next were the Plymouth Works, erected under a lease granted by the Earl of Plymouth in 1765.

The second major improvement in iron making technology in the 18th century was the application of coal to the refining process, i.e., the production of wrought iron. We have seen how great were the quantities of charcoal needed for the production of wrought or bar iron. There were many unsuccessful attempts made in the 17th and early 18th centuries for fining pig iron to wrought iron by using coal. The problem with the use of coal as fuel in heating iron is that the coal releases sulphur, which is taken up by the iron when hot and causes it to become brittle (red-short), so that it disintegrates under the hammer.

The first real breakthrough came when the brothers John and Charles Wood obtained two patents in 1761 and 1763 to produce wrought iron with coal as fuel.[5] They broke sheets of pig iron into small pieces (stamping) and placed them into covered clay crucibles (pots). Between a dozen and twenty pots were put into a coal fired reverberatory furnace and heated. Thus the metal was protected from the sulphuric fumes. The pots eventually broke in the heat and the molten metal was removed to be reheated in a chafery (also coal fired) and consolidated under a forge hammer. The Stamping and Potting process, as this method became known, was the only commercially successful technique for utilizing coal in the production of bar iron before Cort introduced his puddling process in the 1780s. Nearly half the output of bar iron in this country was carried out by this method, which was consistently 50% cheaper than charcoal production.

The Beginnings of the Cyfarthfa Works

Anthony Bacon was the third ironmaster to establish an iron works in Merthyr. He obtained a lease from Lord Talbot and Mr. Richards on 29.8.1765, predated later by five months.[6] Bacon was a rich London merchant, a supplier to the Admiralty and other government departments. He had possessions overseas and important shipping interests, among others in Whitehaven in Cumbria. His partner was Dr. Brownrigg of Whitehaven. Dr. Brownrigg's sister Jemima was married to Charles Wood.[7] Anthony Bacon engaged Charles Wood as his agent to supervise the construction of the Cyfarthfa Works. From the beginning the works were designed as an integrated works, to produce both cast iron in a blast furnace and bar iron, using the Stamping and Potting process. The Cyfarthfa Works therefore differed from the two works already established in the Merthyr area, the Dowlais and Plymouth works, which at that time only produced pig iron.

Charles Wood's Diaries, 1766-67

The activities in establishing the Cyfarthfa Works in that early period have been recorded by Charles Wood in remarkable and very important diaries. They were called by Wood: "An Account of the material transactions at Cyfarthfa in the Parish of Merthyr Tydfil". They commence on 11.4.1766. A fascinating description of a journey to Bristol and London from 1-14 July is included. The diaries continue to record activities in Cyfarthfa until 28.9.1766, when Wood went to his own works in Lowmill in Cumbria. He remained there during the winter until 11.4.1767, when he returned to Cyfarthfa. Entries there continue until 10th May, 1767.A further section of the diaries follows here, with entries from Low Mill and other places in Cumbria, covering an earlier period, namely 7th August, 1752 to 18th September, 1754. These entries are of great importance, as they describe the experiments with the Stamping and Potting Process, which eventually led to the two patents of 1761 and 1763. The diaries are written in a beautiful copper plate hand, as legible now as when they were written. The original document is not available in this country. It belongs to a Wing Commander Wood, who some years ago lived in Australia. He very generously allowed a microfilm to be taken from the manuscript and several copies of this film are in existence.

The first entry each day deals with the weather. This is usually recorded at 5.30 or 6 o'clock in the morning, and often again several times a day, perhaps at 12 noon and 6 o'clock at night. The weather was of extreme importance for the construction of the works, which had to be carried out in the open. None of the buildings had been completed in the early months and in bad weather the workers got wet and went home or did not turn up for work. Furthermore the site of the works was near the river. In heavy rain the river was often in spate and overflowed its banks, and damaged or carried away some of the buildings and watercourses being constructed.

The next group of entries deal with a detailed description of the work carried out each day and the workmen engaged on the different tasks. All the skilled craftsmen are mentioned by name. Sometimes seven or eight are named on a given job. The unskilled labourers are not individually named, only their total number is given. The largest number employed are the masons, supported by several labourers. Next in number were the carpenters, supported by sawyers. Other craftsmen were a tyler, brickmakers, iron ore and coal miners. There were a number of draft animals, horses and oxen and the work they performed each day is recorded. Thus there was a complete record of the progress of the various stages of the construction of the works. Whilst the descriptions are very clear, our understanding is hampered by the absence of a plan. Such a plan existed, as it is referred to in the Diaries, but it is not now available. These records show in a most remarkable detail the early stages of the construction of an important industrial complex at the very beginning of the Industrial Revolution. And they also allow us an insight into the social and economic life at that time in Merthyr Tydfil and the surrounding area.

The Management of the Works

We do not know how and why Anthony Bacon engaged Charles Wood and how far Wood was involved in the early planning of the site. Work at Cyfarthfa had started about a year before the Diaries start and was probably supervised by his brother Sam. A number of craftsmen from Cumberland also worked in Cyfarthfa at that time. They seem to have formed the management team of the site, although they worked as craftsmen, except Wood's brother Sam, who kept the accounts. They were George Ford, Joseph Lucas, George Lyndon and William Postlethwaite. They originally stayed at the village, as they called Merthyr, but on 14th May, 1766, they moved to the farm Llwyn Celyn, which the firm had rented. A name that appears frequently in the Diaries is that of Isaac Wilkinson, who owned iron works in Bersham, near Wrexham. He was also a partner in the Plymouth Furnace. He frequently visited the Cyfarthfa Works and gave advice on many aspects of the works, particularly those connected with the Blast Furnace. We do not know what his official position was and whether he received any remuneration for his advice.

The Location of the Site

The works were situated in the valley of the river Taff, a short distance south of the confluence of the Taf Fawr and the Taf Fechan. The western boundary of the site was the river Taff up to the bend near the Pandy Bridge. The eastern boundary was the bank on which stood the Cyfarthfa Rock. The old furnaces were built against this bank and are there to this day. The valley floor consists of river deposits and below them hard rock. Many of the foundations of the building and watercourses were sunk in this rock. The water which provided most of the power for the plant and machinery was supplied by the river Taff and its two main tributaries or branches, the Taf Fawr and the Taf Fechan. They both rise in the Brecon Beacons, an area of heavy rainfall. Tributary streams on both banks of the two Taff rivers supplemented the water supply. The reason why the ironmasters came to Merthyr in the latter half of the 18th century was the abundance of the water supply but, of course, even more the rich mineral deposits which were readily accessible, namely iron ore, coal, limestone, clay and building stone.

The Construction of the Works

In reading the Diaries it becomes clear that Charles Wood was not only the manager (agent), but also acted as architect and surveyor. He was the expert in the Stamping and Potting process, the new method of making bar iron, as he had invented this process with his brother John. He knew all its stages and the buildings, machinery and methods required. He was also familiar with the construction and the management of blast furnaces. Whilst he frequently consulted Isaac Wilkinson about them, the final decision was his. He understood the construction of water courses and was able to survey them, i.e., to determine their gradients and the height of the water supply above the water wheels.

Charles Wood had to use considerable ingenuity and skill to manage the construction of an iron works, which was a highly sophisticated industrial enterprise, situated in a rural area, where no other industries existed apart from the two already established furnaces at Dowlais and Plymouth. He could, as we have seen, introduce a few key personnel, but had otherwise to employ local labour, unskilled in the new processes which he introduced. Similarly, the materials used had to be obtained locally if at all possible. It was difficult and costly to bring parts and materials from Cardiff in view of the bad conditions of the roads. To obtain goods from further afield, say Bristol or Liverpool, involved a sea journey as well, with additional expense.

It is proposed in the following to deal first with the different types of material used and the persons employed in working with them, and then to proceed to describe the watercourses, buildings and plant constructed.

The Work of the Stone Masons

The most important building material used both in the erection of the buildings and the construction of the watercourses was stone. The stones used were dressed stones, laid down in strong mortar. The stones were available in the vicinity of the works and we hear of two quarries, the High Quarry and the Low Quarry. Occasionally stones were brought from Llwyn Celyn or the Wern. As mentioned, the greatest number of craftsmen employed were the stone masons and theirs was a skill in which the Welsh excelled. The masons had to build the walls and other structures and usually dress the stones they used. Wood uses the word scabbling for the dressing of stones. The breaking of the stones in the quarry was usually done by the labourers, but sometimes it was included in the task of the masons. The work to provide the stones and bring them to the building site was considerable. Here are two examples: 7th August: Labourers: three in the quarry raising stones for weir; two loading them to the masons in hand barrows; one serving them; two making up Mortar. On 11th August: two raising stones in Quarry, six carrying stones out for the carts, two carrying stones to the masons, one at Cardiff and one at Common mortar, four at the mouth of the great race tamping clay, two serving at the stacks, Joseph Lucas and James Mason and one leading stones.

Charles Wood emphasises two aspects of this construction work. One concerns the mortar used. Two kinds are mentioned: the ordinary mortar, which used the local limestone, and the Cardiff Lime. This made a much harder mortar than the local material and was used for all the more important constructions. It seems to have been an early type of cement. On 23rd May one of the workers is quoted as saying that he had some time ago worked on the repair of a race in Cardiff, where this lime had been used some considerable time previously. It was used in mortar to set stones in the race bed. It was found that after a number of years the stones had been eroded by the action of the water, but the mortar stood proud, having been less eroded. Perhaps this Cardiff Lime comes from the Lias beds found in Penarth as well as Aberthaw and used in the manufacture of cement today.

The other aspect of interest was the method of dressing stones. The process in the Diaries is called Scabbling. Wood finds it to be very slow and expensive, far more expensive than the method used in Cumbria, where evidently this type of dressing was not used, or used to a lesser degree. Charles Wood complains, on several occasions, that he tried to persuade the Welsh masons to give up this method, but in vain. One mason told him that he was not prepared to produce shoddy work, as he would only be blamed for it later (10th June).

The two principal methods of remuneration were Day Work, where the workers were paid by the hour or the day, and piece work, where the remuneration depended on the work performed. In this case the payment was fixed by an agreement, the "Bargain". These bargains were sometimes stated in writing and gave the amount to be paid for certain quantities of work carried out. The conditions of these agreements varied. Sometimes the worker had to provide the material himself and take it to the place of work. Sometimes the management would arrange this. Usually the craftsmen provided their own tools, but sometimes more difficult tools would be provided by the management. Where hard rocks had to be worked, the sharpening of the tools could be arranged for the workers. Gunpowder for blasting was always provided by the management. The works site in the early days was exposed to the weather, as no buildings had yet been completed. Charles Wood realized how much work was being lost in bad weather and early on provided simple shelters, called shades. They were often provided where scabbling had to be carried out. The "bargain" was usually entered into with one or two craftsmen, who in turn employed labourers. The wages were paid to the Principals, who had to pay their helpers. This payment often took place in public houses and Wood mentions on one or two occasions that such pay days ended in heavy drinking, possibly brawls and often in the consequent absence from work of the parties involved. It will be readily seen that the masons in the early days formed the largest number of employees. Once or twice, Charles Wood mentions that they were short of masons and once even had to send to Montgomeryshire to recruit further craftsmen.

William Edwards

One of the most prominent masons working on the site was William Edwards, the well-known bridge builder. He built the famous bridge in Pontypridd in 1756. He lived in Groes Wen, Caerphilly, where he was the minister of the Methodist Chapel for 45 years. He worked in Cyfarthfa as a Master Mason when the Diaries of Charles Wood started, and left on 28th June, 1766. He was very knowledgeable in the matter of the Cardiff Lime. His son David worked with him. The most important job he performed in Cyfarthfa was the survey of a race or feeder, which was to bring water to the blast furnace to be erected at the so-called Cyfarthfa Rock. It is clear that he was well able to carry out this skilled survey. Edwards was also asked to quote a price for the erection of the Blast Furnace. His involvement with these two features will be discussed later. Charles Wood records the following assessment of William Edwards. "Edwards knows most of the masons in the neighbourhood and the County and can produce when we cannot and will be able to manage them much better than we can and will I find by experience as well as from information execute the work in a workmanlike substantial manner as he stands partly on his Credit from all the work he undertakes." (Entry of 5th June, 1766.) The last entry concerning William Edwards is on Saturday, 28th June, 1766. "Paid William Edwards five and three-quarter days and his son David one day and took leave upon his going into Carmarthenshire to undertake the building of two bridges." One of these bridges was probably the one in Dolauhirion near Llandovery over the river Tywi.

The Use of Timber

Next to the stone masons, the most important group of craftsmen were the carpenters. Two of them, George Ford and William Postlethwaite, had come from Cumbria and were members of the management team. Postlethwaite was also able to make patterns for the moulds from which cast iron sections and other items had to be cast. It becomes clear in reading the Diaries that the vast majority of the parts of plant and machinery made of wood had to be completely prepared on site. There were no building suppliers to whom one could turn. Thus the first stage in preparing such plant was to obtain the timber in the form of trunks from the surrounding woods. The right to fell and transport trees was an important part of the original lease. It is interesting to note in passing that the lease also gave Bacon & Co. the right to cut cordwood. This was usually used to produce charcoal, but it is clear that in Cyfarthfa there was no intention to use it in this way. Charles Wood wanted to use it for the production of wooden rails for tramroads. The requirements for timber were obtained from large trees which were usually selected and felled by workers and then their price was paid to the owners of the estate. The size of the tree trunks brought to the works is astonishing. Here are two examples: on 4th July, 1766, a tram with six horses and four oxen brought one piece of timber 67 and a half feet. On 10th July a tram with six horses and three yokes of oxen brought four pieces of timber 113 feet. A tram was a wooden sledge. These pieces of timber had to be brought from the woods over rough ground; there were no roads. The tree trunks had to be sawn into sections by sawyers, several teams of which are mentioned. They worked in specially constructed saw pits. Most of the plant used in the watercourses which were not made of masonry, were constructed of wood, such as sluices, penstocks, the frame of a weir. So were the water wheels with their frames and beams. A number of dwellings for the workers were also erected in the works and made of timber. It has already been mentioned that one of the carpenters was a skilled pattern maker, who prepared the moulds for the iron castings for parts needed in the furnaces, such as lintels, fire doors, base plates, iron bars for fire-places, etc. There were also heavy hammers and other parts.

The Site at Pen y Wayn Newydd

We must now deal with some of the other materials used in the works. One site some distance from the works where a number of raw materials were obtained, was a site called Pen y Waun Newydd. This location is shown on the Ordinance Survey map of 1814, where it indicates Coal and Mine Works. Its position is on the Aberdare Mountain, to the West of Heolgerrig. This site was extremely important, as the essential raw materials, iron ore, coal and clay, were found and worked there from an early date of the works. A Brick Kiln was also erected there. (The site has now been destroyed by open cast workings.) A few quotations from the Diary are of interest. On 16th May, Evan William, Sawyer, is making Carrs on Draggs for bringing bricks from the Mountain. 17th May: the flourishing furnace and stack cannot be proceeded with until bricks are burnt and fetched from the mountain. Anthony Wedgewood, Potter and two labourers have been seeking and getting clay for pots for one month past. 19th May: three horses and two men fetched bricks from the kiln. 20th May: William Walter, collier, with three men have been bringing up a level to a four- and five-foot band of coal near the brick kiln. 27th May: Wood went to the mountain to see bricks drawn from a kiln. He found many bricks spoilt because the heat used was too great and the bricks were burnt. The coal was stronger than the brick makers expected. 8th June: agreed with Thomas David to fetch from the Brick Kiln in Penwain every week from this day until first day of November, three m (it means thousand) Brick Common and fire (fire bricks) at 5d per m to be paid for every fortnight and to lend him a Carr and Slade with pair of panniers in good order and he engaged to deliver them back in the same good condition. He engaged also to supply the Brickmaker with sand as much as they may want from this day during the season of making for 5d.

Iron Ore

The indispensable raw material for the production of iron is the iron stone or mine. On 19th May, Charles Wood agreed with Richard Rees to raise 1,500 dozen of mine or ironstone. A dozen of mine is a cubic yard of mine. They agreed the following conditions: to pay him £5 for bringing up a level, to carry off the water, make use of the waste of the soil etc., at 2/6 per dozen and one guinea over in every hundred dozen which will make it 2s 9d per dozen and promised him that if we were ready with our Furnace by the time he had raised the quantity, that he should have one of our collieries to work.

On 25th June Wood discusses with his friend and adviser, Isaac Wilkinson, the location for burning (calcining) of the iron stone. Wood shows him the situation intended for the blast furnace, which he approved. It is clear from later evidence that this situation was where the furnaces now stand, at the so-called Cyfarthfa Rock. Mr. Wilkinson advised to take the field on the other side of the road for a bank to burn iron stone and coke coal, as it will then be down hill to the bridge house across the high road. This field was later rented by the company and it seems plausible to assume that it was located above the furnaces, where the coke ovens and calcining furnaces are still recorded on the maps 100 years later, on a site occupied until recently by Thorn Electrical factory. One of the ways to obtain the mine was by washing, which is also referred to as scouring. In this operation a rush of water is created to wash away the topsoil and expose the iron stone. An entry of 25th August shows this: Mr. Morgan and Zachary Philips with my brother and myself went to the Wern to view the damage complained by Philip David, the tenant, by our washing and laying the mine.

On the same day he agreed with William Lewis, the Mine burner at Plymouth furnace, to burn our mine upon Penwain at 2d per ton. This was to be weighed at the bank where the furnace is to be and 18d per ton carriage. This method saves the carriage of coal, it being within about 60 yards from the Mine stock. One ton of coal will burn about three ton of mine. On 28th August he records that part of the burnt mine is brought down and laid upon the bank, where the furnace is intended. The calcining of the mine at Pen y Waun was probably done in open fires. It was not until a year later, on 18th April, 1767, that Charles Wood set out three kilns for burning mine stone. The location is not stated, but is likely to be on the field behind the furnace, mentioned above. On 9th September, 1766, he agreed with sundry to raise in Penwain Common 200 dozen of mine at 2s 6d per dozen, reckoning a solid yard a dozen or twelve bushel in measure to be taken either way at the option of the company.

Coal

Equal in importance to the iron ore as a raw material was coal. We have shown earlier how the ironmasters had in the past tried hard to replace charcoal with coal, and how the Darbys of Coalbrookdale succeeded in using coke for the smelting of cast iron and the Woods developed the method of refining cast iron with coal. Coal is available in great quantities and excellent quality in the area of Merthyr and the whole of the South Wales coalfield and was destined to overtake and eventually to replace iron ore in importance for the economy of Merthyr. The first mention of coal deposits and the extraction of coal appears in the Diaries in an entry of 20th May, 1766: "William Walter collier with three men have been bringing up a level to a four- five-foot band of coal near the brick kiln for it is one as will save more than great expense in bringing it in the carriage to supply the kiln; which coal is said to be as good as any for air furnaces. If so it will be of great use." There follow several entries concerning a dispute with one of the colliers who dug coal in places where he was not entitled to work. His excuse was that the word pit in his contract, according to local custom, meant any part of the same vein, even if this vein was followed for some considerable distance. The dispute was eventually referred to Mr. Bacon himself, who confirmed that Lewis William John had to confine his workings to the original place.

Another important entry is dated 25th August: "Several of us went to the Wern and from there to the farm Cwm y Glo, which land is very poor but as there is coal and mine it is in the Company's interest to have it. There is a six-foot vein of coal near the house very good which has supplied the tenant with fuel. The house was formerly built by Mr. Davies for Presbyterian Meetings. Father to the present Samuel Davies, the Minister of the Meeting House near the bridge." We learn later that the farm was actually rented by the Cyfarthfa Works. It is also interesting that the coal mine described is probably the one later known as Waun Wyllt, which became the property of Robert and Lucy Thomas, the pioneers of the South Wales Coal trade.

Charles Wood certainly could appreciate good coal when he saw it. However, he did not leave this matter to chance. On 21st April, 1767, he describes a series of trials with four-horse loads each of coal from twelve separate locations. Each location is clearly identified, and details of some of the trials are described.

Several trials were recorded on 21st April, 1767. Here are two examples:

> ***No. 2.*** A coal from Cwm y Glo. A 9 foot band... burns well by blast is a clean sweet coal but dull in a house fire.
> ***No. 3.*** Coal in the mountain above Cwm Y Mine; this band or vein lyes two lifts about 2 feet 6 inches deep; dull in a house fire, but burns well in a Smith fire. A sweet coal.

Another interesting item is dated 30th August, 1766, when he gives an estimate of anticipated coal consumption in the works as follows:

Coal for Blast furnace	100 tons a week
Coal for four flourishing furnaces	80 tons a week
Coal for two shingling furnaces, 20 tons each	40 tons a week
Coal for pots etc.	20 tons a week
Total	240 tons a week

An entry of 25th April, 1767, indicates the large reserves of minerals found. It says: "Mr. Wilkinson walked with me to the brick kiln and to view the Coal and Mine at Penywain, Cwm y Mine and from thence up the Mountain as far as Lewis William Johns old work. By washing it has laid bare several veins of coal and mine; to all appearances they will serve several generations. The coal under the brick kiln is represented to be fine coal of about seven or eight feet thick."

Cast Iron

Cast iron was an important material needed in the equipment of the buildings and the provision of parts in the Cyfarthfa Works from an early stage. A blast furnace, which would have produced cast iron, was however not erected until some time later. It was therefore necessary to obtain cast iron from other furnaces, particularly from the Plymouth furnace. On 15th May, 1766, Charles Wood contacted two partners in the Plymouth furnace, Mr. John White and Mr. Thomas Guest and made them the following proposal:

"Anthony Bacon a Co propose agreeing with John White & Co. for metal in grain of a good grey quality to the amount of 500, 1000 or 2000 tons delivered at the works of the said Anthony Bacon & Co at the rate of 4, 5 Ton long weight, to be paid for every six months, after delivering of one hundred tons. That the said John White & Co. shall make for the said Anthony Bacon & Co whatever cast uses they may have occasion for, at their works now Erecting at Cyfarthfa in the Parish of Merthyr Tidvil at the rate of £5 per Ton long weight, to be paid for at the delivery of every 20 Tons by a bill drawn by that Company's agents on Anthony Bacon payable six months after date. By such agreement the many advantages of which it will be productive is obvious. First it will free John White & Co. from the great uncertainty of procuring carriage to Cardiff, as well as Sale of the metal when at Market. It will lessen your Capital near one third of what it will be necessary to carry your work on; the value of your metal will come in at certain stated periods to answer the demands that will issue from your works & prevent any future calls from the several Proprietors, and as Interest is the strongest tye to persons in the same business this will be productive of that end. All which is offered to your consideration."

It is evident that this carefully-worded and wide-ranging offer had been considered well in advance by Charles Wood and probably agreed with Anthony Bacon himself. On receiving it, the partners in the Plymouth company asked for time to consider it. When their reply came on the next day, it contained a number of conditions. Mr. Wood sent the reply to Mr. Bacon, and nothing further was heard about it. However, it becomes clear that the partners in the Plymouth furnace were anxious to obtain business on a smaller scale. On 27th May we read:

"Just now came Mr. Terry and informed me, that the Plymouth Company were willing to cast anything we wanted that could be done in open sand upon the terms proposed, namely £5-15 per ton short weight, i.e. 112 lb to the hundred and 20 hundred to the ton delivered at Cyfarthfa and if I agreed desired the patterns might be made as soon as we could."

Charles Wood agreed. On 29th May details are given about the castings required. It says that patterns for bearing bars and for furnace bases were sent. Wood also states that a pattern for a hammer is finished. Some particularly large items were delivered on 17th June, namely six stamper boxes, 33 inches by 38 inches by 25 inches, each weighing 23 cwt. Six bottoms for the boxes, weighing 13 cwt each; 14 stamper heads weighing 2 cwt each and three anvils weighing 14 cwt each. We see thus that these castings were required for the air furnaces in the course of erection and for the processes of stamping and potting. Some special metal parts, however, had to be obtained from outside. On 15th June we read that William David was required to go to Pontypool for Stamper Shank Wheel Axle heads and rod iron. To quote Charles Wood: "The best and toughest iron being made there of any in these parts."

By this time the fortunes of the Plymouth Furnace were declining, due to poor management by Mr. Terry, and two partners sold their shares to Anthony Bacon & Co., namely Isaac Wilkinson and John Guest. These two, with Charles Wood, consequently travelled to Bristol on 1st July to have the transfer documents drawn up by an Attorney and Charles Wood then journeyed to London to obtain Mr. Bacon's signature. These journeys took fourteen days. By July it becomes clear that the Plymouth Furnace was losing money. The deliveries of castings continue. On 2nd August, the following were delivered: 2 stamper boxes, 4 plates for washing and 34 small plates for furnace stoke holes and cinder holes, all weighing 4 tons. On 10th August, Charles Wood feels that the Plymouth Furnace should be blown out (that means closed down). In order to be profitable it would require substantial improvements and reconstruction, he feels. On 11th August, Wood visited Plymouth but was unable to conduct any business with Mr. Terry. The workmen came to Mr. Terry so often to demand their money due that Wood had but little time to say anything to him. He remarks: "As the men will not work the furnace must be blown out." An entry on Wednesday, 13th August, says: "Went to the Plymouth Furnace with patterns for Stamp head and box for Clay Mill gudgeons and gave direction for them and one frame. Order should be completed before they blow out, which they promised to do."

On 1st September, Charles Wood gives orders to alter the flourishing furnace for a casting furnace in order to cast the cylinders etc. for bellows and, if he can agree with the Plymouth Company for stock of all their pigs and metal, after the cylinders are cast, etc., the remainder of the metal may be granulated in the furnace and when they are altered into flourishing, this metal will be ready for that operation (i.e., the production of wrought iron).

An agreement to purchase all the stock of the Plymouth Furnace was reached soon after, as the following entry shows:

"On September 18th, Thomas Guest and Mr. Terry came to me and informed me that they wanted money to discharge the Plymouth Company debts and that the Bridgenorth Gentlemen had directed them to sell all the metal in hand and collect the debts due, for that end. That they were willing to treat with me for 95 Tons of Pig, and 9 Tons of scrap metal. I agreed to give them £3.15 for the Pigs and £2.10 for the scrap metal, the former short and the latter longweight delivered here at our Work... I gave them a bill for the amount of £278.15 upon Mr. Bacon at 30 days sight payable to Mr. Thomas Guest. Furthermore, I wrote to Mr. Bacon and advised him of this bill and purchase."

On 6th May, 1767, a year later, Charles Wood agreed with Thomas Davis to come to Cyfarthfa and to cast lintels for the Blast Furnace stack, an anvil block for the forge, etc., at 11s a ton. "This is a very high price," he writes, "but as we cannot get any other person, are obliged to submit to give it." Wood also gave orders to prepare the casting furnace for use. Wood then orders patterns for various parts to be made, to be cast in Cyfarthfa from the pig iron obtained from the Plymouth Furnace, which by now had been blown out. Some of the parts to be cast are quite large. One lintel for the blast furnace was to be 17 feet long and weigh over 16 cwt.

There is no further information concerning the Plymouth Furnace in the Diaries. Bacon acquired it some time later. After his death in 1786, it was transferred to his brother-in-law, Richard Hill.

The Supply of Water Power

The principal source of power for industrial purposes was water power. In Cyfarthfa, the water was taken from the river Taff, somewhere below the confluence of its two branches. The Blast Furnace had its own water supply taken from the Taf Fawr. The first entry in the Diaries shows how far the construction of the various races had progressed, when Charles Wood arrived. To quote from the Diaries:

"Came to Merthyr Tydfil 11th April, 1766, and found the preparations for the several buildings not so forward as expected. The Grand race from the river was brought up, the arching and the walls are taken up. The outer wall from the flood gates to the turn of the river was finished in a workmanlike but very expensive manner. The inner wall to form the pool was brought down which is about 20 feet of the place where the forebay is to be. The arch about the Clay Mill race was made within 20 yards of the house, and part of the race for the Stampers, which is all that is material done."

The broad outline for the plan of the water supply is thus described: the flood gates were probably the forerunner of the later weir, the grand race was the principal leet and its walls and arching were complete. Two walls were built to form the pool, an outer wall from the flood gates to the bend in the river (probably near Pandy Bridge) and an inner wall forming the pool. It ended at the lower end of the pool, near the place where the forebay was to be built. The forebay is a substantial channel which is situated at the downstream end of the pool. The pool tapers towards the forebay. The forebay usually directs a substantial stream of water over a water wheel, which is usually positioned several feet below the forebay. In Cyfarthfa the forebay was a very elaborate construction built of stone, supplying several wheels with water power.

Several of the principal industrial buildings had water wheels to supply their power and each such building and wheel had its own race. The races mentioned in the Diaries are as follows: besides the Grand Race, there were the Clay Mill Race, two Stamper Races, a Chafery Race, two Hammer Races. There was a separate race, the Tai Mawr Cut, bringing water to the blast furnace, and a back race from this furnace to return the water to the river. On 10th August an entry gives the dimensions of the races: the grand race was divided into three sections: the first was 65 yards long and six feet wide, the second was 56 yards long and six feet wide, the third 37 yards long and eight feet wide. The grand race with its several branches was 300 yards.

The watercourses were very solidly constructed, several feet deep, with foundations often cut in the solid rock. They had side walls two or three feet high, built of dressed stones, set in strong mortar. All the races were arched over with dressed stones and covered over with earth and debris, so that they were running below ground. The flow of the water was regulated by sluices and penstocks.

One of the most substantial constructions of the water supply was the weir. It was begun on 17th July and a great number of the workers were employed in its construction. Thus on 18th July the number given is: 16 masons, 32 labourers, 5 carpenters. On 24th July Wood writes: "The masons and labourers work daily in the water, therefore to encourage them I give drink to some and advanced wages to others who do not choose drink." On 28th July he writes: "The labourers have to lay down the remainder of the frame for the weir a third time. It has been washed down by the floods twice." On 6th August he records that the weir is almost finished and was erected in as short a time as any in England, from our first beginning to this day inclusive is nine and a half days and I reckon tomorrow for the dry wall at the end will be ten and a half days."

Buildings, Plant and Machinery

The next group of constructions were the buildings, plant and machinery in which the various operations of the works were to be carried out. They were mainly concerned with the Stamping and Potting process. Thus the first building mentioned, with its water wheel and penstock, is the Clay Mill, situated on the Clay Mill Race. Here the clay for the earthenware pots was to be prepared. The Mixing Room was intended to house the operations which prepared the metal to be put into the pots. The Stamper house was to house the stampers, large hammers to break up cast iron plates into small fragments. There was to be a Washing house and a Drying house, to dry the pots. Other buildings are concerned with the refining processes: the Flourishing house, the Forge, and the all-purpose Smithy. Air furnaces for the various stages of reheating the metal were constructed from the very beginning. It was intended to have nine eventually.

The Blast Furnace and its Water Supply

As I mentioned, plans for the construction of the water supply for the main parts of the works and the location of most of the buildings and plant for them had been drawn up by the time Charles Wood came to Cyfarthfa. However, two important sites were only determined some time after his arrival. They were the location of the blast furnace itself and the position of the water course to bring water to the furnace wheel. The place where the furnace was to be situated is called in the Diaries "The Cyfarthfa Rock". It was situated on land tenanted by Richard Williams (called William Richard by Professor T. V. Davies). His farm was called Tir Hugh Morgan. Two fields were eventually rented from this farm.[8]

The Tai Mawr Cut

William Edwards, the builder of the Pontypridd bridge, was asked to survey a possible supply of water for the blast furnace. He finished his survey on 4th June, 1766. He fixed a point 960 yards up the Taf Fawr. He therefore did not select a point near the works, but went up stream almost as far as the point where the railway Viaduct in Cefn Coed is situated today. The fall to the wheel of the Blast Furnace was to be 27 feet. Edwards promised to ensure that the aqueduct would not lose any water on its passage to delivery upon the wheel. He quoted a price of £300 for the construction of the feeder, with the following conditions: "our smith to sharpen what tools he used in the work, he finding iron and steel for new laying and steeling them and to complete by 1st July, 1767." Charles Wood adopted this route with some alterations. Edwards left soon afterwards and the work was carried out by other workers. The feeder which was eventually constructed started somewhat higher up the valley than suggested by Edwards, at a point where a solidly-built weir spans the river just below the Railway Viaduct in Cefn Coed. This weir, however, was built later. Originally the water was taken from a stone ridge or sill, several of which ran across the river in those days. Charles Wood calls them natural weirs. The water was taken from the right hand side of the Taf Fawr, on land belonging to the farm Tai Mawr. Two fields were eventually rented from this farm on which the feeder was situated. The river bank is steep at this point and a retaining wall had to be built for some 100 yards to carry the feeder from the point of intake. It then enters a tunnel cut into the solid rock. This tunnel is 5 feet wide and 6 feet high, 102 yards long. It emerges opposite the end of the Fingertip and continues into the area of the works.

The work on the cut did not start until the following year. On 14th April, 1767, two separate contracts were let for constructing the cut in the open and a separate one for a tunnel to be cut through the rock, 6 feet high and 5 feet wide, we finding powder, tools and candles. He adds: "The rock is so hard, no pick will stand it."

On the next day he states: "The bargain to drive through the rock has begun and find it so hard that it cannot be performed in any reasonable time without blasting." A few days later he observes that the water that is proposed to be brought from the land Tai Mawr for an overshot wheel may be too little in a dry summer. Isaac Wilkinson proposed that water from the two branches of the Taf might be brought to the furnace wheel, in aid to the other as an undershot, which would make the quantity of water more certain for the furnaces at all seasons.

We know that several more feeders brought water to the wheel, taken both from the Taf Fawr and the Taf Fechan. That happened after the Diaries had finished. It is also of interest that the Tai Mawr Cut has recently been scheduled as an Ancient Monument by Cadw.

The Blast Furnace

The first entry concerning the construction of the Blast Furnace occurred on 4th June, 1766, when William Edwards was desired to give an estimate of the charge or expense he would undertake to build a Stack only without Bridge House, Bellows or Casting House, 36 feet square and supposing it to be 50 feet high, he to be at the charge of getting and carrying of stone, getting sand and paying for the lime upon the same terms as we have it. A. Bacon and Company not to be at any more charge or expense but the price per perch to be agreed upon. William Edwards to clear the foundations and clear and complete the back race for the delivery of the water into the pool. Raise stone, carry them from the present quarry, cleated and squared. If the quarry does not produce sufficient stones for our present need, Mr. Edwards is to clear and open a new one at his own expense. He is to find the sand, mix with the lime and make it into mortar. He is to pay for the lime at the rate we are paying at present. The cast iron lintels for the arch and the çentre that may be wanted for the purpose to be found by A. B. & Co. The fire bricks for the inner wall to be laid near the work by the Company. Mr. William Edwards to be at the expense and charge of all other items relating to the erection of the stack. the work to be finished on 1st July, 1767, for the sum of £550. These are Mr. Edwards' proposals. Mr. Charles Wood then remarks that no decision regarding the stack need be made now, as it can not be built until the water is brought and may be completed in less than half the time that the cut can be made conveying the water to it.

On 22nd June, Wood again refers to the stack. He says that he thinks the bank at Cyfarthfa Rock will allow the stack to be 50 feet high, which in his opinion it ought to be, as the height will be a means to prevent the coal mix falling down too soon, as it often does in low ones before it is sufficiently heated to fuse immediately when it reaches the tyeres, which is the occasion of much bad metal being made at several furnaces. The earthy part, which is the scoria, is then not being separated from the metal part. On 26th June, he states that Mr. Wilkinson cut (out) the form for a furnace and gave Mr. Parry direction to draw a section.

The contract to build the stack was eventually agreed on 18th August with Harry Williams, Edward Thomas John and David John, Masons, as follows: to build a stack for a blast furnace upon the terms following, vizt. me to find them with lime near the place and they to have 3 s per perch, they themselves to provide and bring to the place stones, sand water and all necessary, having the use of the quarry for that purpose. The company to provide them with crows and sledge hammer and to repair the hammer when needed, the same to be returned or paid for if lost. The whole building to be carried on and completed without delay or loss of time, in a strong, solid, workmanlike manner. The Company to erect a shade, near the place allotted for the furnace, for the workers to scabble stones under in rainy weather. Agreed likewise with the three masons, to dig the foundation for the furnace at 4d per square yard for the earth and 8d per yard for the rock and to supply them with powder for blasting the rock if found necessary. Signed by them and witnessed by Samuel Wood. The next entry concerning the furnace is on 6th September: "I am just returned from viewing and letting the back race from the river to the furnace wheel to Rosser Thomas, his brother William Rhys and William Lewis. To be made 10 feet wide and driven up 18 inches below the river as it is now about three inches below the weir, at 3d per earth, sand etc. and for the rock 8d per cubic yard.

On 9th September we read: Leveled (i.e. surveyed) the bank against which the furnace is to be built. It is 47 feet high to the flat part of the field and from thence to the surface of water about 6 inches rising over the weir 19 feet more, in the whole 66 feet. The stack may be 50 ft high the foundation 6 feet and then there will remain 10 feet for the cistern and cut or back race for a flat bottom boat to convey the metal to the flourishing furnace etc. It may be continued for the metal to be put into the boat out of the cistern which will save the room for bins and labour in taking it out of the bins.

On 1st May, 1767, he writes: The furnace is this day brought up to a level in every part and carried on in a workmanlike manner by the masons. An entry on 6th May states: Agreed with Thomas Davies to cast lintels for the Blast Furnace stack and other parts at 11s per ton. The last entry concerning the blast furnace is on 7th May: The carpenters were fixing the centre for the front arch.

Transport

A large part of the internal transport of materials in the works was carried out by manual labour. We have seen how the workers carried stones in several operations from the quarry to the place of work. Sometimes they seem to have used wheel-barrows or were assisted by a horse and cart. The unloading of the pig iron delivered from the Plymouth furnace and its piling had to be done manually,. One important task was to fetch materials from Pen y Wayn: coal, iron ore and the bricks produced there had to be brought to the Cyfarthfa site. On 15th May we read that a sawyer made a sledge to fetch lime from Pen y Wayn. The entry of 28th May mentions: "Waggon at home. Three horses fetching brick on their backs and three men the same in cases with two men brought 1460 bricks and two load of coal for the smith's shop." On 6th June: "One man with 2 horses, one in a carr, brought 600 bricks. David Lewis with 2 labourers were loading clay for fire brick." A contract dated 8th June, to fetch bricks regularly from Pen y Wayn, has been mentioned earlier.

The draft animals used in the works were horses and oxen. They were kept at the farm Llwyn Celyn. they had to perform various tasks required on the farm, ploughing, hay making, assisting in the grain harvest. They were shoed by the works' smith. We have already described how they fetched timber from the woods. They had also to pull waggons bringing goods from Cardiff. They used the old Roman Road via Caerphilly. On one occasion, after heavy rain, the carriage got stuck in the mud and further draft animals had to be fetched to pull the waggon free. The lime obtained from Cardiff was usually brought by a contractor. The cost of transport was high. On 13th May, 1766, Charles Wood writes that the cost of carriage is nearly 4 times the price of the lime. This includes a charge for the turnpike. (10th May, 1767.) Some of the horses were occasionally used for riding. Thus Sam Wood rode to Cowbridge to obtain cash for the payment of wages and expenses from the agent of Lord Talbot.

Workers' Dwellings

Charles Wood arranged for workers' dwellings to be erected over certain buildings, which housed plant and machinery. The first entry relating to this is dated 16th June, 1766, when he orders to raise the roof of the Stamper House and the Forge by three and a half feet, to allow the wheel to run under the rafters. This will be an additional charge of about £8. "But," he continues, "there will be gained as much room as will make four apartments for 4 families, with rooms for four further families over the forge. An entrance gallery may be made from the rock to each apartment. The dimensions of the rooms over the Stamper house will be 42 ft by 33 ft for four families. By continuing dwellings above the several branches of buildings for the workmen belonging thereto will save erecting separate houses for them at much great expense and the convenience of every workman being near his work will be an ease to them and an advantage to the masters, as I have experienced." Later we learn that another set of such dwellings were erected over the Mixing Room and Clay Mill. We can only guess at the noise and dirt created by the machinery in operation below these dwellings.

A Proposal to Grind Corn

A proposal to grind corn in the works is mentioned on 15th September, 1766. It states: "As the millers in the country are very exorbitant in their tolls, which occasions meal much dearer than it otherwise would be, George Ford informs me that he can at a small expense fix a pair of stones to be twined to the chafery wheel, which will grind the corn the workmen may use, without the least detriment to the other work. And as we have stone in our own land fitt for grinding any grain, I have ordered George Ford to provide for such a mill to put up when the occasion calls. It will be prudent to use all the means in the Company power to free their workmen from the imposition of this country, which is very great and unless this can be done will not be any possibility of preventing the Workmen getting into the Company Debt or advancing their wages or losing them as they cannot maintain their families with the wages agreed, unless they can be supplied with their provisions at the market price which they have not been hitherto."

The Role of Anthony Bacon

We know little of the control or supervision Mr. Bacon exercised over Charles Wood. Wood seems to have had a large measure of discretion. He certainly could hire and fire all employees. We know that he worked to a detailed plan as far as the main works were concerned. Certainly Charles Wood made the decision about the location of the Blast Furnace and the course of the race bringing water to the Furnace Wheel. However, he certainly consulted his senior staff and particularly Isaac Wilkinson before coming to a decision. He mentions letters to and from Mr. Bacon on several occasions but never mentions their content. The only time that Mr. Bacon was directly approached was when his Company purchased five shares in the Plymouth Furnace, when Wood travelled to London to obtain the signature of Mr. Bacon to the deeds. On one occasion a workman appealed to Mr. Bacon when he, the workman, was dissatisfied with a decision of Mr. Wood, and Mr. Bacon replied upholding Mr. Wood's decision. On the whole Charles Wood seems to have had a good deal of independence, e.g., when he left Cyfarthfa in the autumn of 1766 to go to Low Mill and did not return until the following spring. We hear on several occasions that Wood submitted estimates of cost of some larger item of plant, such as the cost of building a railway, i.e., a tramroad to supply transport for material in and to the works. Mr. Bacon did not visit the works during the period covered by the Diaries.

Accounts and Finance

Samuel Wood kept the accounts and they were sent every fortnight to Mr. Bacon. The cash necessary for the payment of wages and expenses was obtained from Mr. Thomas Morgan, the Steward of Lord Talbot in Cowbridge. On one or two occasions it is stated that Mr. Morgan visited Cyfarthfa and brought the cash with him. At other times, Mr. Samuel Wood rode to Cowbridge to obtain the cash.

Some Items of Social and Economic Interest

Church and Chapel

Services in the Church, namely Prayers and Sermons, were held every other Sunday in the afternoon in English, at all other times in Welsh. (25th May, 1766.)

An entry on 17th July states that Charles Wood took this day from Mr. Gervas Powell, Vicar of this Parish, all the great and small tithes, vizt. wheat, barley, oats, lambs, wool, geese, hides, kids, pigs, honey and Easter Offerings within the Hamlet of Gellideg – at the yearly rent of £29 and four fat geese, payable in May and November, the first payment to be made in November, 1767. "This Hamlet," he writes, "takes in all our farms as also the whole district of Lord Talbot and Mr. Richards Liberty – therefore I thought it right, to take it to prevent any dispute or trouble from any other person that may lease it..."

The yearly meeting of Mr. Samuel Davies, a Dissenting Minister (of Ynysgau Chapel) took place on Sunday, 20th July. The entry in the Diary of that day states: "After 12 o'clock we all went down to the village and dined before One. This being the yearly meeting of Mr. Samuel Davies, a Dissenting Minister in Chapel, Numbers of that Sect, come from all parts, which occasioned every Public House full of these people therefore we left Edward Morgan (i.e., landlord of the Crown and Anchor), soon after we had dined."

Militia

The entry of 15th September states: "This being appeal day for the Militia, most of our Workmen are gone to Llantrissant to appeal as they have three children each, or more." Next day he writes: "Few hands came in. John Edge, Brickmaker, was taken out of the List for Militia Men, he having served as a Marine and produced his discharge. Aaron Wedgwood potter was also taken out, as a labourer and having three children. But James Mason, an air furnace builder, and William Postlethwaite, carpenter, were continued, as not coming under the section of the Act. Had they appealed as Labourers each with three children, they would have been cleared."

Fairs and Holidays.

The Waun Fair held several times a year near Dowlais Top was a great attraction to the workers and many of them attended instead of coming to work. One fair was held on 24th September. The only public holiday mentioned is the Merthyr Wake on 25th April. Wood says: "It is here called a Revel." The weekly meat markets were held in Merthyr on Saturdays and Tuesdays.

Weights, Measures, Coins

Many units of weight, etc., seem strange today. There is a difference between a Serch, 25 cubic feet of stone and a Perch, with two meanings. Either five and a half yards in length, or thirty and a quarter square yards (also called a square pole). A gold coin is mentioned to the value of 36 shillings. It went out of circulation in 1816. Measures of grain differed in different markets. At Cardiff, Caerphilly, Cowbridge and Llantrissant, which were the chief market towns, there were ten gallons to the bushel. The wheat is streaked (that means kept level with the rim of the vessel), the oats heaped as high as will go. In Brecon, eight gallons is their bushel for wheat and oats, both streaked.

Postscript.

Little is known about Charles Wood's life after the Diaries ended. He remained agent of the Cyfarthfa Works until his death in 1774.[9] His wife survived him. He had several children, of whom Ann was the youngest. She was ten years old when he died. Ann's daughter, Mary Howitt, published an autobiography in which she recalls some reminiscences of her mother relating to Charles Wood. He had a deep detestation of slavery, which he had witnessed in Jamaica, where he had lived for many years. On the outbreak of the American War of Independence, Charles Wood sided with the American people and had a great admiration for George Washington.[10]

Charles Wood took out a Lease from Henry Richard of Coyty and his wife Mary, dated 29th April, 1771, of Limestone at Craigfawr y Gurnos in Merthyr Tidvil.[11]

Charles Wood died in Merthyr on 17th October, 1774, his wife Jemima in November, 1799. They were both buried at St. Tydfil's Churchyard. Their remains were transferred to the Cefn Coed cemetery in 1911.[12]

Notes

1. T. V. Davies: T*he Farms and Farmers of Senghenydd Supra prior to the Industrial Revolution*. Private Edition. Part 1. Pages 263 ff. and 332 ff.
2. *Glamorgan County History*. Volume V. Editors A. H. John and Glanmor Williams. p. 97.
3. *Ibid.* page 98.
4. Charles K. Hyde: *Technological Change in the British Iron Industry 1700-1870*. Princeton University Press. 1977. pp. 7, and 76-93.
5. R. A. Mott: *Henry Cort, the Great Refiner*. The Metals Society 1983. pp. 2-8.
6. J. Lloyd: *The Early History of the Old South Wales Ironworks. 1760-1840*. p. 48.

7. David C. Agnew. *Protestant Exiles from France*. Reeves & Turner. London. 1874. p. 99.
8. T. V. Davies. *Ibid*. p. 401.
9. Chris Evans. *Labyrinth of Flames*. Cardiff, Univ. of Wales Press, 1993. p. 58.
10. *Mary Howitt Autobiography*. Ibister Ltd., London 1889. p. 8/9.
11. J. Lloyd. p. 49.
12. *Merthyr Express*. 27th May, 1911.

The Winter Art Exhibition, Cyfarthfa Castle, 1909-10

by T. F. HOLLEY

Introduction

Cyfarthfa Castle was built in 1825 by William Crawshay and occupied by him and his successors until about 1890. For years the Castle remained unoccupied. In 1908 during the mayoralty of Alderman D. W. Jones, negotiations were entered into between the Mayor and Mr. William Thompson Crawshay. The Castle, its well timbered park, land and plantations, comprising 150 acres, were acquired for £18,500 by the Merthyr Tydfil Corporation.

In October, 1909, the Education Committee decided to hold a small exhibition at Cyfarthfa Castle, of work by students of the evening schools and technical classes, supplemented by a Loan Collection of like work from the Victoria and Albert Museum.

This small Exhibition was a great success and upon the initiative of Councillor Frank Treharne James, then Mayor, a Winter Art Exhibition was held, the principal feature being the works of Penry Williams, a native of Merthyr.

A magnificent Loan Collection of paintings by Penry Williams adorned the Castle walls for some months, together with a Loan Collection of Water Colour Drawings representing the British School, from the Victoria and Albert Museum.

The Cardiff newspapers paid scant attention to this Merthyr initiative but the Exhibition was well reported in the *Merthyr Express* newspaper. Some of these reports are summarised here and furnish a vivid impression of the glittering and exciting event:

A. Letter from Charles Russell James, Hampstead.
B. First account of Exhibition and Exhibits, and details of Opening Ceremony.
C. Second notice of Exhibition and Exhibits.
D. Permanent Museum and Art Gallery proposed.
E. Brief notes on William Williams, father of Penry, and mention of Tomos Glyn Cothi.
F. Winter Art Exhibition drawing to a close.
G. Concert for Winter Art Exhibition.
H. The Museums Act adopted, permanent Museum and Art Gallery founded.

A. Letter from Charles Russell James, Hampstead

"Sir, I am glad to learn that the Merthyr Corporation are about to do honour to one of Merthy's distinguished sons. Probably but few of the younger generation know that PENRY STREET was named after him. I remember Mr. Penry Williams. In my father's time, in the year 1868, he came to stay in Brynteg (House). On that occasion he made a sketch of Merthyr from the dining-room window. I believe that sketch is in the possession of my brother, Dr. Alfred James, of St. Andrews, Biggleswade.

My recollection of Mr. Penry Williams is of a small, dapper little man of the old school. He had a quiet, modest, gentlemanly bearing. I recall him as a singularly unobtrusive, reflective guest, who spoke little, but to the point, a shy little mild-mannered gentleman. He also, on that same visit, made a sketch from the old iron bridge at Merthyr. Your worthy Mayor has written to me asking me if I will lend my specimens of the artist's work. That request I willingly comply with.

"It may be of interest to your readers if I indicate what specimens of Penry Williams's work are in my possession. I have four of his oil paintings:

1. 'The Tambourine Girl', with a girl companion at the foot of some steps. Of this picture I have an engraving which, I believe, appeared in the *Art Journal* some years ago.
2. Another tambourine girl with a girl companion dressing her hair.
3. A mother with a sleeping child on her lap, this I think was a sketch for a larger picture.

4. Landscape, with mountain, trees and waterfall.

"I have three sketches in colour taken out of one of Penry Williams's sketch books, namely:

5. A study of the fore part of a donkey, and two delicate water colour sketches.
6. One of Cefn (Coed) Bridge with the lower part of the village and the River Taff.
7. Old Penydarren Ironworks with the landscape in the background and Penydarren House.

"Besides these I have nine pencil sketches indicating the artist's careful methods of working. Some of these are quite sketchy but their interest lies in the peep they give one behind the scenes.

"They are as follows:

8. Hafodunos, North Wales.
9. Capel Curig.
10. Tivoli, near Rome.
11. Two goats and some human figures (on the back of the Tivoli sketch).
12. Studies of sleep.
13. Study of a young donkey.
14. A man carrying a wild boar, with men beneath, similarly engaged.
15. A landscape sketch of mountain, trees and water.
16. Hanmermeer, with church, lake and rowing boat.

"The history of most of these is this. Some years ago, and in the lifetime of Penry Williams, Mr. Theed, the sculptor, wrote to my late father (Charles Herbert James, M.P.), and doubtless to other Merthyr men, saying he had some of Penry Williams's pictures entrusted to him for sale. My late father bought several oil paintings at Mr. Theed's studio in London. At the same time, I secured a couple of pictures.

"Some of the sketches came out of a sketch book which Charles Herbert James bought from Penry Williams's sister, Miss Sophie Williams.

"Bryan's dictionary of painting (1899) has the following account of the artist. 'Penry Williams was born at Merthyr Tydfil in 1798. His father was a house painter and Penry was sent as a boy to London to study in the Royal

Academy at the charges of Sir John Guest, Mr. Crawshay and some other Welsh magnates who were interested in his talent. Penry first exhibited at the Royal Academy in 1824. In 1827 he went to Italy and settling in Rome continued to contribute constantly to English exhibitions. His works were chiefly Italian landscapes and character subjects, painted in the manner of the Italian School of fifty years ago.

" 'His *Italian Girl with a Tambourine* and *Italian Peasants* had for a time a place in the National Gallery. They have now been relegated, the first to Nottingham, the second to the Leicester Museum.

" 'For nearly sixty years Penry Williams was a familiar figure in Rome, where he was very popular. He died in 1885.'

"Yours, Charles Russell James. Hampstead. 15.11.1909."

(*Merthyr Express*, Saturday 20.11.1909 p.12 col.3.)

B. First Account of Exhibition and Exhibits, and Details of Opening Ceremony.

"During the next six weeks, electoral controversies notwithstanding, Cyfarthfa Castle ought to be the Mecca of thousands of the inhabitants of the Borough of Merthyr who are interested in things beautiful. The Art Exhibition, opened by the Mayor on Tuesday afternoon, 7.12.1909, is a highly creditable production of works of art and articles of historical and antiquarian interest, considering that it has been brought about with very short notice, and in a brief space of time, without much organised effort.

"We believe the idea occurred to the Mayor (Councillor F. T. James) when the exhibition of the Winter Art Classes was held a couple of months ago, and subsequently matured, with the result that there is now in the great hall and the suite of three rooms on the south-western front, a collection of beautiful paintings in oil and water colours, sketches in sepia and pencil drawings, embracing examples from the studios of some of our most eminent artists, all loans by private gentlemen resident in the Borough, or having some family or other interest in it.

"The works of one painter, a Merthyr born and bred boy, Mr. PENRY WILLIAMS, so largely predominate amongst the local contributions that it may also be called a Penry Williams Exhibition, supplemented by works of other artists; but the third gallery is entirely filled by a contribution of lovely exhibits lent by the circulation division of the Victoria and Albert Museum at South Kensington. It is surprising that a large number of the works of Penry Williams are permanently housed in the homes of Merthyr gentlemen, and it is an honour to their patriotic instincts no less than to their artistic tastes that they should have secured so many examples of genuine art by this distinguished son of Merthyr.

"Some of the Exhibits

The Hall is occupied with pictures in oil and water colours, engravings, lithographs, old prints, sculpture, archaeological remains of Merthyr, cases of coins, Egyptian antiquities, etc. Mainly the objects exhibited have some relation to Merthyr, which imparts to them a particular interest. There is a portrait of William Meyrick. Most Merthyr people have heard, sometime or other, of the famous Meyrick, the lawyer who lived at Gwaelodygarth, whose body lies in a vault inside the parish Church, and about whom no end of stories, fabulous or otherwise, circulate, but none of us living today have any idea of what manner of man he was.

"Here we see a faithful delineation of his features, and surely a more unlawlerlike face than this rubiconed country squire we should not have imagined, for the great lawyer who got the better side of so astute a man as William Crawshay.

"Opposite is a large painting of Cyfarthfa Ironworks, in the era anterior to the building of the Pandy Mill, when all the land on the east side of the river was green meadow.

"Here are portraits of Lady Charlotte Guest, drawn by Richard Buckner, engraved by William Walker, lent by Mr. M. Truran; portraits of Lord and Lady Wimborne, about the period of their marriage; a fine portrait, in oils, of the late Mr. Robert Crawshay, lent by Mr. William Evans, Brynteg; another of Sir John Guest; portraits (engravings) of the late Mr. John Nixon, the late Lord Aberdare, the late Dr. Joseph Parry, and a mezzotint of Alderman Thompson. Who was Alderman Thompson? A name very familiar fifty years ago as one of the proprietors of Penydarren Ironworks, and father of that Elizabeth Thompson who married Mr. William Crawshay and became the mother of Mr. Robert Thompson Crawshay.

"We noticed the absence of a picture of that gentleman's wife, surely there are copies of the lithographed portrait of famous Rose Mary in the town of Merthyr, available for loan for this exhibition.

"Then there is the photograph of a bust in marble of the locally-renowned pedagogue, Taliesin Williams, parent of strong sons and daughters, and instructor of many Merthyr boys who have made great names for themselves in various walks of life. Here, we can form our own conceptions of the man.

"Then there are marble busts of men who were famous in their day as those who were tall amongst their fellows, if not quite head and shoulders above them:

Sir John Guest,
Mr. G. T. Clark,
Mr. R. H. Rhys,
Mr. Frank James,

and with them one of Col. Lewis, who, we regret to say, is at this moment prostrate upon a bed of sickness.

"In connection with sculpture there are several beautiful figures by another eminent son of Merthyr, the late Mr. Joseph Edwards, who carved the busts of Sir John Guest and Mr. Clark; also a number of interesting photographs of other sculpture by the same gifted artist, lent by Mr. Washington Morgan. Dr. Webster has lent a beautiful group in terra cotta and a fine bronze statuette after FOLEY. There is a pair of pictures, old lithographs, done in the best style of their day, commemorative of a banquet and ball given at the Castle on the occasion of the return of Mr. and Mrs. Robert Crawshay from their wedding tour, lent by Mr. D. W. Jones.

"Amongst other portraits there are pen-and-ink drawings of Iolo Morganwg, by M. Evans, lent by Mr. Ll. Reynolds (son of Nathan Dyfed); a fine mezzotint engraving (circa 1735) of a portrait by Lely, of the Great Protector, Oliver Cromwell, as he looked in 1653, lent by Mr. F. T. James; a portrait of Edward Williams, of Middlesborough, but born, bred and trained to his craft as an ironmaster, at Dowlais, lent by Mr. Truran; a portrait of John Williams, brother of Penry, lent by Miss Mary Davis, and one of the Rev. Edward Davies, author of *Celtic Remains*, lent by Mr. Aneurin Rees, Town Clerk.

"Roman Remains

Conspicuous objects in this Hall are the two large cases of Roman remains, UNEARTHED IN PENYDARREN PARK TWO OR THREE YEARS AGO, and here arranged and labelled in order by Mr. B. R. S. Frost, who took so much trouble during the excavations. The quantity and variety of these remains are sufficient to testify to a Roman occupation of Merthyr at least eighteen centuries ago upon an important scale, and many of the articles are evidence of the comparatively high civilization which the conquerors brought with them from Italy. All these artefacts have an intensely local interest, because they were found in our own soil.

"Mr. J. T. Vaughan sends an etching of old Merthyr, which enables us to mark what changes have been wrought in seventy-five years. There are also two large cases of interesting and valuable curios, which, though having no connection with Merthyr, find a proper place in an exhibition of this kind, being antiquities from the tombs of the ancient monarchs of Egypt, and numerous examples of Roman, Greek, Etruscan, Persian and Indian art, in pottery, carving and encaustic tiles, lent by Mr. H. H. Southey.

"Mr. Tom Prydderch

Over the doorway leading from the Hall into No. 1 gallery is an effective painting of Calvary by another Merthyr painter of our time and still living, Mr. Tom Prydderch, who, it will be remembered, was discovered by Mr. W. Pritchard Morgan, twenty years ago (i.e. ca. 1889), and sent by that gentleman to London for tuition. Since then Prydderch has done an immense amount of work, and some of a high character, and in the other galleries several pictures from his brush are exhibited, showing that his talents command the appreciation of competent judges.

"This gallery, number one, is practically a Penry Williams exhibition, there being nothing but his work here. The late Mr. Charles Herbert James, Brynteg, was for a great portion of his lifetime upon terms of intimate friendship with Penry Williams.

"Mr. James was a constant visitor to Penry's studio in Rome, and the great painter made his home at Mr. James's house when he came to Merthyr. Mr. James was a great admirer of Penry Williams's productions, and purchased a great many which, upon his death, passed into the hands of different members of his family. Consequently we have a very large proportion of the exhibits in this gallery as loans by members of Mr. James's family.

"The Mayor, Mr. F. T. James, is also the fortunate possessor of numerous examples of Penry Williams's work, and they find their places in this gallery.

"Those who have lent Pictures

The gentlemen who have lent pictures, besides the Mayor, are

Lord Glanusk, who sent two lovely paintings of Italian subjects,
Sir John T. D. Llewellyn,
Sir W. T. Lewis,

Mr. G. C. James,
Mr. C. Russell James,
Mr. J. James,
Mr. H. A. James,
Dr. Alfred James,
Mr. E. P. Martin,
Mr. C. H. James, Cardiff,
Sir T. Marchant Williams,
Mr. Rhys Williams, Miskin,
Mr. R. J. Rhys,
Mr. J. Griffith Jones,
Miss Mary Davis,
Mrs. J. Gwynne Jones,
Mr. Arthur P. James,
Mr. E. B. Nash,
Mr. L. M. Evans,
Mr. Glyn Vivian,
Mr. T. Gilbert Evans,
Cardiff Art Gallery and Swansea Corporation.

"There are not many large pictures, the two largest being the *Feast of the Madonna del Arco at Naples*, lent by the Cardiff Corporation, and *Lancaster*, lent by Sir John T. D. Llewellyn. These are notable pictures of imposing size, but the merits of an oil painting are not always found in the largest pictures, and in this Penry Williams exhibition the real gems will be found amongst smaller subjects.

"There is a conspicuous portrait of a lady of masculine countenance, Miss Sophie Williams. Who was Sophie Williams? A lady who kept a school for girls in the first half of the last century, and in Merthyr had almost as great a pedagogic reputation as Taliesin Williams himself.

"Besides the paintings there are a number of pencil sketches contributed by Mr. G. C. James, which were executed at various times by the painter, as preliminaries, probably, to serious work. These are admirably suited to assist young beginners in drawing or sketching as showing the methods of a great artist in dotting down his ideas before forming his main scheme for a pictorial creation. In the next gallery there is a smaller collection of beautiful pictures by different artists, including several by another Welsh painter of fame, David Cox, but these and the third gallery, which is exclusively devoted to a magnificent collection sent down by the circulation division of the Victoria and Albert Art Gallery, South Kensington, we must leave for notice next week. The exhibition will be open for six weeks, and we hope it will be visited by thousands who can feast their souls on beautiful ideas expressed in the glowing colours of the painter.

"The Opening Ceremony

Amongst those present at the opening ceremony, on Tuesday afternoon, were

The Mayor and Mayoress of Merthyr
(Councillor F. T. and Mrs. James),
Miss Lorna James,
Colonel A. P. James and the Misses James,
The Lord Mayor and Lady Mayoress of Cardiff
(Councillor and Mrs. Chappell),
Sir T. Marchant Williams, Stipendiary Magistrate,
the Misses Lewis, Mardy,
Miss Ira Rees,
Mrs. W. Edwards,
Mr. Taylor, H.M.I., and Mrs. Taylor,
Miss Edmunds,
Alderman D. W. and Miss Jones,
Alderman and Mrs. Morrell,
Alderman and Mrs. T. J. Evans,
Councillor N. P. and Mrs. Hankey,
Councillor R. P. Rees,
Councillor J. W. and Mrs. Lewis,
Councillor Isaac Edwards,
Councillor F. Pedler,
Councillor F. S. and Mrs. Simons,
Councillor David and Mrs. John,
Councillor John and Mrs. Davies,
Councillor W. and Mrs. Marsh,
Councillor D. J. and Mrs. Lewis,
Councillor L. M. and Mrs. Jones,
Councillor William Lewis, and
Councillor H. M. Lloyd;
Mr. T. Aneuryn Rees, Town Clerk,

Mr. J. E. Biddle, Deputy Town Clerk,
Mr. Rowland Harrris, Borough Controller,
Mr. T. F. Harvey, Borough Engineer,
Mr. T. Gilbert Evans, Assistant Overseer,
Dr. Duncan, Medical Officer of Health,
Mr. H. H. Southey,
Mr. and Mrs. W. R. Southey,
Mr. Llywarch Reynolds, solicitor,
Mr. R. J. Rhys, Llwydcoed,
Mr. W. L. Daniel,
Mr. W. Pritchard Morgan, Liberal
Candidate for Merthyr Borough,
Mr. and Mrs. J. T. Vaughan,
Mrs. Dowding, London, who lent some exquisite specimens of old Egyptian work, comprising mummy cloths, jewellery, sandals and shoes, coins, glass and pottery,
Dr. Webster and the Misses Webster,
Mr. Isaac Williams, the Secretary of the Exhibition,
Mr. John Lloyd,
Mr. E. Price,
Mr. Bernascone,
Miss Mary Davies and many others.

"Suggested Permanent Art Gallery and Museum

At three o'clock the Mayor, Councillor F. T. James, who wore his chain and gown, said it gave him intense pleasure to declare the Exhibition open. With the exception of an Exhibition held at the Drill Hall in 1880, there had never been such an interesting function before that day. The Corporation fell in with a suggestion thrown out by himself to hold an Exhibition of Penry Williams's pictures at the Castle, and those present would agree that Cyfarthfa Castle was eminently suited for such a purpose. He trusted that the Council would convert that portion of the building into a permanent Art Gallery and Museum. (Applause.)

"During the last three weeks the Committee entrusted with the carrying out of the arrangements had worked exceedingly hard, and he was sure that all who visited the Castle would enjoy the result of their labours (hear, hear). That they had such a magnificent collection of pictures was largely due to the energetic secretary, Mr. Isaac J. Williams, the art master of the evening and technical schools, and also organiser of the evening continuation classes (applause). No better man could have been appointed to the position, and great credit was due to him.

"He (the Mayor) felt sure that such a collection of pictures, the work of a native of Merthyr, would surprise the public. A great many dealers in England would tell them that they had never heard of Penry Williams, but the pictures on view at the Castle were proof that if he was not a great genius, he was a great artist.

"Another object they had in view in holding this Exhibition was to show that Wales could boast of an artist besides Richard Wilson, and that Penry Williams was a native of Merthyr (applause). The Corporation were deeply indebted to the owners of the pictures produced by Penry Williams for lending them, and also for the loan of other pictures and art specimens.

"He (the Mayor) was very pleased to see the Lord Mayor and Lady Mayoress of Cardiff present that day. The Merthyr Corporation asked the Cardiff Corporation for the loan of Penry Williams's picture entitled *Festa of the Madonna del Arco at Naples*, and the Lord Mayor willingly granted the request, and wrote that he was delighted that that famous picture was to be exhibited in the town of the painter's birth.

"In conclusion, the Mayor expressed the hope that people of the Borough and the adjoining districts would pay the Exhibition a visit of inspection, for they would find ample enjoyment from an artistic point of view. The Mayor also reiterated the hope that the Corporation would keep these rooms for the purposes of an Art Gallery and Museum (applause).

"The Lord Mayor of Cardiff, Councillor Chappell, who was received with applause, said he was delighted to have the opportunity of being present at that ceremony. He trusted that such Exhibitions would be held every year, because no one could estimate the great amount of good they did. It was often said that the character of a family was portrayed by the pictures on the walls, and these Exhibitions would stimulate people to take an interest in art and do away with the specimens 'made in Germany'. (Laughter and applause.) There was something in the work of a good artist that was noble and elevating, and he was sure that future Corporations would continue the Exhibition so successfully started (applause). Councillor Chappell promised that at some future time the Cardiff Corporation would lend other pictures for the Merthyr Exhibition.

"There were many ladies and gentlemen who owned pictures and who were fond of telling their friends, 'I have in my house a picture of which there is no copy.' 'How many people would love to see those pictures,' was his reply. 'It would do your hearts good to lend them for an Exhibition such as this.' (Applause.)

A Revelation

Sir Thomas Marchant Williams, Stipendiary Magistrate, then moved a vote of thanks to the Mayor of Merthyr for his efforts in establishing such an interesting Exhibition. Sir Marchant said it was a revelation to most of those present, as it was to himself, although he was quite familiar with pictures, that so many of Penry Williams's pictures should be got together and placed in Cyfarthfa Castle. A hope had been expressed that this portion of the Castle would be permanently used for an Art Gallery and Museum. He (Sir Marchant) did not know of any better place in Wales for such a purpose. He spoke with bated breath in the presence of the Lord Mayor of Cardiff, but he honestly believed that Merthyr had given birth to a larger number of distinguished Welshmen than any other town in Wales.

"Taking away Richard Wilson, the immortal, they had remaining the two greatest artists, the living excepted, Joseph Edwards and Penry Williams, both born in Merthyr. Sir Marchant also drew attention to the picture entitled *Festa of the Madonna* and also the landscape of Lancaster, lent by Sir John Llewellyn. He sometimes used this simile, he referred people to the lines of Keats on the nightingale –

> 'Thou was not born for death, immortal bird,
> No hungry generations tread thee down.'

He asked his friends the meaning of these lines, and they could not tell him. Looking at the ladies present, he saw some beautiful costumes, lovely hats and beautiful frocks. 'Offer these ladies,' said Sir Marchant, 'all those dresses and hats next year, and they would not have them. They are hungry for a change.' (Laughter.) But the nightingale sang to Julius Caesar two thousand years ago, and to Ruth three thousand years ago, and the nightingale was like the pictures, they lived for generations, and Penry Williams's pictures would, if preserved, be admired in many generations to come (applause).

"Penry Williams was the son of a house painter, and Wilson was a mason, so that this Exhibition was a working-man's gallery. It showed what the sons of working-men could do if they were only given the chance. Nearly all the artists of Wales were sons of working men. It had been the dream of his (Sir

Marchant's) life to have an art gallery in his native town, ABERDARE. He admired the Mayor of Merthyr for the great work he had thrown into this Exhibition.

"He trusted these rooms at the Castle would be preserved for an Art Gallery and Museum, so that the working-men might benefit thereby.

"In conclusion, Sir Marchant Williams coupled with the vote the name of the Mayoress, who had materially assisted his Worship in getting together such a valuable collection of pictures.

"Alderman E. Morrell seconded the vote, and also referred to the valuable assistance rendered by Mr. Isaac Williams. He hoped in the near future that a secondary school, second to none in Wales, would be established in Cyfarthfa Castle, but at the same time he re-echoed the hope that that portion of the Castle would be reserved for an Art Gallery.

"The vote was carried with acclamation and the Mayor suitably replied.

"The visitors then followed the Mayor and Mayoress on a tour of inspection." (*Merthyr Express* 11.12.1909.)

C. Second Notice of Exhibition and Exhibits

"We are glad to be able to report that there has been a large attendance during the past week at the Art Exhibition, at Cyfarthfa Castle, and most of the visitors have been both surprised and pleased with the extent and quality of the exhibition. Since it was opened it has become evident that it would have been possible to have got very many more objects of interest of an artistic nature had the project been more widely known at first.

"That fact must give the Corporation encouragement for a repetition of their enterprise upon a larger scale at some future period, let us hope not very far distant.

"We would call attention to a small case of interesting objects, No. 10 in the catalogue of exhibits, in the hall, amongst which will be observed a china tea pot bearing the name of Clement Morris, Merthyr, 1788. It is lent by Mr. D. T. Alexander, of Cardiff, and a note states that it was made at Merthyr. This is the first time that we have heard of pottery of this kind, or any other, being made at Merthyr, but the name and date are burnt in the enamel surface, and whether that of the maker or a mere vendor it would be interesting to know.

"At the bottom of the case is a miniature portrait of Mr. George Scale of Llwydcoed lent by a descendant, Miss H. G. Scale. This was the Mr. Scale who brought a considerable amount of capital into Aberdare, which he invested in the iron trade and founded Llwydcoed Ironworks. His memory is commemorated in the name of an important hostelry at Aberdare, the Scale's Arms, and one of his descendants, the late Mr. E. W. Scale, who lived so many years at Troedyrhiw House, held the Office of registrar of births and deaths at Aberdare and died about twenty years ago (i.e., about 1889).

"In the Penry Williams gallery there is a picture, No. 15, of Mr. Scale's house at Llwydcoed. It stands alongside the public road and fifty years ago was in the occupation of the late Mr. R. H. Rhys.

"A picture of pathetic interest is a small water colour No. 24 of *My Father's Cottage in Merthyr Tydfil, South Wales*, the writing being in Penry's own hand. Nobody could identify the spot now, as it is a cottage in open country with no other houses near it. This picture was lent by Sir W. T. Lewis.

"No. 30 is a picture of *Merthyr Riots* bearing the date 1816 when Penry would be eighteen years of age. It is a crude work and its interest lies in its illustrating the degree of the painter's knowledge of his art at that time and as a pictorial record of the state of the 'Pentre' then. Most of the buildings in High-st., from Glebeland to Castle-st., had not been laid down, and opposite was an open field with a grand old withered oak tree, which old Merthyrians recently passed away remembered well. There were soldiers here on that occasion, so that the events must have presented some alarming features, though not so serious as those of a quarter of a century later.

"No. 38 is a charming little water colour, a view of Merthyr Valley from Cyfarthfa Castle, the perspective extending to Troedyrhiw, lent by Dr. Alfred James of Biggleswade. Two pictures lent by Mr. Rhys Williams of Miskin, No. 5, water colour, *Nymphs* done entirely in greens of different shades and a smaller one in oils *Steep Holmes*, No. 43, are a couple of gems. Many of the pictures are Italian subjects and show all the warmth of colour and national life peculiar to Italy. Amongst the local subjects are three very effective small paintings of waterfalls, Nos. 86, 89, 91, lent by Mr. J. W. Price of Neath. Mr. Charles Russell James has sent several; indeed as we remarked last week the James family together are the largest contributors to the gallery, their loans including some of the choicest oil paintings as well as water colours and pencil sketches. A pencil sketch of Mr. Huskinson, No. 39, lent by Mr. H. A. James is remarkably life-like; No. 83, portrait of Edward Williams and his wife (1825) are quaint miniatures lent by Miss Mary Davis.

"Number two gallery is devoted to other works and amongst them are three small Turners, Nos. 1, 5 and 10, lent by Mr. D. T. Alexander. They are so small that some people may wonder that the mighty painter of the gorgeous pictures of Venice and Carthage could bestow his time upon such trivialities, but the genius is in these tiny things the same as in the great ones.

"No. 2, *Edw Rocks*, by Tom Prydderch, lent by Mr. W. T. Rees, Aberdare, is a beautiful picture, that strikes one at once. The same artist has an *Old Abbey*, No. 16, lent by Dr. Webster, and another, No. 17, *Mountain Scene near Dolygaer* lent by himself, both fine pictures.

"No. 12, *Polperro, Cornwall* by E. M. Ward, R.A., lent by Dr. Webster, is a particularly fine painting, and so is No. 4, *Head of Loch Lomond*, lent by Mr. W. Griffiths.

"There are several admirable examples of David Cox's work, No. 20, lent by Mr. D. W. Jones, No. 33, *Carnarvon Castle*, lent by Mr. F. T. James, No. 34, *Scene in North Wales*, lent by Mr. F. T. James, and No. 35, *Moorland Scene*, lent by Mr. D. T. Alexander, all of which have remarkably beautiful sky effects.

"No. 24, *A Village Scene* by Peter Watson, lent by Mr. W. Griffiths, is a picture with much life in it. No. 25 is a picture of a Welsh woman by Mortimer Mempes, lent by Mr. F. T. James, Nos. 27 and 31, lent by Miss Mary Davis, are two small pictures of Napoleon, one a full-length portrait, standing, the other, representing the general on horseback crossing the Alps, a favourite subject of painters of the age.

"Mr. C. H. James of Cardiff has contributed several fine pictures to this room of which *The Clothes Basket*, No. 3, by Mrs. Allingham, is one that will stand looking at; but a finer picture is his *Capel Curig*, by David Cox. *Old Westminster*, No. 42, is another picture by Cox, of a different type, lent by Mr. F. T. James.

"In the next gallery we have the National Collection of water colour drawings from the National Gallery of British Art, Victoria and Albert Museum, South Kensington.

"These are noble pictures, not of large dimensions, but having such a wide range of subjects and treatments that every picture seems to represent something new. There are some Clarkson Stanfields, some belonging to the Townshend Bequest, and the Parsons Bequest; other gifts by different gentlemen to the Museum as examples of the finest work of British artists in water colours.

"A special descriptive catalogue is sold at a penny and it is well worth the while of the visitor to have this catalogue with him that he may know something of the history of the pictures.

"There are half a dozen glass cases occupying the window recesses of these two galleries, filled with objects of archaeological interest, lent by Mrs. Dowding, who is a collector enjoying special facilities for obtaining such objects. The curios are from Egypt, Palestine, Syria, Greece and Italy and illustrate art from its earliest stages of crude origins in the Stone and Bronze Ages, down to the fifth and sixth centuries A.D.

"An inspection of these relics of civilisations past inspires strange thoughts of the tremendous secrets lying at different parts of the earth's surface, buried, maybe, not so far beneath our feet as we may suppose, of the life and works of mighty races of whose existence we have no conception until these remarkable evidences come to light.

"The latest mystery of all is the unfolding of the gates of the tomb upon a race of men who flourished in Peru thousands of years before the Incas, and whose physiognomies and works point to a close family relation with the same races that flourished in the valleys of the Tigris and Euphrates about the same period, from seven thousand to ten thousand years ago.

"Fancy that! Where were boastful Britons then?"

(*Merthyr Express* 18.12.1909 p.9 col.3.)

D. Permanent Museum and Art Gallery proposed

"At a meeting of the Merthyr Corporation on Monday, the following letter was received from Mr. Isaac J. Williams, secretary of the Cyfarthfa Castle Exhibition and organiser of evening classes:

> " 'Gentlemen, I beg to report as follows:
>
> " 'The Exhibition was opened on December 7th, 1909, and up to today has been visited by 6,105 people, and 1,093 programmes have been sold. The total receipts to date amount to £38. The total number of exhibits is 376, including 101 pictures from the Victoria and Albert Museum, London. Having regard to the weather, the time of the year, and the General Election, I venture to think that the attendance is extremely satisfactory, and clearly shows the need of utilising the rooms at present used for the Exhibition for a permanent Art Gallery and Museum. The entrance hall and four rooms have been suitably coloured and fitted up in such a way as to enable them to be used as a permanent Gallery and Museum without any further initial expense.
>
> " 'The pictures and other items, lent by the various owners will, ere

long, have to be returned, AND I WOULD SUGGEST THAT THE CORPORATION SHOULD NOW CONSIDER THE ADVISABILITY OF CONVERTING THE PRESENT EXHIBITION INTO A PERMANENT ART GALLERY AND MUSEUM FOR THE TOWN BY ADOPTING THE MUSEUM'S ACT.

" 'In my opinion, the Corporation will have no difficulty in obtaining the consent of a large number of owners of the exhibits to leave the same on loan for an indefinite period, and apart from this, the Victoria and Albert Museum authorities are prepared to allow their existing collection to remain until the 1st of March 1910, after which date another loan collection can be obtained for a period of twelve months, provided the Corporation determine to maintain a Museum upon the lines mentioned, they will also obtain a grant in aid towards the purchase of approved objects of art. In fact, every inducement is offered by the Board of Education to encourage local authorities to provide this public need. I would also point out that in the event of Cyfarthfa Castle being converted into a Municipal Secondary School, an Art Gallery and Museum would be an additional and very important adjunct.

" 'I have been fortunate enough to secure the transference of two valuable pictures by Penry Williams, from the Nottingham and Leicester Art Galleries to Merthyr. These pictures, which are the property of the trustees of the National Gallery, and are worth £250, may remain on loan if we have a permanent Gallery, and I (Isaac J. Williams) have no doubt that we can obtain further assistance from the same source.

" 'As a further nucleus the following are already in the possession of the Corporation:

1. Two cases of Roman remains found at Penydarren Park.
2. One case of fossils.
3. One case of Egyptian relics, given by Mr. H. W. Southey.
4. Bust of Sir John Guest.
5. Bust of Col. D. R. Lewis.
6. Engravings of Joseph Edwards's works, given by Mr. Washington Morgan.
7. Monumental model by Joseph Edwards, given by Mr. Washington Morgan.
8. Two engravings of work by Joseph Edwards, given by Mrs. William Harris.

9. Views of old Merthyr, given by Mr. D. T. Alexander.
10. Portrait of Mr. Thomas Evans.
11. Portrait of Mr. Henry Richards.
12. Collection of medals by Mr. Chas. Morgan Davies.
13. Pictures by Penry Williams, donated by Mr. E. B. Nash.
14. Collection of butterflies, moths and insects, Mr. G. Fleming, M.A.
15. Model, Death of Achilles

and many more have been promised.

" 'The following are by way of loan for an indefinite period:

1. Two paintings by Penry Williams, National Gallery.
2. Painting by Penry Williams, Mr. Frank Treharne James.
3. Engraving by Penry Williams, Mr. I. J. Williams.
4. A set of Cruickshank etchings, Mr. I. J. Williams.
5. Enamel, I. J. Williams.
6. Coloured print, Cyfarthfa Ball, F. T. James.
7. Coloured print, Merthyr, Mr. J. T. Vaughan.
8. Case of coins, Mr. B. R. S. Frost.
9. Case of coins, Mr. C. M. Davies.
10. Two cases, Egyptian and Greek vases, etc., H. H. Southey.
11. Persian tiles, H. H. Southey.
12. Case of medals, C. M. Davies.
13. Old prints of Merthyr, C. M. Davies.
14. Old manuscripts, C. M. Davies.
15. Engraving of Merthyr, I. J. Williams.
16. Pictures by Mr. T. Prydderch and many other promises.

" 'In conclusion I can only hope that I have made a very clear case, and trust that the Corporation will take advantage of the opportunities they possess, and thereby encourage all who are interested and proud of their town to come forward and adorn Cyfarthfa Castle with their interesting and valuable possessions, thereby giving pleasure to the whole community.

" 'I am, gentlemen, your obedient servant, Isaac Williams, secretary.'

"The Mayor, Councillor F. T. James, said he thought the report very satisfactory, and he was not sorry for the part he had taken in the Exhibition. Notwithstanding that the Exhibition was opened in the winter months, it had been highly appreciated.

"*Councillor W. Lewis, Treharris*: The receipts do not come to much.
"*The Mayor*: We do not look upon it as a paying concern.
"*Alderman D. W. Jones*: Some people have not got any ambition above £..s..d.

"The Mayor said the time had come when the Council must utilise the suite of rooms, now used in the Castle for the Exhibition, for the benefit of the inhabitants of the Borough. He, therefore, gave notice to move that the Museums Act, 1891, be put into force (hear, hear).

"Mr. Isaac Williams will be glad to hear from readers who have works of art or specimens suitable for the Museum, which they will be prepared to lend or give to the Corporation." (*Merthyr Express* 22.1.1910 p.9 col.2.)

E. Brief Notes on William Williams, Father of Penry, and Mention of Tomos Glyn Cothi

"Now that every man, woman and child has an opportunity of inspecting the splendid collection of paintings by the eminent artist Penry Williams, I take it that every item connected with the life of the painter may be of interest.

"It is not generally known that William Williams, the father of Penry, was not only a house painter, but a sculptor of no mean repute. In the vestibule of the Old Meeting House, Aberdare, a fine marble tablet has been put up to the memory of the Rev. Thomas Evans, generally known by his bardic name, Tomos Glyn Cothi, who died on the 29th January, 1833. On the lower right hand corner of the tablet may be seen the name of the sculptor, 'W. Williams, Fecit'.

"W. Williams may be supposed to be an expert in his profession, as this tablet was erected at the expense of a few friends of the noted bard, and it is only natural to think that the subscribers would look about for the most competent man to execute the work.

"Tomos Glyn Cothi was a very remarkable man. As his name implies, he was born in a small cottage on the banks of the Cothi, near Brechfa, Carmarthenshire, on the 20th of June, 1766. He was brought up as a weaver, but being a man of more than ordinary abilities, he read widely both in English and Welsh, and soon became known as the most accomplished man in the locality.

"About the year 1797, as Tomos was strongly suspected of having espoused the teachings of Tom Paine, he was closely watched and, furthermore, for having sung a song which savoured of the spirit of the

French Revolution, the bard was arrested by the spies who patrolled the neighbourhood. Tomos was taken to Carmarthen, where he was placed in the pillory, afterwards he was sent to gaol, where he remained three years.

"Tomos was a voluminous writer, and a good hymn writer, several of his works having been written by him during the term of his incarceration.

"It is said that while he was compelled to stand in the pillory on one of the squares of Carmarthen town, his two daughters walked all the way from Brechfa, about twelve miles, and stood by their father, one each side of him, for many hours.

"When about forty-eight years of age Tomos was invited to take charge of the Unitarian Church at Aberdare, and there he remained until his death.

"Penry's father executed this beautiful tablet to perpetuate the memory of one who showed great zeal in promulgating his opinions amidst trials and discouragements, and who was indefatigable in his devotion to the cause of civil and religious liberty." (*Merthyr Express* 15.1.1910 p.6 col.6)

W. Williams, Fecit, 1911

"This legend is now, among other places, at Gellionen, at the bottom of the following inscription:

> 'This marble is dedicated by a few friends to the memory of the Rev. Thomas Morgans, for more than thirty years Pastor of Protestant Dissenters at Blaengwrach; who in his benevolence of heart, humility of mind, and purity of doctrine, exhibited the character of a sincere follower of Jesus Christ. Rejecting all human creeds, he believed in one God, and one Mediator between God and man, the man Christ Jesus. He died, not leaving many equals behind him, October 17th, 1813, aged seventy-six.
>
> W. Williams, Fecit.'

"The Rev. T. Morgans was ordained on the same day as Edward Evans (1716-1798), Aberdare, at Blaengwrach, July 1st, 1772.

"W. Williams, I believe, was the father of Penry Williams, the eminent painter. S.N.S." (*Merthyr Express* 26.8.1911 p.12 col.1.)

F. Winter Art Exhibition drawing to a close

"We would remind our readers that the greater portion of the magnificent collection of pictures, sculpture etc. now on view at Cyfarthfa Castle will ere long have to be returned to their respective owners.

"Therefore everyone should take advantage of the short time remaining to pay a visit to what may rightly be termed the people's Art Gallery and Museum, which they will find to be extremely instructive, artistic and comfortable.

"The gem of the Penry Williams collection, *The Festa of the Madonna* was painted by the gifted artist at Rome in 1872, when he was over eighty years of age.

"On Thursday, January 28th, there will be a promenade concert, further particulars of which will be found in our columns next week. Up to the present the Exhibition has been visited by 5,400 people."

(*Merthyr Express* 15.1.1910 p.10 col.1.)

G. Concert for Winter Art Exhibition

"On Thursday night a promenade concert was held at Cyfarthfa Castle in connection with the Winter Art Exhibition, and proved a great success. The entertainment was organised by the hon. secretary of the Exhibition, Mr. Isaac J. Williams, who is deserving of praise for his efforts to please all tastes. In the absence of the Mayor, Councillor F. T. James, the Deputy-Mayor, Councillor Isaac Edwards, presided, and on behalf of the Corporation thanked the artistes for their services, which were given gratis. These concerts, Mr. Edwards said, had done much to popularise the Exhibition.

"The following was the programme:

Overture, *La Flanders*, Mr. Llewelyn's orchestra;
song, Miss Anita Powell;
concert solo, *Cleopatra*, with orchestra accompaniment,
Mr. H. Llewelyn;
piccolo solo, *Tarantella*, with orchestral accompaniment,
Mr. J. Bollen;
overture, *La Diadem*, orchestra;
violin solo, *La Traviata*, Mr. P. H. Llewelyn;
song, Mrs. Willis;
pianoforte solo, Mr. Ll. Nicholas;
song, Mr. D. Daniels, accompanied by
Mr. E. M. Davies, Balaclava Road, Dowlais;
selection, *White Queen*, orchestra;
solo, *Lost Chord*, Mr. H. Llewelyn;

violin solo, *Salut d'Amour*, Mr. P. H. Llewelyn;
selection, *William Tell.*". (*Merthyr Express* 12.2.1910 p.6 col.6.)

H. The Museums Act Adopted,
Permanent Museum and Art Gallery Founded

"On Sunday last, the day being fine, no fewer than 1,117 persons visited the Art Gallery at Cyfarthfa Castle. Now that the Museums Act has been adopted by the Corporation steps are being taken to procure additional gifts or loans of art treasures, and the secretary, Mr. I. J. Williams, will be pleased to receive offers. Letters should be addressed to Mr. Williams at the Town Hall or Cyfarthfa Castle." (*Merthyr Express* 5.3.1910 p.10 col.2.)

Discussion

A major Art Exhibition was organised at the Drill Hall, Merthyr Tydfil, in 1880. This Exhibition was referred to in *Merthyr Historian*, Volume Seven, 1994, in the context of William Menelaus's contributions to it.

Shock waves were experienced in Merthyr Tydfil when Menelaus donated many of his paintings from the 1880 Merthyr Art Exhibition to the newly formed Cardiff Free Library, Museum and Schools for Science and Art, in 1882. At that time, there was no Art Gallery, Free Library, Museum or Town Hall available in Merthyr Tydfil, in which to house and display such a collection of paintings.

The next major Art Exhibition in Merthyr was this 1909-10 Winter Art Exhibition, held at newly-acquired Cyfarthfa Castle. It was an outstanding success and this success built up an unstoppable movement for the foundation of a permanent Museum and Art Gallery.

The Corporation adopted the Museums Act, which came into operation on the first of April, 1910.

The Victoria and Albert Museum Authorities sent down an entirely new Collection and, with generous help from a few patrons, a good start was made towards establishing a permanent Museum and Art Gallery.

Councillor Frank Treharne James made a major contribution towards the establishment of Cyfarthfa Castle Museum and Art Gallery. He was Chairman of the Cyfarthfa Castle Museum Committee in 1914.

Major Frank Treharne James, M.B.E., V.D. (1861-1942), was a member of the Council of the National Museum of Wales.

A bronze head, eleven and a half inches high, of F. T. James, sculpted by Sir William Goscombe John, was exhibited in the Royal Academy of

1936. This bronze head was presented to the National Museum of Wales by Mrs. Dalzell Rees.

The fascinating story of the first ten formative years of Cyfarthfa Castle Museum and Art Gallery is the subject of ongoing research.

The Wealthiest Place and the Poorest Ministry

by ROGER L. BROWN

Some notes on the history of the parish of Merthyr Tydfil before Disestablishment from the files of Queen Anne's Bounty and the Ecclesiastical Commission

The parish of Merthyr Tydfil, by the 1900s, was probably the wealthiest living in Wales, if not in the whole of the Church of England. Bishops suspected its wealth, but because this was hidden in glebe rentals and incomes its value was never adequately revealed. Throughout the whole of the 19th century the parish was served by four incumbents. George Martin Maber had been appointed rector in 1795 but for much of his ministry he was an absentee incumbent living at Swansea. His successor, the Scot James Colquhoun Campbell, who served the parish from 1844-59, was believed to have owed his appointment to a relationship with the second Marquis of Bute, the patron of the parish. His ministry was a remarkable one during which the parish was built up after years of neglect, and his success was partly measured by his appointment to the bishopric of Bangor in 1859. Lord Derby, who claimed the right of patronage to Merthyr as the prime minister who had elevated Campbell, appointed John Griffith of Aberdare in his place. A man with a national reputation, a strong and assertive controversialist, Griffith continued Campbell's work, and perhaps all the more so because of his passion for social justice and his concern for the Welsh people of the parish. His death was deeply mourned, and though the parish wished his son Charles to be appointed, the Bute trustees, W. H. Clever and Lewis Jones, Anglo-Catholics to a man, preferred Daniel Lewis, who remained in the parish until his death in 1920. Under him the parish stagnated and almost disintegrated, and his ministry, or rather lack of it, in the parish, became a deep embarrassment to the diocesan and church authorities on the eve of disestablishment.

This paper takes note of the correspondence and files of Queen Anne's Bounty and the Ecclesiastical Commission. As such it is selective in subject, though rich in detail, and forms a contribution to, rather than a definitive study of, these four incumbencies.[1]

Queen Anne's Bounty was founded by the queen of that name. Informed by interested parties that she was in receipt of income confiscated from the Church, namely the first fruit and tenths income, which the clergy had paid to the Pope before the Reformation and which had been regarded thereafter as part of the royal income, the Queen gave it back to the Church. A survey was made of all the livings in the country and their incomes, and those who were under a certain figure, starting off with £10 in annual value but increasing as the years went by, were augmented by lot with £200 each. This money was invested in land and the income from that land became part of the income of the clergy of that parish. However, a prior claim was given to those livings which were augmented by a private individual with £200 or more, and which received [at first] an equal grant from the Bounty. The same requirement also applied to these livings that the money be invested in land. At a later date the governors were permitted to lend money by way of mortgage for the building of parsonage houses.

The Ecclesiastical Commission was established in 1835, and one of its tasks was to reform the finances of the Church. It did this, in part, by equalising the episcopal incomes, and by regulating the incomes of the cathedral bodies. Although life interests and existing leases were respected, a substantial sum became available each year from the surplus revenues. This income was applied by the commission to populous parishes in industrial areas. The income of the clergy of these parishes was increased by augmentations and grants; grants were given for the building of parsonages and [in the earlier days] churches, and for the stipends of assistant curates. The assistance given by the commissioners to this parish and others in south Wales was crucial in the development of the Church during the 19th century.

The Parish in 1832

A Parliamentary enquiry into the revenues of the Established Church took place in 1832. It led to the creation of the Ecclesiastical Commission, and the gradual reform of the Church's financial and administrative structures. Each incumbent was sent a printed questionnaire. G. M. Maber, incumbent of Merthyr Tydfil since 1795 thus duly reported that his living was a rectory in the patronage of the Marquis of Bute. A population of 26,000 was served on one curate who received a stipend of £143. In addition Maber mentioned a stipend of £20 paid towards the salary of a cleric who served the chapel of ease which was "patronised" by the owner of the Dowlais Ironworks. The parish church held 2,000 people, the chapel of ease at Dowlais 450. There were full Sunday services in each church, and these services alternated between the English and Welsh languages. The rectory house had been used by the curate for the previous three years, but was now let to a respectable tenant, one Mr. Lewis. By this Maber made clear he was an absentee, though he was happy to declare his income at £884 gross and £675 net. Merthyr Tydfil was thus one of the wealthiest parishes in the diocese as well as one of the most neglected.

This substantial income was made up of the tithe income of £448, income from the rents of the built-up parts of the glebe land, £270, the "butchers' shambles" which produced £40, and the letting of a field and gardens at £45, £20 in Easter offerings and £60 in surplice fees. The outgoings consisted of the poor rate of £128, collection of tithe and rent at £60, repair of chancel £3 and other rates and taxes which brought the total to £209. Maber, in response to the question about the future prospects of the parish, mentioned that if the depression in the iron works continued then his income would be much diminished as the poor rate would increase substantially. In all it might mean a drop of ten per cent in his net income.

A more substantial loss to the parish of Merthyr came in 1837 when the new parish of Dowlais was formed from it. In order to endow the new parish, one fifth of the tithe and glebe income of Merthyr was settled on the rector of Dowlais. It was a situation which was to give rise to considerable difficulties at a later date.

The rector of Merthyr also lost part of his income when new districts or parishes were formed from the mother church, whose incumbents became entitled to the surplice fees rather than the "rector". Campbell thus inquired in a letter to the commissioners regarding the new district of Cyfarthfa on 7th May, 1857, as to whether any compensation for the loss of these fees might be provided for himself and his successors. One may well feel it was a cheeky request judging by the income of the parish, but nevertheless it was made. Claiming that his average fees were £118 for the six years to 1857, he alleged that since the consecration of Cyfarthfa church these fees had been reduced to £98, a loss of £19. But Cyfarthfa's fees only amounted to £3.17s.6d, though John Howell, its incumbent, noted in a letter of 25th February, 1859, that his poor congregation expected more from him than he could obtain from them, hinting thereby that he sometimes ignored charging fees to his poorer parishioners. It seems Campbell, removed from them in every way, allowed no such concession. The matter appears to have been dropped thereafter.

St. David's Church

St. David's Church had been consecrated on 8th September, 1847, as a chapel of ease to the parish. The site had been conveyed to the commissioners from the glebe of the parish by Campbell and Rector Jenkins of Dowlais. Jenkins was required to give his consent as he was entitled to part of the income of the parish of Merthyr. The site had been reserved originally for a rectory house, but one W. Davies of Merthyr, a local solicitor, writing to a Treasury official in June, 1844, noted that since the previous incumbent's death the present rector wished to build elsewhere, but Maber's conveyance of the site to the Commissioners for Building New Churches for the purpose of building a rectory could equally stand for the building of a church.

Nevertheless, the site was reconveyed to the Ecclesiastical Commissioners as noted above. The church cost £4,109, to which the Church Building Commissioners had granted £1,150 on condition it had 1,200 seats; £150 came from the drawback on the import duty paid on the timber used in the building; the Incorporated Society gave £700; Alderman Thompson, a London industrialist with substantial local interests offered £200; and a local committee raised £1,497, leaving a large amount to be found. Separate estimates were requested for the main church and for the building of the tower, due to these financial difficulties. Thus S. Daniels of Crickhowell tendered £3,832 plus £671 for the tower, and Thomas Brooks of Bristol £4,630 and £400 for the tower. Daniels won the contract. Half the seats were required to be free and unappropriated for ever. The completion of the church brought to an end a very stormy period in the history of the Church in Merthyr.

The building of the church had been first suggested in 1842 when a committee had been set up with one Thomas Williams as its secretary. This committee concluded that a church seating 1,000 people was required which could be increased if necessary to 1,240 by use of galleries. The cost was estimated at £3,520, and of that sum the committee itself had obtained £1,950, but this seems to have included the promise of two large sums from various interested societies. The Incorporated Church Society had offered a grant of £500 on the understanding that half the seats would be free, and a further grant of £1,000 was promised by the Church Building Commissioners on condition that seating was available for 1,200 persons. It also appears that various, but vague, promises of financial assistance had been made by some of the local ironmasters, which were conditional upon various details being allowed, such as the number of people the church would seat. The site, of course, was free of charge, being part of the parish glebe. The committee, however, soon began to realise that the cost of the building would leave a substantial deficit, and it expressed considerable concern on this account. In addition the architect, Thomas Wyatt, wished to have a spire and seating for 1,500 people, but these items would cost an additional £1,200. The parish church, the committee noted in one of its applications for grant aid, could seat 855 people on a basis of eight inches per person but could not be extended, while the chapel at Dowlais seated 450, but had become a separate parish in 1839. This was the total church accommodation for a parish of 25,000 people. The Marquis of Bute, as patron of the living, in a letter of 2nd August, 1843, expressed considerable annoyance that the promoters of this new church were ready to spend £3,400 on a building which would only seat 1,200 people. As an evangelical, he was clearly concerned that sufficient accommodation should be found for people in the churches of his patronage. Furthermore, as a magistrate, he believed that church attendance helped establish a moral society. Bute thus argued that the planned seating accommodation should be doubled, although even then there would still be insufficient space for the needs of the parish. The promoters, he wrote, should knock off every ornament and have a plainer style of architecture than the decorated style. Such economy would enable them to build a church seating at least 1,500 people. "It may be observed," he concluded, "that there is hardly any place in the Kingdom where a showy building would be so entirely thrown away as in Merthyr."

Wyatt's design allowed for the seating of 1,038 people in the main church and in a western gallery, but in a letter of January, 1844, he noted the pressures being placed on him via the Church Building Commissioners and the Incorporated Society by two of the local ironmasters. They had threatened to withdraw their subscriptions unless galleries were added to the transepts in order to increase the seating to 1,200 people. Beyond that, he argued, the design would admit of no further increase. To the arguments of Lord Bute and Mr. Hill, one of the ironmasters, that he should have a design allowing 1,200 on the ground floor and an additional 300 seats in two galleries, Wyatt responded by saying that the necessity of such an increase should be proved to exist. There was disagreement too about the need for a spire, and Wyatt rebutted that one by stating that he believed the subscribers preferred a tower. All this was taking place against a backcloth of industrial depression in the iron trade, as Thomas Williams reminded the Building Commissioners on 1st April. The requisite funds were not available and he felt that the plans had to be reduced and modified. Wyatt disagreed, feeling that the depression meant that tenders might be lower than otherwise and savings would be made on that account, though he was prepared to cut out the south porch and vestry from the plan. At the same time it was noted that there were other costly proposals before the parishioners which would require equally generous giving, namely the building of a new parsonage house and the extension of the churchyard, the existing one not being "commensurate to the wants of the place".

Campbell, now appointed rector, pointed out a further argument in October, 1844, which does not appear to have been mentioned beforehand. It was the great desire, he wrote, to separate the Welsh and English congregations. "This is universally agreed upon by all the clergy and competent persons connected with the District. At present we are obliged to have four services each Sunday in the parish church, two of which are at inconvenient times." He noted, too, that some, probably the Welsh congregation, felt themselves "ill-considered", and this was causing "great dissatisfaction and jealousy". The new church would be for the English congregation and the parish church for the Welsh. The query as to whether this new church was to be the basis of a new parish was answered by saying that it was built too near the "mother church" to be suitable as a new district or parish church, and in any case the rector of the parish ought to provide for both services. Furthermore, this division of languages would work more effectively than any local division "by God's blessing". Quoting his bishop he suggested that this new church would be far fitter for the superintendence of the incumbent than the old parish church. Jenkins, the rector of Dowlais, he added in a later letter of 7th February, 1845, indicating that the matter was being given ample consideration by the Board, also felt that this was not the site for a district church. If that was required they were prepared to exchange this site for one at a greater distance from the parish church. The Board eventually accepted all these arguments, Campbell clinching the arguments by writing as late as 23rd July, 1847, that Lord Bute was most agreeable to the recommendations that St. David's should be a chapel of ease in the parish of Merthyr Tydfil rather than a district church. It was also agreed that the right of nominating a minister to serve it should be vested in the incumbent of the parish, for the Marquis was "most anxious that the two churches should be as far as possible under the same management". This, however, was theoretical, for in effect the minister of this church was also the incumbent of the parish!

At the end of the day the estimated costs exceeded the amount raised by £532, and consequently modifications had to be made to the plans. The spire was abandoned. Omitting the doors to the pews saved £60; using one coat rather than two of oak stain on the roof timbers saved £58; a bell turret instead of a wooden lantern reduced costs by a further £20, and in all the work was reduced by a sum of £341. However, the church was duly consecrated and opened, though not without one mishap. Wyatt noted in March, 1848, that an accident had nearly destroyed the vestry, but the builder had made it good at his own expense.

The Burial Ground

A vestry meeting held at eleven in the morning of the 6th May, 1845, empowered the churchwardens of the parish to raise a loan of £1,500. This was in order to purchase two acres of land at £500 per acre and pay the necessary costs of enclosing this land and making it a burial ground. This money was borrowed from one Edward Morgan, a local merchant, and repayment was to be made over a period of ten years from the church rate, at £170 per annum capital and interest of five pound per cent. A later vestry increased this loan to £1,700. This churchyard was almost redundant by the time this debt had been paid, for it was closed by an Order in Council of 7th April, 1854, having been fully utilised.

Curates for the Parish

John Griffith, writing on 12th January, 1863, from the rectory which was still known as Gwaelod y Garth, applied to the Ecclesiastical Commissioners for a grant for a curate, understanding that they now gave such grants. He hoped that this favour would be extended to him as it was already being received by his neighbours at Dowlais, Aberdare and Gelligaer. He had four curates for his vast parish. Two gentlemen subscribed £50 between them towards the cost of one of these curates, and another £50 came from what Griffith described as a precarious source which might be ended at any time. A further sum of £50 came from a church society [probably the evangelical Church Pastoral-Aid Society], in order to meet that £50 given by the two gentlemen, but he had to find £20 as a return grant to that society, and if he failed to do so he had to make up that sum from his own pocket. This was at a time when the incumbent of a parish was legally obliged to find the stipends of his curates, rather than his parishioners.

The commissioners replied that such grants were only given from year to year, being known as temporary grants, and as the salaries of the curates appeared to be provided for they could make no grant. In their favour it may be argued that applications for these grants always exceeded the monies available. It seems to be a case, too, where Griffith offered too much information! The matter consequently dropped, but in June, 1866, Griffith requested a grant to meet the cost of three curates. He offered a sum of £160 in return for an equivalent grant; the arrangement being with these grants, if allowed, that the parish was required to find by some means or another half the sum of a curate's stipend, and sending it to the commission, who would meet that sum with an equal amount up to £60 per person, sending quarterly payments to the incumbent concerned. He noted that two curates were supported by grants of £50 each by the Church Pastoral-Aid Society and the Assistant Curates' Society, but with a population of between 28-29,000 he needed more staff than just four curates, for the anticipated ratio at this time was at least one clergyman to every 2,000 of population. His letter of the 21st June, 1866, continued to describe in graphic detail the circumstances of his parish:

> "The mother church has a class of population peculiar to itself, being the centre of a mining district comprising about 200,000 people. All the thieves and vagabonds of this huge district make Merthyr their headquarters. The great mass of them always return home before Sunday, to attend the Merthyr Market, and leave again by Tuesday. They live in three well known quarters entirely by themselves, namely severally 'China', Riverside and Cledrew. I have long wished for a

curate who had nothing else to do Sundays and weekdays but to work among this class."

Neither he nor his curates had time to do anything in these areas, having four churches to look after. But he believed from his "intimate acquaintance with them" that a curate, "a wise shepherd", devoted to the work he had described, would mean that "great good could be done among them". Griffith also laboured the point that while all his clerical neighbours received such grants, he did not.

His plea was successful, and he received a grant of £180 per annum to meet his equivalent benefaction – as it was termed. Although he had requested this grant for three curates, the commissioners were later to point out that the number was never specified, only it was to be not less than three. One imagines that even "China's" reputation was known in the Ecclesiastical Commissioners' board room at Dean's Yard. In his reply of deep thankfulness, Griffith noted that three curates would be paid at the rate of £100 to £120 each per annum, but he had difficulty in finding a third man, as curates were "very scarce in Wales".

This third curate did not materialise until June, 1868, two years later, and he received a stipend of £100. These three stipends cost in all £320, of which Griffith found half from the parish or his own resources, and the commissioners an equal half. This meant that their grant was £20 higher than what was actually paid. Rather than lose this sum Griffith requested the commissioners to allow him this amount as part of the stipend of a fourth curate who was paid £80 per annum, this stipend deriving from a grant given by a society which required a return grant or collection of £30 per annum, a recent increase of £10, as he noted with some annoyance! It was difficult to get any man for £80 but he could get a good man for £100, and in any case this additional sum for the curate serving the Tydfil Well district would be a great boon to him. Thankfully, because of the special condition of the grant already noted above, this was allowed.

Two years later Griffith wrote that the Society which gave him the £80 grant, the Assistant Curates' Society, was about to reduce it from that sum to £50. Its secretary, Edward E. Cutts, had written to him to say that the committee had 250 good cases pending and had been forced to practise the most rigid economy, and as his was a parish with "large claims upon the Ecclesiastical Commissioners" they hoped he would obtain the additional funding he required from them instead. This letter threw Griffith into a near panic for, as he wrote to the commissioners, in his present situation it was tantamount to withdrawing the grant altogether, though he needed that curate to minister to the Tydfil Well and Penydarren districts in order to work the parish properly. It would mean that in those two districts with a population of 5,000 he would be unable to hold any services whatsoever.

Griffith anticipated the commissioners' refusal to his request for this additional funding, for writing on the last day of 1870 he stated that he had told Cutts that he could not expect them to do more than they were doing already. He would have to pay the difference himself out of the income of living, which "though it is a heavy pull, yet such are the spiritual wants of this parish I must submit to it". And so he did. In 1874, for example, his four curates cost £420, one at £120 and three at £100. He had £180 from the commissioners' return grant, £50 from the Assistant Curates' Society, and he was forced to find £190 from his own resources or through subscriptions from his parishioners.

Not only did Griffith have difficulties funding his curates' stipends, he also had major problems finding suitable men. The problem was particularly acute for Welsh-speaking clergy. Always a champion of the underdog, it is not surprising that Griffith's needs as well as his charity encouraged him to assist clerical "lame ducks". This happened on a number of occasions. One was in 1869, when he wrote to the commissioners on the 5th October about one J. Peters Parry. Two years before, he wrote, Parry had "transgressed" [it was probably a drink problem], and the bishop had revoked his licence. But five months ago the bishop allowed him to resume duties provided he could find an incumbent ready to take him on a three-month trial. Griffith was prepared to assist, and had been told privately by Bishop Ollivant that if Parry was satisfactory he would licence him at the end of this probationary period. Welsh curates were scarce, continued Griffith in his letter, and there were some good points about this young man: "I fully believe him penitent and anxious to reinstate himself". But he wondered if the commissioners could accept this man as one of his grant-aided curates, for their rules specified that all such men had to be duly and properly licensed by the bishop of the diocese in which they worked. Parry was prepared to accept whatever Griffith could pay him if the commissioners refused Griffith's request, but in fact they surprisingly consented to this arrangement.

Alas, on 7th December, Griffith had to write to them again about this young man. "It is a sad business," he wrote. Notwithstanding the kindness the bishop had showed him he had had to be dismissed. It was a double pity for Griffith as Welsh curates were so scarce. He had to wait until February of 1870 to find a replacement. But this man, J. Lloyd Jones, only lasted until April. A letter of May, 1870, from Griffith to the commissioners noted that the bishop had stopped him from acting as curate in that parish for "the most urgent reasons", but without any further explanation. Clarification came later. Jones turned out to be a bad character to whom the bishop had only given temporary permission to officiate pending enquiry. "Nothing could have been ostensibly better than the way he behaved here," wrote Griffith, but the way he behaved after his dismissal "amply justified" the bishop's action. Both men had left behind debts, and Griffith asked if the commissioners would be willing to let him have any outstanding amounts of the stipend owing for their services as "it would be an act of justice and charity" to pay the poor widow with whom they lodged, "for I am grieved to say they both left her greatly in debt". The commissioners obliged, and the £14.7s.6d. which they sent just covered these debts. Griffith later wrote to say how pleased he was to hand over this money to this poor widow.

Other difficulties presented themselves. Welsh curates were not only scarce, but also demanded good stipends. This meant that sometimes a curate was not replaced for some time, and other arrangements had to be made about staffing the parish. The position was made more difficult still by the commissioners' ruling that for the purpose of a grant, continuous service had to be given, not just a locum provided for Sunday services. This ruling meant, for example, that between one July and December Griffith lost a portion of the grant, as a replacement curate could not be had until the December ordination. This particular man, Samuel Jenkins, was immediately given the charge of the Merthyr Vale district, five miles from the parish church, with a population of 5,000, including within its boundaries what Griffith described as a number of the largest collieries in England. One wonders what training he had before his ordination, and whether his rector was able to give him any effective help afterwards?

These grants were temporary grants, and incumbents were required to re-apply for them at the end of each year. There was no guarantee that a grant would be renewed, and incumbents often lived in fear that if the grant was lost they would have to find the additional monies required from their own scarce resources. As no reminders were sent it is not surprising that on many occasions incumbents forgot to re-apply for the grant, although the commissioners were often sympathetic to their pleas for forgiveness! Griffith thus had to excuse himself in 1875, although his apology was more a statement of fact than anything else. He had been feeding daily 5,000 children during the great lock-out of that time. He felt no apology was needed for his remissness, for this fact "will plead for me this time", he wrote. Indeed, one wonders if he did not anticipate some assistance from the commissioners' staff in what had become a national scandal. The great distress of 1878 also provided another excuse on a similar occasion.

By April, 1884, Griffith's own son, Charles, was curate in the parish. Later he was to become dean of Llandaff. A serious illness meant that he needed three months' rest, this having been recommended by the eminent London physician, Sir Andrew Clerk, whom he had consulted. The bishop had agreed to this leave of absence and had also agreed to the arrangements made for covering his duties, for Griffith was unable to find a resident locum, stating that the problem of finding a bilingual man "increased the difficulty much". The weekday duties of the invalid curate, consisting of three weekly services, the vitiation of the sick and surplice duties, as well as his turn every six weeks at the workhouse services, would be taken by Griffith himself or his curates. But his Sunday duty, including one sermon, would be covered by the vicar of Penydarren, an ecclesiastical district technically in the parish of Merthyr, for one guinea a week. Requesting the commissioners to sanction these arrangements, Griffith pointed out that by substituting his fourth curate – who was not grant aided – for his son he was still able to fulfil the conditions of the grant.

The commissioners declined. The arrangements proposed for the Sunday services were not sufficient to justify them paying the grant in order to reimburse the vicar of Penydarren for his services. A resident curate taking the Sunday services was essential before the grant could be paid. Griffith's action was swift. He recalled his son from leave, arguing that he could not risk losing these three curates' grants or closing down one church in his parish. He would not have consented to this arrangement had not the bishop sanctioned it, on the grounds that his son had so over-worked for the previous two years amongst the lowest class of people in the parish that his health had suffered. Charles thus returned after an absence of twenty-three days, but as he returned the commissioners wrote to say that Griffith had misunderstood their letter. There was no danger whatsoever that even one of his three grants would be at risk because of this temporary absence, and there was little doubt they would be renewed. What they had meant was that the portion of one grant for that particular leave of absence would not be paid. With gratitude Griffith dismissed his son for a further leave of absence in this almost ecclesiastical snakes and ladder game, and he was able to regain his health over a further period of six weeks' rest.

Daniel Lewis, the new rector, a Lampeter man and former vicar of Brynmawr, appointed by the Bute trustees because of his tractarian sympathies, endeavoured in the December of 1885, the year of his appointment, to obtain a further grant of £60 from the commissioners. This was for a man who would be based at Treharris. Here, Lewis argued, were some 4,000 people, four large nonconformist chapels, a school built by the local School Board for 750 children, but no clergyman. The local church people had obtained a temporary loan of a room for church services, and he felt they could raise among themselves about £30 each year towards the curate's stipend. The commissioners could not assist. They were not offering any new grants as they were increasing the value of those already given. Lewis re-applied for this additional grant in 1887, noting this time that the population of the parish was 24,000 while his income had been reduced through the fall in the value of the tithe [we notice later that while this was true it was hardly the full story!]. To show the commissioners the needs and wants of his parish Lewis sent them a printed report of the St. David's National Schools and a page from his parish magazine. This detailed the work and services of the parish.

The National Schools' report indicated that there were 700 children on the books with an average attendance of 492. The cost per head for running this school, based on this latter figure, was £1.11s.3d., compared with £1.15s.9½d. for voluntary schools generally and £2.5s.4d. for board schools. Lewis, having shown that he was running an economical parish, indicated that the government grants brought in £433, school fees £233, subscriptions £81 and the proceeds of a concert £20. The magazine extract noted the Sunday workhouse service, young communicants' classes, a ragged Sunday School, weekday services with sermons, St. Tydfil's Mission House [otherwise 2, Old Church Place, which Lewis noted elsewhere had been previously used by both Chartists and Mormons] with its two East Grinstead sisters, and his five curates and one licensed and probably stipendiary lay reader.

Impressed or not, the commissioners gave another negative response. Lewis tried again in 1888, stating that the curate was required for the Treharris part of the parish, where the mission church, seating 400 people, had been functioning since 3rd January, 1887. In this application he again stressed his loss of £70 in tithe income, the £250 he had to find from his own pocket to help support his five assistant clergy, while he added that he could not continue this number of curates indefinitely unless he received outside assistance. Once more the commissioners declined to assist him.

1890 came, and Lewis wrote to the commissioners in his annual application for the three curates' grants already in being that he now had six curates, but he would have to discontinue the services of one as he could not afford the cost. He was now paying £250 per annum towards their stipends so that his own stipend was hardly more than that of a senior curate. As this appeal failed to produce any effect, Lewis spelt out the position even more clearly during the following year. He now requested the additional grant for the district of Twynyrodyn where a church was about to be erected for its 3,000 population. The diocese had already voted him a grant of £25 towards the cost of a stipend. There were now five places of worship in the parish besides the workhouse chapel. The parish was twelve by five and a half miles in size, and had a population of 24,000. His stipend in 1887 was £647 gross and in 1889 £632, but after paying £270 in stipends and £163 in other outgoings he claimed that his own stipend was under £200 per annum in actual value. It took all his energies to raise the £2,300 required for the parish budget. His people were scattered, bilingual services were required, and more clergy needed to serve the parish. Another printed leaflet accompanied his request. This was an appeal for £12,000: £3,500 was required to restore the old parish church, £4,000 to build a new district church at Trelewis and £1,500 for its vicarage, £1,600 for Twynyrodyn, and £1,500 for school buildings.

Unsuccessful once more, Lewis reapplied the following year, 1892. He now had two grants from two diocesan societies for a clergyman at Twynyrodyn of £25 and £30, but more was needed. It was obviously grossly unfair, he inferred, that his parish with a population of 24,000 had only three grants, while the parish of St. John's, Pentrebach, whose incumbent William Green had recently died, had two churches, three curates and a population of between 8 to 10,000. One of these curates was supported by an endowment of £200 per annum given by the late Anthony Hill, and the other two received commissioners' grants. He clearly hinted that one of these grants should be transferred to his parish. The commissioners' reply indicated that Lewis had been given inside information. They could not take on any new grants but in the event of a lapsed grant in some other parish of his diocese they would reconsider his application. Alas, Bishop Lewis of Llandaff did not support this particular application for a transfer of grants.

Next year came, and with it the annual renewal of his request for this fourth grant. All the usual arguments were employed, population, language, size of parish and number of churches, although now he also specified a falling off in the surplice fees of the parish because of the opening of a registrar's office in the town for marriages and the opening of a new public cemetery. The following year, 1894, found Lewis with a novel argument. He now advocated a local claim as the commissioners had royalties from the Plymouth Coal and Iron Company, via the Llywel glebe, but the commissioners declined to accept this as a local claim for the parish of Merthyr. Although in 1896 Lewis could hardly plead poverty, having placed £2,500 from the sale of his glebe land with the commissioners in trust for his benefice, he still maintained he found it difficult to make ends meet, having to spend £400 on repairs to the rectory. A negative answer was returned as usual by the commissioners. In the following year Lewis fell into some trouble about the existing curates' grants. An alert bishop noted that one of the curates whose stipend was fixed at £120 had only received £100. Lewis argued that he had deducted the missing money for the board and lodging he had provided for that curate at his rectory, but this, he was told, was a private arrangement that had nothing to do with the grant money. The certificate sent to the commissioners, countersigned by the bishop, had to show that the full amount of the promised stipend had been paid to the curate.

Treharris became a separate parish in 1900, and the bishop persuaded the commissioners to transfer one of Merthyr's three grants to this new district. Merthyr, he noted, had a population of 17,000 but a gross income of £600 [in fact it was much more], while the new parish had a population of 10,000 of whom 7,000 had been taken from Merthyr. This new agreement must have come as a rude shock to Daniel Lewis, who was being answered back in his own coin in respect of his suggestion for Pentrebach, and who had already re-applied for this fourth grant earlier that year. By this time he probably received little sympathy from the commissioners, for they had to send out constant reminders for him to renew the grant applications, and Lewis sending back to them outdated cheques for redating which he had failed to bank in time.

But further tribulations were to come for Lewis. In November, 1905, D. T. Griffith, vicar of Llantrisant, requested the renewal of his three grants from the commissioners and an additional grant. The commissioners were favourable, for the parish of Llantrisant extended into the Rhondda valley, but they felt this additional grant could only be allowed if another grant had lapsed in the diocese. Checking their references they discovered that Lewis had made no further applications for the renewal of his grants since November, 1902; one suspects that the hard-pressed clerks had simply given up the task of reminding him. He had failed, too, to send in the certificates of employment since 1903, although he was still receiving two grants. Statistics showed that Llantrisant had eight places of worship compared to Merthyr's five, though Merthyr had almost twice the population. Yet Llantrisant had one telling point about it, namely that it was in public patronage, while Merthyr was still in private patronage, that of the Bute trustees. By this time the official mood about private patronage had changed, and the commissioners along with many bishops were clearly unsympathetic to its continuance, also feeling that such patronage involved duties as well as privileges, particularly in providing financial assistance to the parishes concerned. They were also influenced by Bishop Pritchard Hughes' statement that "Llantrisant is a much more needy case". Perhaps they forgot he was a former incumbent of that parish! And so Lewis found himself after 1905 with but one grant for a curate from the commissioners. And for this situation he could only blame himself.

The Subdivision of the Parish

During May 1859, Rector Campbell wrote to the Church Building Commissioners requesting financial assistance in order to build a new church in his parish. This was for Troedyrhiw. He offered to give up his legal claim to the surplice fees of the district if it became a separate parish. The church, designed by John Pritchard, would have 305 seats, of which two-thirds would be free, and would cost £1,295 plus the ten per cent fee for the architect. The site had been given by the Hon. Robert Henry Clive, who had purchased it from the Plymouth estate, in which he probably had some interest. Subscriptions and grants, of which two of £50 each had come from diocesan societies, amounted to £783. By July, Clive was threatening to withdraw his offer as the commissioners were creating difficulties about the mineral rights, insisting that these should be included in the offer of the site, whereas Campbell pointed out that as the workings were at least 250-300 yards under the surface they could not affect the stability of the surface buildings. Eventually the matter was resolved by the commissioners conceding the point. The new church was thus consecrated on the 6th January, 1853, as a chapel of ease in the parish of Merthyr. Three years later the commissioners permitted a schoolroom to be built on a corner of the site, as this area had not been consecrated. Campbell had hoped that a parsonage would be erected on the same site, and that its cost would be met by the liberality of a gentleman. One wonders if this was Clive?

During 1865 Griffith, reading his church newspaper, the *Guardian*, noted that the Ecclesiastical Commission had devised new regulations for the endowment of new districts or parishes. Accordingly he wrote to them regarding the district of Penydarren in his parish. The church, seating 600 people, had been built by the present Bishop of Bangor, his predecessor, on land given by William Henry Forman, Esq., an iron merchant of Cheapside, London. A district containing a population of 6,000 had all but legally been assigned it, and a stipend for a clergyman had been provided from local sources and a grant from the Church Pastoral-Aid Society. Although the church had been built to the required standards of the commissioners, it had not been consecrated, and an endowment would be needed to provide an income for the new "vicar". There were considerable hold-ups with regard to Mr. Forman's title to the land, but eventually the commissioners were prepared to accept the 999-year lease he had passed over to the parish, and the bishop was thereby able to consecrate the church and the commissioners to endow Penydarren as a new district. And thus a new parish came into being.

By 1914 it was planned to establish two new districts from the existing parish of Merthyr. These were the areas of Merthyr Vale and Tydfil Well. Merthyr Vale had a population of 5,000. The services were held in a former coffee tavern which had been licensed for public worship. Land for a new church had been offered by the Rt. Hon. Amelico Lockwood, C.V.O., M.P., of Romford, a local landowner, and an appeal for £4,000 to build it had already been launched. Tydfil Well, also called All Souls' after the church it was proposed to build there, had a population of 3,000. Its church members met in a hired hall. But Bishop Hughes stated in 1910 that there was little prospect of any church being built in the latter area while it remained part of the parish of Merthyr Tydfil, a reflection, one feels, about the then incumbent, Daniel Lewis. Lewis had previously offered the commissioners the sum of £150 per annum to each district as an endowment. This money would come from his tithe rent charges and from the glebe rents, and was given subject to the provision that he could retain the patronage of these new parishes in his own hands. However, he had hitherto declined to sign the necessary deeds. Indeed, in 1913 Bishop Hughes had endeavoured to find out how these districts could be established legally without requiring the rector's consent and, finding there were ways and means, he probably brought some influence to bear upon Lewis. As a result, Lewis repeated his offer in 1914. At that time his income was assessed at £1,800 per annum, although £355 per annum would be taken from that sum at the next avoidance [vacancy].

By that date, however, the Disestablishment Act of 1914 had been passed, which disendowed the Church of all its property, save of its church buildings and contents, which it had obtained prior to 1662. Although the Act was postponed until the end of the War, which had broken out as the Act was passing through Parliament, its effects were immediate. It was thought that the glebe lands of the parish of Merthyr had belonged to the Church before that magic date of 1662, and so would be confiscated, as would the tithe rent charges, and the Act, moreover, prohibited any existing interests from being alienated. All that the commissioners were able to do, therefore, was to accept the sites offered for the churches, but not to form new districts, and they advised the rector to use the income he had promised, while it was still available [for he had a life interest in it], to employ curates instead. It was obviously unreasonable to form two new districts which might have to be dissolved within a few years' time, and such problems could only increase the difficulties of the Church in Wales when the Act came into force. It was felt better, all round, to leave the areas as part of the parish of Merthyr Tydfil.

After the War, however, the commissioners felt able, perhaps having taken expert legal advice, to endow new districts if this was accomplished before 31st March, 1920, the date of disestablishment. The Bishop of Llandaff pressed the case of these two districts, and the commissioners got on with the legal work involved. However, in the case of Tydfil Well they met difficulties. The land had been gifted to the Church by the South Wales Estates Company on condition that the promoters paid the legal costs of the conveyances. But in spite of many applications the promoter, the rector of Merthyr Tydfil, had not replied, and until these costs were paid the conveyance could not be sealed by the commissioners or the district established. Merthyr Vale was inaugurated, happily, but Lewis's prevarication lost the people of Tydfil Well both a church and a separate parish.

The Rectory Glebe and Income

Each year the rectors of Merthyr were required to pay to Queen Anne's Bounty the sum of £2.1s., being the annual "tenths". This represented the ancient tax once paid by the clergy to the Pope, but which Henry VIII had alienated into his royal coffers, and which Queen Anne had given to the Church, forming with these and other revenues Queen Anne's Bounty. Originally the tax represented ten per cent of the income of the parish, but the amount had been fixed by the King's Book of 1535 and, thereafter, in spite of inflation and the increase in the value of livings, it remained a static annual sum. It was the duty of the Bounty governors to collect, as much as it was the duty of the assessed clergy to pay their dues. We have seen elsewhere how this money was used to the good of the Church and the welfare of its clergy.

In view of what has already been written, it is hardly surprising that Daniel Lewis received reminder after reminder about these payments. However, in his latter years he arranged for these monies to be paid by what he described as his glebe estate office. A number of firms from time to time were entrusted with the handling of the glebe estate of the parish, now built over, and each one was described in official correspondence as the Merthyr Glebe Estate. In 1900 this business was handled by the Court Estate Office, in 1910 by one W. T. Jones, and from 1919 by Lewis Jones and Company, all of whom described themselves as Lewis's agents in these concerns.

Some examples of the rentals obtained from this estate are noted in the files of Queen Anne's Bounty. The Vulcan Hotel, part of the glebe estate, and which building had probably come into the possession of the glebe through the surrender of its lease, was leased for an annual rental of £200 in 1900 for 99 years – a good bargain for the lessee in any case, while the Castle Hotel and other sites were leased to A. J. Withers of New Hall, Bargoed, a theatrical proprietor, on a 99-year lease of £300 per annum for the first 21 years, and thereafter for £400, the lessees to keep the property in repair. It was probably the Vulcan Hotel which was mentioned in correspondence between the town clerk of Merthyr and the commissioners during January, 1915. The town clerk wrote that the churchyard, which had been closed in 1854, had had an entrance to it that had been "stopped up" in 1871 or thereabouts by an extension to a public-house, with the permission of Griffith. The responsibility for these closed churchyards had recently passed to the town council by transfer from the local government board, and his council was desirous of having the entrance restored to its original state. The commissioners replied that they did not agree that Griffith had either the power to give that permission or they the power to order what was requested by the council.

In 1896 freehold land belonging to the glebe was sold to the local [school?] Board for £2,500, and this money was handed over by Lewis to the commissioners to be held in trust for the benefice. He asked that the interest on this money, which probably went back to the date of the original agreement which had only just been ratified, amounting to £360, should be returned to him, as he had promised several subscriptions to the various funds in the parish on the strength of this income. He had promised £100 to the parish church tower and the same for its chancel and £50 towards the new church at Merthyr Vale. The agreement of 1839, by which one-fifth of the income of the parish was paid to the rector of Dowlais, operated here as well. The money was placed in stock and the dividends were sent half-yearly to Lewis, from which he was required to pay the appropriate share to the rector of Dowlais. But these dividends were sometimes cashed late or not at all, so that the poor rector of Dowlais continually wrote to the commissioners complaining he had not been paid and even suggesting he was being defrauded of this money by Lewis. In April, 1905, he wrote that he had had to go to the High Court to obtain payment. Between 1908-11 there was a substantial exchange of letters between Dowlais and the commissioners, with the rector of Dowlais making his usual complaints, and between London and Merthyr, with the commissioners stressing to Lewis the great inconvenience he was causing to them and others by not attending to his business. Cheques dated to July, 1903, were still uncashed in 1911, and on Lewis's death in 1920 a vast number of vouchers were forwarded by his executors to the commissioners for payment, dating from 1912 onwards.

The income from the glebe estate was considerable, but was hardly ever notified in the official returns. In 1856 the income was returned as follows: glebe land rented out £375, tithe income £429, and fees £80, and while this equalled £884, one-fifth of the regular income had to be given to the rector of Dowlais by the agreement of 1839. This reduced the Merthyr gross income to £707. The outgoings were equally considerable. Rates took £73, the collection of the tithe £40, the payment to the curates £180, the mortgage payment on the rectory £45 and the rates on the house £14, plus £2 for chancel repairs. The net income was therefore £353 net, although as the church authorities did not allow such items as house rates and curates' stipends to be regarded as legitimate deductions, the "official" net figure was correspondingly higher. The 1885 figures, based on a tithe rental of £427 and ground rents of £268, plus the rent of £12 from the twelve acres of land on the farm called Cwmsaybran near Treherbert, Rhondda,[2] were a little lower. However, the renewal of leases and the steady growth of building on the glebe estate brought Lewis a considerable income, but it was very difficult to find out its actual value, as Lewis kept matters close to his heart. For example, he returned only his tithe income to the commissioners, but not that of the glebe land. No wonder the rector of Dowlais felt defrauded. After disestablishment the capital value of the Merthyr glebe estate was said to be in the region of £100,000. At the then current rates of return Lewis must have received at least £3,000 per annum from this estate, plus his other sources of income, as compared to a bishop who received £5,000 with far more substantial outgoings. Thus the parish of Merthyr Tydfil was one of the richest livings in the whole of the Church of England.

In 1913 thc commissioners were undoubtedly surprised by an offer from Lewis to make an apportionment of the income of his parish, which would come into effect on either his resignation or death. This was on the eve of disestablishment and one wonders, cynically, if Lewis was really making an empty gesture to ease his conscience, for much of this money would be lost through the disendowment clauses of the subsequent legislation. On the other hand, Bishop Hughes had been putting great pressure on Lewis regarding the subdivision of his parish, and possibly had discovered that the income of the parish was far, far greater than he or anyone else had imagined. The bishop would have regarded the retention of such an income by a single individual as immoral when compared with the poverty of many local incumbents.

The rules only allowed Lewis to favour benefices in the same patronage as his own parish, that is, of the Bute trustees. And thus it was agreed that at the next vacancy of the parish, three of the other Bute parishes would benefit. Aberdare would benefit to the tune of £160 per annum, Roath by £130, and Neath by £50, bringing all these livings to an average annual income of £400. In addition the two districts were to be established immediately, requiring another £300. In spite of these deductions the value of the living would still be considerable, although how much of this income would survive disestablishment was never certain. As Lewis died in October, 1920, after the date of disestablishment, this scheme was lost in the general financial restructuring of the Church in Wales.

Problems and Disputes

Lewis had other problems besides these financial ones! A letter of his to the commissioners of November, 1887, noted that the Liberationists had appointed a parish warden at the previous Easter vestry who was demanding a say in the disbursement of the offertories at St. David's Church. The commissioners ducked. It was not a matter on which they could comment. A further dispute occurred in this church during 1893-4. One Mr. Dunstan of Penydarren Park complained to the commissioners about the pew rents in this church. Were the wardens correct in placing the free seats on the worst side of the aisle? In fact there were only 110 rented pews, and the income of £70 which they provided in 1891 was used to pay for the verger and organist. When the commissioners replied they could offer him no information, Dunstan wrote back stating that their answer was most unsatisfactory: "I do not think the Commissioners can realise the harm that is done to the Church in this part of the country by the nebulosity of the laws governing it." Answer was returned that the commissioners were not responsible for such matters at all.

Queen Anne's Bounty had been given the task of administering the dilapidation Acts which governed the repair of the parsonage houses. These Acts required that the houses were to be kept in good repair, and at every vacancy they were to be professionally surveyed, the cost of repairs to bring them into order established, and the outgoing incumbent or his executors required to pay these costs. As this system imposed considerable and sometimes unforeseen hardship on clergy and their widows, modifications were later introduced whereby, after an inspection had been carried out and the stipulated repairs done, a five-year exemption certification against dilapidation charges was given.

An initial survey for dilapidations after the death of John Griffith had revealed a substantial number of houses had been built on the glebe, and C. E. T. Griffith, as his father's executor, paid over the considerable sum of £202 to the new rector, which Lewis was required to place in the governors' dilapidations' account. He was told he could draw on this money and in 1891 he requested that it be invested for him. Although not all this money had been assessed on the rectory house, some of it had and, in 1902, the Archdeacon of Llandaff made a formal complaint under Section 12 of the 1871 Ecclesiastical Dilapidations' Act about the state of this property, and the Bishop ordered Lewis to carry out the required work. Though some work appears to have started, Lewis having complained about the darkness of the dining room whose window was close to a high boundary wall, it was a token gesture. Although in 1904 it was reported that there was £295 in the dilapidations' account on behalf of Merthyr, and Lewis had requested a loan of £308 for repair work, the first was never withdrawn and the second never finalised. By 1915 the amount in that account, now increased through interest to £416, but in unsellable consols, was transferred to a war loan of £277, but at a much higher rate of interest, and this sum helped offset the then enormous sum of £750 assessed for dilapidations when Lewis died. He lived for a number of years prior to his death in a local hotel, the *Castle*, and had totally neglected the rectory house.

*****

The vigour of two incumbents, utilising a number of hard-working and now long-forgotten curates, had rescued the parish of Merthyr Tydfil from its 18th century slumber. Campbell received his reward of a mitre, Griffith had to make do with the tribute of a nation, for he never received any ecclesiastical preferment, although he was probably the unmitred leader of the *gwerin* clergy of the diocese. But both built up the parish to a state of efficiency and provided a clear spiritual ministry to its inhabitants. This work was slowly but ruthlessly lost under the ministry of Daniel Lewis. It is impossible to know what really happened. He may simply have given up when faced with the multiplicity of tasks facing him, but there seems to be no record of him being a sick man. His ministry in that parish was a liability, not simply to the parish but to the whole Church in Wales. And nothing could be done about it, for the parson's freehold protected him absolutely. His curates did the work of the parish as best they could, but the want of an efficient administration and leadership clearly handicapped their work. He treated atrociously his two sisters who looked after him for many years. Lewis's litigatious temper – he seems to have had some training as a barrister – seriously delayed the development of the town centre, especially by his refusal to allow the roads to be widened near the old parish church, which at least he had rebuilt in 1897. His high church activities alienated many and almost decimated his congregations – though to obtain others he requested gifts of clothing to enable poor people, especially men, to attend his services, while his poor relationship with the local authorities meant that the church schools were replaced by board schools in 1914.[3] It needed all the energy of his successor, Canon John Richards Pugh, to rebuild parochial life in that area. But that is another story.

1. I am grateful to the Secretary General of the Church in Wales for enabling me to use these files, now lodged with the Representative Body of the Church in Wales, and to its archivist, Mrs. Jan Price, for facilitating their use.
2. The second Marquis of Bute presented this rent charge to the incumbent in 1847, but the Bute solicitors wrote to the commissioners in 1915 to say that the annual rental had not been claimed since 1901.
3. David Lee in Victor Jones *et al.*, *Merthyr Tydfil: A Valley Community* [Merthyr Tydfil 1981], p. 448: Rebecca Lee, *A History of St. David's Church, Merthyr Tydfil*, [Merthyr Tydfil nd.], pp. 17-20. The parish magazines for 1887 and 1890 in Glamorgan Record Office, P/4/CV/20. J. E. Holliday, *Llandaff Church Plate* [London 1901], p. 65, notes that Lewis had refused to co-operate in his inquiries.

Literary Associations of Merthyr Tydfil, 1909

by A. J. Perman

Introduction

The new Intermediate or County School at Merthyr Tydfil started work in October 1896 and was formally opened by Principal Viriamu Jones, of Cardiff University, in January 1897.[1]

The first Headmaster of County School was Mr. Charles Owen, M.A., who died in 1904.[2]

Mr. C. Owen was succeeded as Headmaster by Mr. A. J. Perman, who had been an Assistant Master at County since it opened in 1896.[3]

Dr. C. H. Herford, M.A., Professor of Literature at Aberystwyth University College, had this to say of A. J. Perman:

"Mr. Perman is an able English scholar with wide reading, AND A GENUINE LITERARY TALENT OF HIS OWN, completely acquainted with the history of the language and its literature in all periods. From his unusual variety of attainments in classics and modern languages, Mr. Perman is peculiarly fitted to conduct Intermediate education of the better kind, while his long experience of practical work in a Welsh school is evidence that he is competent in this respect also."[4]

A Naturalists' Society existed in Merthyr from 1889-1895.[5] The Society then ceased to exist, but was resuscitated in 1908 by B. R. S. Frost. The reborn Society did not survive beyond 1909.[6, 7]

This Naturalists' Society should fairly be described as a Scientific and Literary Society, lectures were delivered on

"Lepidoptera of the Merthyr District",

"The Geology of South Wales",

"Numismatics",
"A Dissertation on Pictorial Art".

Mr. A. J. Perman, M.A., delivered a lecture to the Merthyr Tydfil Naturalists' Society in 1909, on the subject of "Literary Associations of Merthyr Tydfil." This interesting history is here reproduced in full.

Text

"When we remember that 150 years ago Merthyr Tydfil was nothing but a small village inhabited by shepherds and farmers, a village which must have seemed to the polite inhabitants of Neath or Brecon much as Cwm Taff or Torpantau appear to us, it will seem almost presumptuous to speak about the literary history or literary associations of Merthyr at all. The thought will immediately arise: What time has there been for such things in this short career? What can have been produced here to vie with the literary product of the historic towns of our land? How can it be expected that in this short life Merthyr should have given to the world, or have attracted to itself, men who can compare with the poets, the historians, the philosophers whose names are linked for ever with the history of cities like London or Edinburgh, Bristol or Oxford?

"And not only has the time been short; the circumstances of the town have been on the whole unfavourable to literary activity. 'It cannot be expected,' says Malkin, 'that literature should have been much cultivated or the arts of elegance and civilisation been held in much price in a town which owes its existence to rough, unpolished industry.' The cultivation of literature has generally needed a leisured class, and a state of life the opposite of feverish industrial activity. Few soils have shown themselves so barren to literature as those of the mine, the forge and the factory. But even when Malkin wrote, there were signs of a dawning interest in literature. 'Literary improvement,' he says, 'has begun to put out some buds of early promise, and we have only to hope they may be brought forward to that state of ripeness and utility which science has attained in other places, originating in similar causes and blessed with similar prosperity. There are many of the inhabitants who apply themselves to the study of mineralogy, chymistry, and other branches of natural knowledge in a regular train of scientific initiation,' and Malkin proceeds to record a fact which is of especial interest to the Merthyr Naturalists' Society as showing the first beginning of our present work; 'There are several book societies at Merthyr Tydfil, and I am told that a Philosophical Society is in its infancy, though I augur but indifferently of its general success among a people whose pursuits are little favourable to any branch of science but such as may be immediately connected with the advancement of their own manufactures.' "

"Poetry and Romance

"But whilst we may freely grant the truth of the assertion that neither Merthyr's circumstances nor the shortness of its existence as an important town has been favourable to literary activity, still there are one or two considerations on the other side which are to be remembered. And, first, it is true I think to say that Welsh literature has been singularly independent of towns, and of the surroundings which town life supplies. The poetry and romance which are the chief glory of Wales from the literary point of view, have sprung up oftenest from amidst mountain and wood where flowers and birds and rushing streams have fed the poet's imagination and kindled his eye for the beautiful. And not seldom have the sweetest strains of poetry, the most captivating stroke of romantic fancy, come from the seclusion of some humble cottage, or of some lonely hill-side farm. And, further, it is indisputable that in Wales there has been an interest in literature far greater than that shown in England. The interest has been more wide-spread and more continuous. It has penetrated more deeply into Welsh life than into English. It has reached the humblest as well as the highest. Interest in literature has been in Wales what it has seldom shown itself in England, a permanent influence upon national character.

"For these reason there is the less unreasonableness than might appear, in looking for a cultivation of literature in a town which has in a century and a half been transformed from a mountain village into a busy centre of industry. Both in its obscurity and its prosperity, it has had around it the traditions of a literary nation, and to these have been added, as we shall see, the fruits of culture and leisured investigation.

"The Farmer Poets

"The literary records of the eighteenth century give us but scanty gleanings. If we may extend our view so as to include Vaynor and Pontsticill, we find about 1740 the farmer-poet, Hywel Rhys, whose most important poetical work was called *The Badger Hunt*. And his son, Rhys Hywel Rhys, who combined many different occupations, stone-cutter, bard, astronomer, botanist, fortune-teller, was also himself a fluent and skilful writer of englynion and penillion.

"A little later in the century we find John Thelwall, a Londoner, and also a man of varied occupations (he is described as tailor's apprentice, law student, man of letters, and radical) visiting the Merthyr valley, and celebrating it in blank verse evidently imitated from the verse of Thomson in the *Seasons*.

"The following lines quoted in Mr. Wilkins's' *History* are said to have been written in Merthyr, and they illustrate the feeling which has come perhaps to all of us, that the Taff Valley, now in so many ways hideously disfigured, must have been at that time of rare beauty:

> 'The blackbird whistles from the pendant groves,' sings Thelwall,
> 'That fringe thy banks, meandering Taff,
> And every spray is vocal. Thro' thy vale
> Smiles green fertility, and on thy heights
> Of hoar sublimity, in varied form,
> Romantic grandeur sits. Each object blends,
> Wild wood and cultured farm and rocky bank.'

"Several local poets (if we may call them so) are mentioned by Mr. Wilkins's as having flourished about the beginning of and during the nineteenth century. Amongst these are William Moses (Gwilym Tew), who was a lock-keeper on the Glamorgan Canal, and published a collection of poems displaying humour and spirit; William Evans (Cawr Cynon), who was a Dowlais miner, who attracted the attention of Sir John Guest, and who wrote a large number of odes, translations, englynion which give him rank with bards not absolutely of the highest class; Nathan Dyfed (Jonathan Reynolds), who died as recently as 1891, and who was celebrated as the winner of more than two hundred prizes during his bardic career; D. T. Williams (Tydfylyn), who was not only a prolific author of Welsh verse, but also an able composer; and David W. Jones (Dafydd Morganwg), whose works include a *History of Glamorgan*, a poem on *Creation* and an essay on the *Manufacture of Iron*, and who was said to have surpassed all records in the gaining of eisteddfodic prizes.

"Merthyr Eisteddfod

"These names are sufficient to show that in the field of native prose and verse, Merthyr was during the last century not without its honoured representatives. And the history of the Merthyr Eisteddfod shows that for a long series of years, local interest in literature was strong and living, and that creative ability was far from being absent.

"From an able examination of the records of this institution published in the *Merthyr Express* a few years ago, it appears that, putting aside a small meeting held in 1822, which scarcely appears to have been regularly organised, the first Merthyr Eisteddfod took place on New Year's Day, 1824, at the Boot Hotel. The subject for the chief prize, the Chair, on this occasion was *A mighty view of Merthyr Ironworks*, twelve englynion being required to be composed on this theme.

"The Chair was awarded to Mr. William Moses, who has been already mentioned, and whose bardic name (Gwilym Tew) was given him in jest, he being a man preternaturally thin. To show how much an eisteddfod at this period differed from those we are acquainted with (in 1909), it may be mentioned that there was only one other prize, and that for harp playing.

"There were two other Merthyr Eisteddfodau in 1824 and two in 1825. The meeting of the Spring, 1826, was apparently a failure, but one was held in July, and it is interesting to note that it began by a sermon in the Parish Church in the afternoon, and that the members then went to the Vulcan Inn for the Eisteddfod itself. In 1827 we find records of two eisteddfodau, and in 1828, 1829, 1830, 1834, the meetings were continued.

"In 1831 an Eisteddfod was held by the Society called 'the Merthyr Free Inquirers', and in subsequent years we find frequent mention of their meetings side by side with those of the 'Merthyr Cymmrodorion' and those of the 'Cymdeithas Cadair Merthyr', already spoken of.

"In 1835, the first Eisteddfod at Dowlais was held, and with varying intervals and under varied names we find the series continuing up to 1869, when a specially large and successful gathering of two days was held under the presidency of Lord Aberdare (then Mr. Bruce), and in 1901, when the National Eisteddfod was held at Merthyr.

"Early Eisteddfodic Programmes

"It is very interesting to note the items which formed the programmes of these early Merthyr Eisteddfodau, and to compare them with the programmes set forth in our own days (i.e., 1909). Take, for example, the annual meeting of the Merthyr Cymmrodorion Society held in 1834 at the White Horse Inn, Twynyrodyn. There were prizes for reading and spelling; for an englyn on Charity; for an englyn on The Back Biter; for an awdl In Memoriam to the late William Wilberforce, the emancipator of slaves; for an essay on The

Objects of Cymmrodorion Societies and for a poem on The Patience of Job. There is nothing frivolous about this, and it reads strangely beside a programme (which I take at random from this year's announcements), in which we have a chief choral competition, second choral, third choral, male voice, girl's voice, boys' choir, brass band, piano solo, vocal solos, ambulance, mining, recitation and, lest literature be altogether forgotten, a prize for an elegy. Very often I think even the elegy is left out, and although literature may be represented, it is not thought of sufficient value to be advertised. There is evidently a swing of the pendulum in these things, just as in politics, and probably neither the old nor the modern Eisteddfod lover would understand the enthusiasm of the other.

"During the first half of the nineteenth century, it is unquestionable that these Merthyr Eisteddfodau were of immense value to the town. When books and newspapers were fewer; when ideas penetrated society much more slowly than at present; when education was much less widespread, they kept alive a love for poetry, for reading (since creative work implies familiarity with the masterpieces and models of great writers), for sober, serious intellectual occupation, for the things which endure when the petty traffic of every day has vanished. And the men whom we find deep in the composition of odes, and elegies and essays, were no Oxford scholars, no leisured dilettanti. They were the iron-workers, the miners, the tradesmen and the farmers of the district. It pleases me [Perman] to think that Gwilym Tew was a lock-keeper; Cawr Cynon a working miner; and that the officials and main supporters of these early Eisteddfodau were men whose days were well filled with the labours of ordinary business.

"A Child of the Eisteddfod

"Such a man also was Thomas Stephens, whom we may look upon as the most considerable writer Merthyr has yet produced, a man who found in the pursuit of literature that wider interest which gives salt and savour to the common occupations of every day. Stephens, too, was a child of the Eisteddfod (and that much criticised institution may well be proud of its son), for his early efforts were stimulated by and directed towards the honours to be gained in Eisteddfodic competitions. The life of Thomas Stephens was in the highest degree uneventful. Born at Pontneathvaughan in 1821, he was educated at Neath, in the school of a Unitarian minister, and at fourteen was apprenticed to a chemist of Merthyr Tydfil named Morgan. Before he was twenty-one, he became head of the concern, and he remained a diligent and successful man of business in the same shop (the one we know so well) until the time of his death in January 1875. In 1846 he actively promoted the establishment of the Merthyr Library; in 1849 he enjoyed a prolonged tour through the principal cities of Europe; in 1856 he made a journey through Ireland; and in 1858 he was High Constable. In 1862 he showed himself a devoted friend to the afflicted as Secretary of the relief fund raised after the explosion in the Gethin Pit, in which forty-nine men were killed. In 1866 Stephens married Miss Margaret Davis, who still survives him. In 1868 he supported Mr. Bruce in the memorable election of that year; and on Mr. Bruce's defeat, he gave up, to a great extent, his former interest in public affairs. In 1870, whilst walking at Vaynor with Mrs. Stephens, he was seized with a severe attack of paralysis, and though he recovered, he was never the same man again.

"Such were the incidents of a life singularly placid and untroubled. But the real life of this able, acute, even-tempered, diligent, earnest, upright man was in his books. And we shall see in them how clearly a title to fame he possesses. To the general public, Stephens has always been a man of one book, *The Literature of the Kymry* and although this reputation puts aside, perhaps unfairly, many essays and discussions of singular insight and weight, still it is true that this book is his greatest effort, and displays to the fullest advantage all his characteristic qualities. It aims to be a history of Cambrian literature from 1080 to 1350, a period, as the author observes, 'amongst the most stirring in the history of man', and its main purpose was to remove the ignorance existing in the minds of English people (and consequently of other nations as well) of the real literary worth of Wales.

"To Remove a Reproach

" 'I for one,' Thomas Stephens exclaims in his preface, 'will no longer bear the too just reproach that we are continually boasting of literary wealth which we never produce for the public inspection in an intelligible form; for how can we reasonably expect our neighbours to appreciate our literature until they are made acquainted with it in a form which they can understand?'

"After a survey, therefore, of the poetical remains of bards earlier than the eleventh century, Stephens proceeds to a systematic description and criticism, with copious translations and illustrations, of the work of the poets, the chroniclers and the romance writers included in the period between that date and the beginning of the fourteenth century. His subject was one in which previous work had been scanty and fragmentary. He was, therefore, obliged to attack obscure points of literary history, and vexed questions of literary criticism. He could not avoid digressions upon topics allied to his main theme. Thus Stephens discusses Welsh music and the musical instruments used by the Welsh in the early centuries; he finds that the harp and the crwth were the truly Welsh instruments, and that the bag-pipes, although introduced from Ireland in the twelfth century, never became really popular, and were always disliked by the bards; investigates the curious words occurring in an account of a feast given by Gruffydd ap Rhys in 1135, 'and there were performed all sorts of plays of illusion and phantasm', and arrives at the interesting conclusion that Wales had in the twelfth century most probably 'such miracle plays as were known to other nations'; examines the general character, position, numbers and influence of the Bards; inquires into the origin, real authorship, credibility and general literary value of the stories contained in the famous *Chronicle* of Geoffrey of Monmouth; and considers in detail the many fascinating but ever-unsettled questions which circle around the *Mabinogion* and the mysterious figure of Arthur.

"Cherished Legends Sacrificed

"And Stephens's whole treatment, not only of these side issues, but also of his main subject, the work, style and literary value of the Cambrian poets and prose writers, is wonderfully acute, clear and weighty. His judgments are founded upon laborious investigation and exact knowledge. They are sympathetic, for the literature he was examining he loved; but they are honest, the true expressions after full inquiry of what the author believed. He was no blind hero-worshipper, and if truth required it, he sacrificed without scruple cherished legends and venerable traditions. Many of the commonly accepted notions as to the early Bards he dismissed as based on no certain fact; many of the poems concerning Taliesin he assigned to the thirteenth century instead of the sixth; he disproved the well-known story of the Massacre of the Bards by Edward the First; he showed that the story about Ysgolau (or Scolau), who is said to have burnt in the Tower of London a vast collection of Welsh manuscripts gathered there by captive Welsh chieftains, is entirely unauthentic; he resigned the tale, dear to childhood, of Llewelyn and the hound; he exposed (as we shall see further) the unfounded belief that Prince Madoc discovered America before Colombus; and he subjected Gildas Nennius, Geoffrey of Monmouth, to a criticism as keen as it is merciless. Indeed, his determination to follow historic truth wherever it might lead brought upon him no little detraction; he was thought to be a traitor to the Welsh cause.

"But Thomas Stephens was unmoved. As he once said, 'Wales is endowed with sufficient true greatness to be independent of the fictitious and the unreal'.

"Stephens's style has the characteristics of his mental attitude. It is clear, dignified and forcible; not eloquent, not fascinating by wealth of imagery or illustration; but in all points a suitable medium for the expression of the temperate, judicial mind of the writer. It may be readily allowed that it is deficient in charm; that it is in a sense dry. No tinge of the vivid colouring of the poetry he was commending to the English-speaking world fell across his own pages. He has not that irresistible, hammer-like force which makes Macaulay's pages so memorable. He has not the burning enthusiasm which glows in the pages of Green. But perhaps Stephens had just those qualities of intellect and style which were at that period most needed. Vague rhetoric however poetical, repeated assertion however positive, would have failed to create the impression left by this calm, unimpassioned, but masterly work. 'The nonsense talked at Welsh gatherings,' wrote Mr. G. T.. Clark, the well-known antiquarian and critic, 'makes an English man of business ashamed to support them. But you have done so much to introduce common sense and the principles of sound criticism into Welsh Literature that an Eisteddfod promoted by yourself will be an exception.' And this judgment, harsh though it is as regards the Eisteddfodau, may well be extended to Stephens's work generally, and may show clearly enough the qualities most required in a Welsh writer to ensure a more than local reputation.

"A European Reputation

"Thomas Stephens desired above all things to give a 'rational account' of the literature which had often been treated irrationally; and there was no doubt of his success. From the day in 1848, when at the Eisteddfod at Abergavenny a young man of twenty-eight rose to accept the award of the Prince of Wales's Prize, Thomas Stephens has enjoyed a national, a EUROPEAN reputation. The work was quickly translated into French and German, and was accepted as authoritative by all Celtic scholars. Matthew Arnold recognised its value and used it in writing his famous *Lectures on Celtic Literature*. Stephens became at once an authority upon matters connected with early Welsh literature and history. It may be interesting to run over the names of his other chief works, many written, in the first place, for Eisteddfod competitions, and many still unpublished [i.e., in 1909]. We have

A History of Remarkable Places in the County of Cardigan;
Heraldic Poetry of Wales, an essay;
Advantages of a Resident Gentry, an essay;
Biographical Account of Eminent Welshmen since the Accession of the House of Tudor;
Summary of the History of Wales;
History of Cardiff;
History of Welsh Bards;
History of Trial by Jury in Wales, remarkable and learned;
Analysis of the Writings of the Welsh Poets from the Earliest to the Present Times;
Discovery of America in the twelfth century by Prince Madoc ap Owen Gwynedd.

"The latter famous essay, with which Stephens closed his efforts for Eisteddfod prizes, was written for the Llangollen Eisteddfod in 1858. Stephens wrote this masterly essay (it was published in 1893, with an introduction and notes by Mr. Llywarch Reynolds) designed to prove that Prince Madoc never went to America, and consequently did not discover it; that he died at home; that the story of the discovery does not appear in Welsh Literature until after Columbus; and that the story of Welsh Indians descended from Madoc was quite unsupported.

"Although Stephens's essay was manifestly the best, the Committee (disregarding the opinions of two of the three adjudicators) refused him the prize, on the ground that it was 'not on the subject'. Stephens made a forcible and manly protest, but without avail, and he henceforward competed no more.

"Besides the works mentioned, he contributed also largely to the *Archaeologia Cambrensis*, and engaged in voluminous correspondence upon Celtic questions with learned men all over the world.

"Such, then, was the literary work of Thomas Stephens, a man of whom Merthyr may well be proud. He was eminently a truth-lover and a truth-seeker; critical, but not captious; judicial, but not unsympathetic; not sentimental, but yet animated with deep affection for all that is beautiful and strong in the literature of his native-land.

"Lady Charlotte Guest

"The *Literature of the Kymry* was published at the expense of Sir John Guest, and it is to his wife, Lady Charlotte Guest, that we now turn as the next notable figure in the literary history of Merthyr Tydfil.

"She was Lady Charlotte Elizabeth Bertie, daughter of the ninth Earl of Lindsey, and was born at Stamford in 1812. Marrying in 1833 Mr. (afterwards Sir) John Guest, this versatile and extraordinary woman threw herself ardently into the life of her adopted country, and of her husband's home. Lady Charlotte took a deep interest in the Dowlais Schools, and in the welfare of the Dowlais workmen. She visited their homes and gave wise counsel to their wives. She aided in the successful management of the works after her husband's death, and she learnt Welsh so thoroughly as to gain an enduring reputation as the translator of some of the most characteristic of the Celtic romances. Her versatility was as remarkable as her industry. Between 1877 and 1880 while her son-in-law, Sir Austen Layard, was Ambassador at Constantinople, she actively aided the fund for the alleviation of distress among Turkish women and children.

"Lady Charlotte collected china, earthenware, fans and the playing cards of all nations. She published two magnificent folios on fans, three on playing-cards. She was given the honorary freedom of the Fanmakers' and Playing-card Makers' Companies. In her later years Lady Charlotte was blind.

"But her wider title to fame is that she translated into English the *Mabinogion*, the famous collection of "Tales of the Prentice Bards', going back to the twelfth century, and perhaps 'in circulation years, if not centuries, before'. The Tales are of two classes, 'one,' as Lady Charlotte Guest remarks in her preface, 'celebrating heroes of the Arthurian cycle, the other referring to personages and events of an earlier period.' The latter are much the older, and are such stories as those of Branwen, the daughter of Llyr; of Math, the son of Mathonwy; with the 'Dream of Maxen Wledig'.

"The Arthurian stories are such as *Kilhwch and Olwen*, *Owain and the Lion*, *Peredur*, and *The Dream of Rhonabwy*. The translation was published in three large volumes (1838-49) with the Welsh text, a large number of valuable explanatory notes, and several parallel versions, partial or complete, in French, German, Icelandic and Swedish. The patriotic feeling with which the work was composed may be seen from the interesting dedication to the translator's two sons, Ivor and Merthyr, the present [1909] Lord Wimborne, and Mr. Merthyr Guest, who settled in Somersetshire and married Lady Theodora Grosvenor, sister of the late Duke of Westminster. 'Infants as you yet are, I feel that I cannot dedicate more fitly than to you these venerable relics of an ancient lore, and I do so in the hope of inciting you to cultivate the literature of Old Wales, in whose beautiful language you are being initiated, and amongst whose free mountains you were born. May you become early imbued with the chivalric and exalted sense of honour, and the fervent patriotism for which its sons have ever been celebrated. May you learn to emulate the noble qualities of Ivor Hael, and the firm attachment to your native country which distinguished that Ivor Bach after whom the elder of you was named.'

"Warm Praise

"The translation has won the warmest praise on all hands. Thomas Stephens, in his judicial way, says 'The version correctly mirrors forth the spirit of these antique stories, and is as much distinguished for elegance as fidelity. Her ladyship's good taste led her fully to appreciate the charm contained in the simplicity of the original, and she has been eminently successful in producing a version at once simple, animated and accurate.'

"And Mr. Nutt, who re-edited the translation in 1902 with learned notes, praises her warmly for the mingled strength and grace of her style, the unerring skill with which she selects the right word, the right turn of phrase which suggests an atmosphere ancient, remote, laden with magic, without any resort to pseudo-archaism, to Wardour-street English.

"The great success of Lady Charlotte Guest in this very difficult and delicate task has naturally led to the inquiry whether she was not aided by Welsh scholars, whose knowledge of the language must necessarily have been deeper and more accurate than her own. And there seems no doubt that she was helped over difficulties by Taliesin Williams, the famous schoolmaster of Merthyr; by Mr. Jenkins, also a schoolmaster, in Dowlais; and by Rev. John Jones, known as Tegid, a Fellow of Jesus and Precentor of Christ Church, Oxford, afterwards Rector of Nevin, Pembrokeshire, who stayed frequently at Dowlais House, and whose accomplished scholarship must have been of the greatest service to the translator.

"The style, however, is one and the same throughout, and without doubt it must be Lady Charlotte's own. She achieved a fame as remarkable as it is unusual, involving as it did the conquest of an alien tongue, the assimilation of the inner spirit of a far-remote period and of a foreign literary form, and the presentation of these in a manner acceptable alike to the enthusiastic Welshman and to the critical Englishman. Lady Charlotte remains a notable, somewhat enigmatical figure.

"Where Welsh literateurs have captured their thousands, she, an

Englishwoman, has captured her tens of thousands for a real appreciation and admiration of these Celtic tales. But the why and wherefore of her triumphant excursion into Welsh literature are obscure, and we cannot picture her, place her, or realise her surroundings as we can picture the chemist-historian of the *Literature of the Cymry*, busy one moment in the preparation of a draught or prescription, and the next at his desk deep in the obscurities of Taliesin or the problems of the Welsh Triads.

"A Different Figure

"We turn now to a very different figure, that of the scholar, critic and antiquarian, George Thomas Clark, known from the place of his retirement in later life, as G. T. Clark of Talygarn. He was the son of the chaplain of the Royal Military Asylum at Chelsea, and he showed his filial piety by printing, in 1872, a collection of his father's sermons.

"Devoting himself to engineering, he became a pupil of Brunel, and lived for some time in India. Here he became interested in railway construction, and took a leading part in establishing the earliest lines in the Bombay district. He also prepared for the home Government a comprehensive report upon the drainage of the city of Bombay. Returning to England he became, in 1852, co-trustee with Mr. Bruce (Lord Aberdare) for the Guest estates, and for a number of years was the resident trustee at Dowlais, devoting his working days to the cares of management and oversight, and his leisure time to literature, and antiquarian research. Clark was indeed a man of extraordinary diligence. Besides the massive works to be noticed later he wrote exhaustive reports for the General Board of Health upon the sanitary condition of Bangor, Brecon, Brynmawr, Coity Lower, Llanelly, Welshpool, Tenby, Towyn and Wrexham, and he contributed innumerable articles to the *Builder*, the *Archaeologia Cambrensis*, and other antiquarian journals. Clark was Chairman of the Merthyr Local Board of Health from 1860 to 1869; was Chairman of the Board of Guardians [his bust is in the Board-room, i.e. in 1909]; and took a very active part in the life of the district, being at all times energetic in promoting any movements for the improvement of the condition of living and for the spread of education and culture. An article which Clark contributed to the *Westminster Review* on the state of the homes, the lives and general conditions of the inhabitants of Merthyr and Dowlais attracted considerable attention.

"Sixty Years Ago

"Amongst other things Clark says: 'The houses are badly built and planned without any regard to the comfort of the tenants, whole families being frequently lodged, sometimes sixteen in number, in one chamber, sleeping there indiscriminately. It is fortunate that fires are rare, since the miners are accustomed to keep a certain quantity of gunpowder under their beds, as being a dry and secure place.'

"Whatever we may say of housing conditions today [1909], it is clear that in the middle of the nineteenth century they were infinitely worse. It is however upon his antiquarian works that Clark's fame rests and more particularly upon his *Mediaeval Military Architecture in England.*

"This book, published in two large volumes in 1884, is made up of material printed at various times in the transactions of learned societies, and in different journals, it contains first a series of inquiries into the earthworks of the period from the departure of the Romans to the Conquest; into the political value and influence of Norman Castles. And second, a detailed description, minute and as far as was possible, scrupulously accurate, of most of the chief castles in England, a good many in Wales and one or two in France and Scotland. In all, one hundred and two castles are dealt with, and in most cases the descriptions are accompanied by elaborate maps, plans and pictures. To give an idea of the extent of the work it may be said that Morlais Castle occupies eleven large closely printed pages; Dover, twenty-four; and Cardiff sixteen. The style in which the work is written is clear and concise without any pretence to fine writing or elaboration of phrasing. The author aims at providing trustworthy materials for the use of the historian. 'Although my work,' he says, 'has been rather that of a quarryman or brickmaker, I am sometimes led almost to regard myself as sharing in the glory of the architect.' And it is undoubtedly true that such work as this is an essential preparation for historical writing, which may be more picturesque and may make more appeal to the popular imagination. What Clark did was done well, and in all important respects was done once for all. He did for England and Wales what Viollet-le-Duc did for France, and just as Professor Freeman said of the *Decline and Fall*, 'Whatever else is read, Gibbon must be', so we may say for any student of military architecture in Great Britain, 'Whatever is read, Clark must be.'

"Other Historical Works

"Another work, the value of which can hardly be realised by the general public, because it belongs, so to speak, to the foundations of history rather than to history itself, is the four volumes of *Cartae et Alia Munimenta quae ad Dominium de Glamorgan pertinent* (Glamorgan Charters), and *Contributions towards a Cartulary of Margam*, i.e., a complete collection of the Charters relating or belonging to Margam Abbey, is, though on a smaller scale, of the same kind. Clark published also *Genealogies of the Older Families of the Lordships of Morgan and Glamorgan*; and a *Topography of Glamorgan*, all filled with the results of laborious research and minute learning.

"An excursion into quite another field is Clark's *Some account of Sir Robert Mansel, of Margam and of Admiral Sir Thomas Button*, interesting enough to make one wish that Clark had devoted himself more to biographical work. His pictures of Mansel, treasurer of the Navy and Vice-Admiral of England, 'probably the ablest and most distinguished public man whom Glamorgan has produced', and of Button, Arctic explorer and gallant Admiral, 'the one considerable man whom the town of Cardiff can claim as her own', are full of vivid, picturesque detail, and have a human interest not found everywhere in Clark's work.

"Clark retired to an estate at Talygarn, and died there in 1898 at the advanced age of eighty-nine. Few men have done more solid literary work. His work has no popular qualities, no appeal to sentiment or the fashion of the moment; but it is honest and thorough, based upon sound investigation and precise observation. It will last when more showy productions have vanished for ever.

"And now that I have presented to you the Merthyr antiquarian, the translator, and the literary historian of the nineteenth century, you will expect me to produce a Merthyr poet, and it is pleasant to be able to gratify you. In 1827 appeared *Cardiff Castle: A Poem, with explanatory remarks, and historical extracts*, by Taliesin Williams. The author was the famous schoolmaster, son of Edward Williams (Iolo Morganwg, a celebrated bard) whose school in Merthyr was attended by many boys who have since become notable. Of these, two at any rate may be mentioned, Mr. Charles Herbert James, M.P. for the Borough, and Sir W. T. Lewis. Taliesin Williams, or Ap Iolo, to give him his bardic name, was a constant and successful competitor at Eisteddfodau. He won special praise for a treatise on the Bardic Alphabet; he wrote much Welsh poetry, which is greatly admired; and he devoted much time to the arrangement and publication of valuable materials left by his father. Taliesin Williams died in 1847 at the age of sixty. Of his first English poem, *Cardiff Castle*, he says in the preface, 'About a third of the following little piece was composed a few weeks before Christmas, and spoken by one of my pupils at an annual recitation on the eve of the vacation. Should this little publication,' he goes on, 'be deemed worthy of encouragement, I purpose directing my attention to the other castles which became the spoils of Norman rapacity.' It is a poem of about three hundred lines in metres like those of Scott's poems, and it is clear that the Scott series so enormously popular between 1805 and 1813 had largely influenced the author. 'Why not do for Wales,' he may have reasonably asked, 'what Scott has done for Scotland?' Unfortunately, the Scott metres are dangerously easy for a man of any poetical faculty, and Taliesin Williams was hardly a Welsh Scott.

"The chief subject of the Cardiff poem is the storming of Cardiff Castle by Ivor Bach (the redoubtable Lord of Upper Senghenydd, who is reputed to have lived at Morlais Castle) and his men in the time of the second Norman Lord, Robert of Gloucester, and the temporary release of the surrounding country from the Norman vasselage. The poem begins:

" 'The Norman long has ceased to sway
In fair Glamorgan's Vale.
Fitzhamon's race have passed away,
Their deeds as transient as their day;
Whate'er their might, no minstrel lay
Perpetuates the tale;
But old tradition through the land
Still speaks of rapine's fearful hand
That followed in their train.'

and contains several interesting and forcible passages. For example, the couplet on Liberty:

" 'None, none, possess except the free
Th' elastic spring of Liberty.'

the reference to Ivor:

" 'And bright his deeds while ages roll,
Brave Ivor of the giant soul;

Who drew his sword in freedom's cause
Asserting Howell's liberal laws.'

and the reference to Robert of Normandy:

" 'That gateward Tower, Oh! could it tell
Of all the miseries that befell
To Royal Robert there;
Doom'd to its awful prison cell
In anguish and despair;
Deprived of sight by cruel hand,
His sceptred brother's stern command,
And lost to nature's page,
He withered on thro' manhood's prime
And bow'd beneath the hand of time
And found decrepit age.'

"On the whole it may be pronounced a pleasing and spirited poem, not disfigured by any glaring deficiencies, but at the same time not in any way original or rising to anything more than the second rank.

"Glamorgan Traditions

"The *Doom of Colyn Dolphyn: A Poem with notes illustrative of various traditions of Glamorganshire*, published in 1837, is a much more ambitious work, and on the whole a less successful one. It is founded on a story found in the records of the family of the Stradlings of St. Donat's. It is said that a certain Sir Harry returning once from the English side of the Channel, was taken prisoner by a notorious sea thief (hailing from Brittany), named Colyn Dolphyn, and obliged to pay a ransom of 2,000 marks, which was raised by the sale of several manors.

"Sir Harry then had a watch tower built on the coast, and one stormy night Colyn, having mistaken the light, was wrecked with all his crew on the Nash sands near by, and being captured, was tried by Sir Harry, and hanged in the Castle. The poem is in three cantos called respectively, 'The Vase and the Huntsman', 'The Trial', 'The Execution', and the narrative is supposed to be given by an old huntsman, Howell (another reminiscence of Scott), at a Christmas festival given by Sir Edward Stradling (grandson of Sir Harry) in St. Donat's Castle somewhere about the middle of the sixteenth century.

A great deal of the first canto is taken up by a description of a vase on which are pictured figures illustrative of Welsh myths and mythological heroes. Sir Edward then says to Howell:

> " 'Recall thy youthful years, relate
> The tale of Colyn Dolphyn's fate.'

The wreck is described with some vigour. One of Sir Edward's men says:

> " 'Ho! Colyn! Satan's tough compeer,
> At last his victim, thou art here?
> Bear up, old Dreadnought, hail, what cheer?
> Come, clear this pool, nor fume nor fret,
> Exalted fate awaits thee yet.'

Colyn is thus described:

> " 'Fierce Colyn of resounding tread
> Whose frame athletic, stature tall
> Like Saul in Israel towr'd o'er all.'

"In the trial canto a long and rather dull dialogue takes place between Colyn and Sir Harry, and the third canto describing the execution, the hanging of Colyn and his men, is gruesome without being specially striking. The octosyllabic couplet is managed with ease and smoothness, but the narrative is a little confused and laboured, and the descriptive passages are not of any special beauty. If *Marmion* and *The Lord of the Isles* and *Harold the Dauntless* have all been more or less forgotten by the modern reader [1909], we can hardly be surprised if *Colyn Dolphyn* shares the same fate. *Cardiff Castle* on the other hand, is worth preserving, and in a popular form would serve admirably for use in Welsh and especially South Welsh Schools.

"Local History

"As we approach in our survey the records of our own times, the difficulty of choice increases. The Press, for example, offers a theme for investigation fascinating enough. But the history of the Press in Merthyr, although near to our subject, must on this occasion be passed over. The bards, too, who in recent times have upheld the poetic traditions at the Eisteddfod, in the Press and in private, must be left with but scant notice.

"There is a general literary activity in our days which almost makes of every educated man and woman something of an author. And the present writer [A. J. Perman] knows only too well the impossibility of presenting any account of his subject which could be aught [anything] but incomplete. There are, however, a few names which stand out, and with some slight mention of these the present sketch may be brought to a close.

"Among contemporary writers must be mentioned the veteran historian of Merthyr, without whose assistance any such effort as this would hardly be possible, Mr. Charles Wilkins. Mr. Wilkins has, with an assiduity and perseverance beyond praise, devoted himself to the accumulation of historical material, and in his *History of the Coal Trade*, his *History of the Iron, Steel and Tinplate Trades*, his *Literature of Wales*, his Wales, Past and Present and in many scattered articles and essays, HE HAS LAID ALL FUTURE WRITERS UNDER IMMENSE OBLIGATION TO HIS LABORIOUS EFFORTS. It is safe to say that his books are indispensable to those who study local history. They show doubtless less power of selection than of accumulation, but the facts are there in abundance, and whoever will may take what he requires. Such men as Mr. Wilkins are worthy of all honour. Investigations such as his may often seem parochial and trifling. But history is catholic in the full meaning of the word, and it is this patient gathering of local annals which makes the wide generalisations of national history possible.

"Mr. Charles Herbert James, for a number of years Member of Parliament for the Borough, published several valuable lectures on economic subjects of which those upon 'Capital and Labour' and upon 'Wages', may be mentioned.

"The present head of the Bradford United College (Congregational), Principal Griffith Jones, was born in Merthyr, and may, therefore be claimed amongst its literary men. He has published several theological works, one, *The Ascent through Christ*, which have given him more than a denominational reputation.

"And the versatile Stipendiary Magistrate for Merthyr, Sir Thomas Marchant Williams, has shown the lighter as well as the more strictly patriotic side of his nature by publishing a volume of Welsh Lyrics, and he has accomplished what may be thought somewhat of a literary feat in translating a number of the quatrains of Fitzgerald's *Omar Khayyam* into Welsh verse.

"Merthyr as Borrow Saw It

"The allusions to Merthyr in the works of English writers are naturally few. There is, however, a reference to the town in George Borrow's glorified guide book, *Wild Wales*, which has always seemed to me interesting and worthy of notice. Coming at the end of his journey into the Swansea road from Hirwaun he describes how he saw the glare and blaze of the forges before him as he approached the town. 'I had blazes now all around me,' he says. 'I went through filthy slough, over a bridge, and up a street from which dirty lanes branched off on either side, passed throngs of savage-looking people talking clamorously, shrank from addressing them, and finally found myself before the Castle Inn.' The next morning Borrow explored the town. 'What shall I say,' he asks, 'of Cyfarthfa Fawr? I had best say but very little. I saw enormous furnaces; streams of molten metal; millions of sparks flying about; an immense wheel impelled round with frightful velocity by a steam engine of two hundred and forty horse-power. I heard all kinds of dreadful sounds. The general effect was stunning.' Then turning to other parts, he says, 'The houses are in general low and mean, and built of rough grey stone. Merthyr, however, can show several remarkable edifices, though of a gloomy, horrid Satanic character. There is the hall of iron, with its arches, from which proceeds incessantly a thundering noise of hammers. Then there is an edifice at the foot of a mountain half-way up the side of which is a blasted forest, and on the top an enormous crag. A truly wonderful edifice it is, such as a painter might have imagined had he wanted to paint the palace of Satan. There it stands, a house of reddish brick, with a slate roof, four horrid black towers behind, two of them belching forth smoke and flame from their tops, holes like pigeon holes here and there, two immense white chimneys standing by themselves. What edifice can that be of such strange and mad details?'" 'After strolling about,' he concludes, 'for about two hours with my hands in my pockets, I returned to my Inn, called for a glass of ale, paid my reckoning, and departed.' The story which immediately follows of the Irish woman Borrow met at Troedyrhiw is one of the most extraordinary in his works (which is saying a good deal), and I can recommend it to anyone who has not read it. 'The house of reddish brick with four horrid black towers' is not easy of identification now. Could Borrow refer to the iron works at

Penydarren just opposite the County School?

"This sketch of Merthyr literary history, which I have now given, has no claim, as I have said before, to completeness. It represents the impressions of one who approaches the subject without the advantages (or disadvantages) of much previous knowledge, and certainly without any prejudice or bias in favour of any one writer or class of writers. But it is clear that, as regards the past, Merthyr can look back upon what belongs to her literary annals with the just pride that springs from the attempt and the achievement of able work. There are few towns with so short a history that can boast of a literary historian so famed as Thomas Stephens, an antiquarian so able and accurate as G. T. Clark, a translator so skilful in interpreting the thoughts of one language in the forms of another as Lady Charlotte Guest. If we cannot boast of a philosopher, a great essayist or a world-renowned poet; if Merthyr has not yet produced a novelist (a strange thing in these days) then we must look to the future to redress the balance, to fill up the gaps, and the best promise of greatness in the future is the remembrance and in the due appreciation of the worthy traditions of the past."

(*Merthyr Express*. Four parts. March-April, 1909.)

References, Introduction.

1. Foundations, *Merthyr Historian*, Volume Seven.
2. Obituary, Charles Owen, M.A., *Merthyr Express*, 17.8.1904 p.8 col.3+4.
3. A. J. Perman appointed Headmaster, *Merthyr Express*, 10.9.1904.
4. Newsletters, Merthyr Tydfil and District Naturalists' Society, 1992, 1993, 1994. *Merthyr Historian*, Volume Seven.
5. Suggested resuscitation, Merthyr Naturalists' Society, Letter. *Merthyr Express*, 4.4.1908 p.9 col.2+3.
6. Naturalists, *Merthyr Express*, 27.6.1908 p.6 col.6.
7. A.G.M., Merthyr Naturalists, 1909. *Merthyr Express*, 13.11.1909 p.10.

The Gilchrist Lectures

by T. F. Holley and V. A. Holley

Introduction

When, in the course of one month, were three scientific lectures delivered at Dowlais, by Fellows of the Royal Society?

In Spring of 1890 parallel courses of scientific lectures, by eminent lecturers, were delivered at Dowlais and Aberdare. These were known as the Gilchrist Lectures, and were arranged by the GILCHRIST EDUCATIONAL TRUST. The first three Gilchrist Lectures were delivered by Fellows of the Royal Society.

The dates, subjects, lecturers, Chairmen and newspaper references for the various Gilchrist Lectures delivered at Dowlais in the Spring of 1890 are listed in Appendix One.

The sequence of events leading to the granting of this first set of Gilchrist Lectures to Dowlais is not well documented in local papers but a correction in the *Merthyr Express* throws some light on the subject:

> "It has been pointed out to us that we were under a misapprehension last week in assuming that the Committee formed for the purpose of arranging a series of Gilchrist Lectures is a Church Committee. The Committee is and must be a representative one; and accordingly the invitations sent out for the first meeting were not confined to any party or creed whatsoever, two Nonconformist members of the School Board out of four invited having attended. The Rev. Robert Williams consented to act as secretary upon the understanding that he should receive assistance. Thereupon Mr. James Griffiths was elected co-

secretary, so as to render any assistance required."
(*Merthyr Express* 17.8.1889 p.5 col.5.)

Dowlais led, Merthyr followed, and in the Winter of 1890 a course of six Gilchrist Lectures was delivered at Merthyr. Details of these Lectures are summarised in Appendix Two.

The Committee meetings which preceded this second series of Gilchrist Lectures were well documented in the *Merthyr Express* and these very informative reports gave an insight into the aims and objectives of the Gilchrist Educational Trust.

In this essay we study the life history of Dr. John Borthwick Gilchrist, the fruitful investments which enabled the Gilchrist Educational Trust to be set up, the local organisation of the Gilchrist Lectures, and the over-all objectives of the Gilchrist Educational Trust, disclosed by Dr. R. D. Roberts in a preliminary visit and talk at the Abermorlais Hall, Merthyr.

Another set of Gilchrist Lectures was sought, but not obtained, in 1895 and it was not until 1902 that parallel sets of five Gilchrist Lectures were delivered in Dowlais and Merthyr Tydfil.

Details of the Dowlais Lectures appear in Appendix Three, and the Merthyr Lectures are summarised in Appendix Four.

We have found no further mention of Gilchrist Lectures at Dowlais or Merthyr in newspaper searches extending to 1914.

Dr. Gilchrist, Biographical

John Borthwick Gilchrist was born on the 19th of June, 1759, at Edinburgh; his father, Walter Gilchrist, having also been a native of Edinburgh. J. B. G. received the greater part of his early education at Heriot's Hospital, to which institution he presented £100 in later life as a small testimony of his gratitude for the instruction he had received there.

In 1775 Dr. Gilchrist paid a visit to the West Indies, where he remained for two or three years; upon his return he was apprenticed to a surgeon at Falkirk, and afterwards pursued his medical studies in the University of Edinburgh; and early in 1782, when not yet twenty-three years of age, he went to India, having received the appointment of Assistant-Surgeon on the Bengal Establishment of the East India Company.

Almost immediately upon his arrival, Dr. Gilchrist's serious attention was directed, by incidents that occurred to himself, to the importance of the possession, on the part alike of the civil and the military servants of the East

India Company, of a knowledge of the native languages. Before he had been two months in the country, he found himself obliged, for self-preservation, to assume the command of a small party of native troops, who, while escorting a valuable convoy of ammunition and grain, were suddenly attacked, in the casual absence of the European Officer, by a large body of Pindarees; these, however, were soon dispersed, under the orders of Dr. Gilchrist, communicated to the Sipahecs through his groom, who fortunately understood a little English, and happened to be on the spot when the skirmish began.

Not long after this occurrence, Dr. Gilchrist was sent alone as Assistant-Surgeon, with a considerable detachment, which had orders to storm a Mahratta camp in the neighbourhood. In this action a few lives were lost, and several native soldiers were badly wounded; and Dr. Gilchrist, being at that time entirely ignorant of Hindostanee, and having no interpreter with him, found himself quite unable to render to these unfortunates the medical assistance he would have been most glad to afford them. It was, as he himself stated, the moral suffering he underwent while continuing for several years to perform Assistant-Surgeon's duty, through finding himself so little able to discharge his duty to his patients, that first prompted him to the acquirement of their language, of which he afterwards became a fluent speaker.

On the establishment of a College at Calcutta by the Marquis Wellesley, Gilchrist was appointed to the Hindostanee Professorship, with allowances so liberal as to enable him to liquidate all his debts, and, if he had continued to hold the Professorship, to retire with a handsome fortune. Unfortunately, however, he was compelled by a dangerous illness to resign this appointment after five years' tenure of it; and returned to England in 1804, with a very strong recommendation from the Marquis Wellesley to the Home Government which, however, was only sufficient to obtain for him a pension of £150 per annum.

From 1804 to 1806, Dr. Gilchrist was in the constant habit of giving lectures, in or near London, to gentlemen proceeding to India; and among his pupils were several who afterwards distinguished themselves as Oriental scholars. Although these lectures were gratuitous, Gilchrist seems to have drawn considerable returns from the sale of his Hindostanee dictionary and grammar, as well as of other books he had published on Oriental languages.

The degree of Doctor of Laws was conferred upon him in 1804 by the University of Edinburgh, as a former alumnus of the University, who had greatly distinguished himself in the study of the Oriental languages.

In 1808 Gilchrist married Miss Mary Ann Coventry, and purchased a house in Nicholson Square, Edinburgh, where he resided (with a half-caste family whom he had brought from India) until 1816, when he was obliged, through pecuniary difficulties, to break up his establishment in Nicholson Square, and to retire to Inchyra House in Perthshire. His stay in Perthshire was not of long duration, for in June 1817 he left Scotland to take up his permanent residence in London.

During the four years from 1821 to 1825, Dr. Gilchrist engaged in various occupations in London; he became a director of the European Insurance Company; he also endeavoured to obtain the appointment of director in the Beacon Insurance Office and was energetic in attempting to establish a Joint-Stock Bank of England and Scotland, in the management of which he proposed to take an active part. At the same time Gilchrist was an ardent promoter of popular education, and took part with Dr. Birkbeck in the establishment of the London Mechanics' Institution, now [1890] known as the Birkbeck Institution.

Dr. Gilchrist was obviously a man of untiring energy and ardent zeal for the welfare of mankind. Speaking from personal recollection, Mr. Latimer said of him, "A more earnest and unselfish friend of humanity rarely existed." But Gilchrist was also self-confident to the utmost degree, and was thus too ready to measure the ability and even the honesty of other persons, by their greater or less accordance of his own views. Gilchrist had great faith in any scheme of his own suggestion, and readily entered into new undertakings, which he as readily abandoned if he found that he could not have absolute control over them.

During the last years of his life, Dr. Gilchrist paid frequent visits to the continent and it was in Paris that he breathed his last, on the 8th of January, 1841.

Dr. Gilchrist's many publications are listed in the *Dictionary of National Biography*, Volume Twenty-one, Editor, Leslie Stephen, London, 1890.

Dr. Gilchrist's Investments

Having previously made such provision as he deemed suitable for his surviving half-caste daughters (a son, on whose education Gilchrist had expended much money, having pre-deceased him), he left a Will by which the bulk of his property was placed in trust for Mrs. Gilchrist (who took as her second husband the Neapolitan General William Pépé) to receive the income of it during her life; and in a codicil he directs that the trustee or trustees of his Will shall at Mrs. Gilchrist's death appropriate the principal fund "in such manner as they my said trustees or trustee shall in their absolute and uncontrolled discretion think proper and expedient, FOR THE BENEFIT, ADVANCEMENT, AND PROPAGATION OF EDUCATION AND LEARNING IN EVERY PART OF THE WORLD AS FAR AS CIRCUMSTANCES WILL PERMIT."

It is remarkable that the property of the Trust was mainly derived from two singularly fortunate investments, the "Commercial Bank of Scotland" and the "Balmain Estate", adjoining Sydney, New South Wales.

The history of Dr. Gilchrist's Australian property is very singular. The "Balmain Estate" was a barren tract situated on Sydney Harbour, which was granted in 1800 by John Hunter, the then Governor of New South Wales, to Dr. William Balmain, who is believed to have been a naval surgeon who had gone out in charge of convicts. This property Dr. Balmain conveyed in 1801 to Dr. Gilchrist (as the records of the Colony show) for the sum of £17.10s. How Dr. Gilchrist was led to make this purchase, as there is no evidence that he ever was in Australia, is not known; but he was assured that the property, if held long enough, would come to be of great value, as the town of Sydney MUST extend in that direction. This prediction has been most fully realized. Just before Dr. Gilchrist's death, some of the best part of the estate, with water-frontage had been sold by his agents in Sydney for about £4,000; yet the residue was considered of so little value by the trustees who then held it, that they hesitated even to incur the expense of fencing to keep off squatters, and seriously considered whether they should not abandon it altogether as worthless.

During the tedious progress of the Chancery suit, however, the estate being under the management of the Court, further sales were made to the value of about £32,000.

When the estate came into the possession of the Gilchrist Educational Trust, the whole of the residue was disposed of, the proceeds being about £34,370. Thus the property for which Dr. Gilchrist paid £17.10s. in 1801 brought to his estate about £70,000.

For several years past a sum averaging £1,000 per annum has been spent in obtaining the delivery, by distinguished professors, of courses of scientific lectures suited for working-class audiences, in London and the principal provincial towns of England. (*Merthyr Express* 13.9.1890 p.3.)

The Merthyr Gilchrist Lectures, Autumn, 1890

These lectures, by scientists with national and international reputations, were organised for the benefit of working-men. They were not lightly bestowed on a town.

A detailed account of the preliminaries associated with obtaining the course of Gilchrist Lectures held in Merthyr in Autumn 1890 gives an appreciation of the thorough foundation laid to ensure the success of the Lectures.

At a Committee meeting of the Merthyr Tydfil Library held on Tuesday evening, 1st April, 1890, Mr. Charles Henry James, as president of *the Merthyr Naturalists' Society*, asked the Library Committee to co-operate with them in making an application to the Gilchrist Educational Trust for the delivery in Merthyr during the ensuing winter of a course of lectures.

It was thought best that the application should emanate from *the Merthyr Tydfil Library*, inasmuch as it was the oldest educational institution in the town, and that it should be supported by memorials (i.e., letters) from the Naturalists' Society and *the Merthyr Chamber of Trade*.

A resolution to this effect was passed, and the two bodies referred to very willingly acquiesced in the requisition of the Library Committee, and forwarded their respective memorials in support of the application. The local secretary was also appointed at this meeting, and the character of the application defined.

A letter was read from Mr. Charles Herbert James, offering to render any assistance in his power to make the lectures a success.

In accordance with the instructions of the Committee the secretary wrote to Dr. Roberts (the secretary of the Trust), pointing out among other matters the great boon that would be conferred upon a large industrial population such as our town, by the granting of these lectures, and he received an acknowledgement from the secretary of the Trust, promising to lay the application before the Committee when they met in June. A further letter was written to Dr. Roberts informing him that Mr. Charles Henry James had generously come forward with £25 as the nucleus of a guarantee fund.

On the 27th June the following letter was sent to the local secretary by Dr. Roberts:

"4, The Sanctuary,
Westminster, S.W.
27th June, 1890

Dear Sir,

I have the pleasure to inform you that the trustees have decided to grant a course of Lectures to your town, to be given in the autumn. Particulars will follow in a few days.

Yours truly,
R. D. Roberts.

A. Edmonds, Esq."

This was followed on the 15th July by another, in which the dates are given. The names of the lecturers have not yet arrived, but all other information has been sent for the guidance of the Committee.

In addition to the above correspondence the secretary stated that the previous Wednesday he had received the following communication from Dr. Roberts:

"The Sanctuary,
Westminster, S.W.
29th July, 1890

Dear Sir,

The Gilchrist trustees are extremely anxious that the local arrangements in connection with the courses to be given in South Wales in the coming autumn should be such as to secure the thorough success of the Lectures, and they have desired that I should meet the local secretaries and members of the local Committees of all the towns to lay before them the objects of the trustees and the methods to be adopted for attaining the end in view. As it will be impossible to pay a separate visit to each town, I propose to visit Merthyr and to invite representatives of the Tredegar and Mountain Ash Committees to attend the meeting there. I shall be glad to know if Friday evening, September 19th, would suit you for a meeting at Merthyr. In order to create as wide an interest as possible in the lectures, it will certainly be advantageous to form as representative a Committee as possible. I would suggest that you should secure the High Constable to take the Chair at the meeting, and summon to it by circular those in the town likely to be interested in the movement, the ministers of various denominations, leading business and professional men, representatives of different sections of working people, of shopkeepers, elementary school teachers, and others. I shall be prepared to lay before them the whole matter, and endeavour as far as is in my power to rouse an interest in the objects we have in view. Everything depends upon the way in which the Lectures are brought before the public. I shall be glad to learn whether the date suggested is a convenient one.

Yours truly,

R. D. Roberts

Alfred Edmonds, Esq.,
Merthyr Tydfil."

Eloquent Merthyr Address by Dr. Roberts, Secretary, Gilchrist Educational Trust, September, 1890

On Thursday, 18th September, 1890, a meeting was held in Abermorlais Hall, Glebeland-street, Merthyr Tydfil. It was convened by the local Committee to adopt a scheme by means of which the forthcoming course of Gilchrist Lectures might result in some permanent addition to the educational facilities of Merthyr Tydfil.

Mr. W. Morgan, High Constable, presided, in the absence of Lord Aberdare. Also present were leading inhabitants of Merthyr Tydfil, and deputations from Mountain Ash, Tredegar and Ebbw Vale, and several representative working-men.

Dr. R. Roberts addressed the meeting as follows:

> "I am anxious to lay before the meeting what has been the experience at other places, of the best means of securing the success of the Lectures, and to press strongly the desire of the Gilchrist trustees that the Lectures should be made instrumental in adding something permanent to the educational facilities of Merthyr Tydfil.
>
> "The trustees had, in accordance with Dr. Gilchrist's wish, applied the income in supporting various educational movements. They founded scholarships in India and the Colonies, as well as in England. Some of these last are scholarships for women, and only this summer one of them was gained by a student at the Cardiff College, Miss Thomas (applause).

"The trustees have also organised courses of Lectures by distinguished scientific men at great centres of industry in different parts of the country. Until this year, however, the Gilchrist Lectures had not been given in Wales. In Spring 1890 a course was given at Dowlais and Aberdare, and this Autumn Merthyr Tydfil is one of the five Welsh towns to which the Lectures have been granted. The Gilchrist Lectures are intended mainly for working people, and large halls, holding a thousand or two thousand people, have been regularly crowded where the Lectures have been given.

"Experience has shown that one of the most important conditions for securing success has been the formation of a band of earnest workers, including working men, who will canvas and press the sale of tickets at the great Works, and by their personal efforts rouse an interest in the Lectures. It is an advantage also tó sell as many tickets as possible for the whole course at the outset.

"The trustees are anxious that if possible some permanent educational result should flow from the Lectures, and they have suggested a number of objectives, any one of which might, with advantage, be adopted by the local Committees.

"The suggested objectives are the establishment of

1. a Free Library (applause);
2. science classes;
3. technical education;
4. continuation evening schools;
5. reading circles in connection with the Home Reading Union;
6. some form of higher education, such as University Extension Lectures.

"It may be asked how Gilchrist Lectures can aid the attainment of these objectives? When crowded audiences already interested in educational objects are gathered together at the Lectures there is an unequalled opportunity of bringing to their notice, through the Chairman or someone appointed for the purpose, the advantages of the particular objectives which it is desired to promote, and an effective organisation may be formed while the Lectures are in progress, to attain that end.

"The trustees merely suggest these objectives as samples; each town is left quite free to decide what is best for itself, and to take its own way of proceeding. *The trustees believe that it is of the greatest importance just now to encourage the fullest and freest educational experiment in all directions.*

"Consider for a moment how matters stand at the present time. We have been for the last twenty years perfecting our system of primary education, and whatever the faults of that system may be, it is large and comprehensive, and brings the elements of education to every child born in this country.

"Just at the time when the Education Act was passed another most important educational event occurred, namely, the abolition of religious test at the Universities (loud applause), which threw them open to Nonconformists, and rendered them, in a more real sense, national institutions.

"At the same time a few ladies were quietly working to secure the admission of women to the Universities, which resulted in the establishment of the two great women's Colleges at Cambridge, Newnham and Girton, and similar institutions at Oxford.

"Outside the Universities there was also going on a movement for the establishment of local Colleges, and we remember with pride that Wales took the lead in that matter by the establishment of the University College of Wales at Aberystwyth (applause). There are now [1890] eight such Colleges in England and Wales. Thus at the bottom and at the top of the educational ladder facilities have been largely extended, but while at the bottom in our elementary educational system every individual of the nation is provided for, at the top in our University system, in spite of all its advances, it is only a small section of the people, some five or six thousand young men and young women, who possess the leisure and means to avail themselves of the opportunities offered.

"How about the great bulk of the people who have early to enter upon the business of life and earn their daily bread? Are there to be no increased facilities for higher education for them (applause)? Something, but very little, has no doubt been done. On the one hand there has been the movement for providing technical education that will afford special training for the business of life. On the other hand there has been the University extension movement, bringing higher teaching in history, literature and science within reach of the people. In all our towns and rural districts there are men and women, living obscure lives, eager for knowledge, using their leisure time in the evenings as they can in reading and following up some subject in which they are interested. But how great their difficulties are! We have not even fairly grasped the importance of the problem of providing for that class.

"It is clear that we cannot begin to speak of a complete system of national higher education until there is some adequate provision of a systematic curriculum of study for evening students of this kind, with the incitement of *a University diploma or degree to be attained at the end* (applause). Thus we find that at the bottom of the ladder in elementary education and at the summit in the Universities the lines of progress are well defined and clear. We know what we want and how to attain it, but in the intermediate region the case is quite different.

"The provision of a system of technical education and a national system of higher education for the whole people means something new. We have no precedent to guide us, and *our only hope of solving the problem successfully is to make experiments freely*, so to learn by experience what are the best means to adopt (applause).

"In Wales in particular, there is an unequalled opportunity for trying such educational experiments. The interest in education is keen and widespread. The funds of our Welsh Colleges have been largely made up by small subscriptions from comparatively poor people, the majority of whom could hope for no kind of benefit, either for themselves or for their families, from the establishment of these Colleges.

"But must it always be so? At our three Colleges there are about five hundred young men and women receiving higher education. No very great result surely, out of a population of between one and two millions. Cannot something on a larger and more comprehensive scale be attempted? We are in danger of following too slavishly the precedents of the past (hear, hear). We must strike out on new lines, boldly follow our own bent, and create a new type of University, a real University of the people – (applause) – bringing within reach of the great mass of people who are engaged in business occupations, but are willing to devote the evenings to study, the opportunities of higher education (loud applause). This will assuredly come before long. I am not without hope that the new University of London, which will shortly come into existence, may move in this direction.

"The question for you is, shall Wales be in the van or in the rear in this great educational movement.

"Dr. Roberts then urged that the Committee should spare no efforts to make the Gilchrist Lectures a success. He expressed the hope that they would find it possible to add something to the town of Merthyr of permanent educational value as the result of the Lectures.

"Dr. Roberts resumed his seat amid loud applause.

"Dr. J. W. James, president of the Merthyr Chamber of Trade, then proposed 'That it is the opinion of this meeting that the Public Libraries Act should be put into operation forthwith.'

"Mr. Peter Williams and Mr. D. Morgan, checkweigher, Abercanaid, also spoke.

"Mr. Alfred Edmonds, secretary of the Committee organising the Gilchrist Lectures, in an effort to defuse emerging controversy associated with adoption of the Public Libraries Act, said that in order to prevent any misconception arising as to the object of the meeting, he should like to explain that the Committee had only suggested the subject of a Free Library as a matter for discussion at that meeting, and not as a definite objective to be attained through the medium of the Lectures.

"He thought it would be very unwise to enter upon the question with any degree of definiteness without first taking into counsel the inhabitants of the outlying districts and the large Companies around them, who contributed a large portion of the rates (applause). If it were possible to secure the co-operation of the Companies, and in addition to this, arouse an active interest in the matter on the part of the working-men themselves, the thing would be practically accomplished (hear, hear).

"Dr. Roberts was thanked by Mr. Charles Henry James, by the Rector of Merthyr, and by the Official Receiver, Mr. W. L. Daniel.

"Mr. Alfred Morgan said that it was the intention of Mountain Ash to adopt the Free Libraries Act as the outcome of the educational movement set on foot by the Gilchrist Lectures.

"Dr. Roberts said that inasmuch as the meeting did not seem to be unanimous on the Merthyr Free Library, he thought it would be wise not to press it, and Dr. J. W. James's proposition not finding a seconder, this course was adopted.

"The meeting then terminated."

(Condensed from *Merthyr Express* 27.9.1890 p.3.)

Discussion

The movement to obtain Gilchrist Lectures in South Wales was initiated in 1886 by E. M. Hann, Aberaman (*Merthyr Express* 23.1.1886 p.5 col.4), there was also input from Merthyr Library Committee. However, the first Gilchrist Lectures in Wales were not delivered until 1890.

There was a slowly-emerging realisation at the end of the 19th century that the future prosperity of Great Britain required a scientifically educated workforce. Two of the Gilchrist lectures referred to this.

> "Dr. Dallinger in replying to a vote of thanks proposed by Mr. C. Herbert James, said he had been engaged for nearly seventeen years on the Gilchrist staff of lecturers, and he had noted with the profoundest interest the deep desire for knowledge which was spreading among the masses. The future of the country largely depended upon the working men of England and it was to be hoped that the working men would realise the fact and by seeking for technical knowledge, make the future a noble one."(*Merthyr Express* 22.2.1890 p.3 col.3.)

> "Dr. Wilson in concluding his lecture expressed a hope that the Gilchrist Lectures would stimulate them to literary and scientific pursuits. He condemned the over devotion to politics of the nineteenth century, and pointed out that if they paid more attention to technical education there would not be so many complaints about Germany and other continental nations shooting ahead of them [i.e., England]. Dr. Wilson urged his audience to study science, which would have the effect of making them better citizens, and more charitable to their neighbours." (*Merthyr Express* 5.4.1890 p.3 col.1.)

A need was expressed for opportunities to obtain qualifications, including degrees, by part-time study, anticipating by many decades the present day [1995] Open University, Harold Wilson's great achievement.

This need had perhaps been partly catered for in 1858 when London University began to examine external candidates as well as its own internal students. It was made possible for private individuals or students of other Institutions to take London University examinations and obtain its degrees.

Popular interest in Science in 19th century Merthyr Tydfil manifested itself in many various ways.

On a cultural, non-practical level, Societies such as the Cardiff

Naturalists' Society (formed in 1867), the Aberdare Naturalists' Society (formed in 1888), and the Merthyr Naturalists' Society (formed in 1889) flourished, and there was a Naturalists' Society in Rhondda. Some history of this early Merthyr Naturalists' Society appeared in *Merthyr Historian*, Volume Seven, 1994.

These Societies were middle-class in origin, the famous James family figured prominently in the Merthyr Naturalists' Society. Activities included lectures, field trips and a visit to Brittany. The James family also interested themselves in procuring the Gilchrist Lectures.

An example of a Literary Society taking an interest in scientific matters was provided when Mr. Daniel Davies, Pond-street, read an essay on "Gases in Coal Mines" to Dowlais Cymmrodorion Society.

(*Merthyr Express* 22.11.1890 p.5 col.7.)

Charles Robert Darwin (1809-1882) developed his theory of evolution and proposed the principle of natural selection. After research in South America and the Galapagos Islands, Darwin published *On the Origin of Species by Means of Natural Selection or the Preservation of Favoured Races in the Struggle for Life* (1859). This theory aroused bitter controversy because it disagreed with the literal interpretation of the Book of Genesis in the Bible. This generated an ongoing interest in Nature and Natural History among members of the religious community.

The Rev. Dr. Dallinger, F.R.S., lectured at Dowlais on 12th February, 1890. The following eulogy appeared in *Merthyr Express* 8.2.1890 p.5.

> "Dr. W. W. Dallinger, Wesleyan divine and eminent scientist, relinquished his position as principal of the Wesleyan Theological College, at Sheffield, a year or two since for the purpose of devoting greater attention than was possible to him before, to his microscopical and scientific researches.
>
> "A gain to the Christian world at large, this step has proved a good one for the large number of provincial Churches which have since been favoured with the special sermons which Dr. Dallinger has delivered, for with consummate skill HE TURNS OVER A FEW PAGES OF NATURE WHICH HE HOLDS UP AS THE SISTER VOLUME TO REVELATION, and reads for the delight of less favoured mortals a wondrous story concerning Nature's God.
>
> "It is not, however, as a preacher, but as a lecturer and scientist that Dr. Dallinger makes his first visit to Dowlais, to tell us of various

'Contrasts in Nature'. I can only say with the reporter of John Gilpin's immortal ride, when Dr. Dallinger comes to Dowlais, 'may I be there to see' and hear."

Many marvelled at the wonders of Nature and perceived the hand of a Creator in their existence. This notion was simply expressed in the hymn, "All things bright and beautiful, All creatures great and small, All things wise and wonderful, The Lord God made them all."

The apparently idiosyncratic choice of subject for a lecture, "Thomas Edward, the Scotch Naturalist", delivered in Beulah Baptist Chapel, Dowlais, by the Rev. D. J. Hiley, Merthyr (*Merthyr Express* 15.2.1890 p.5 col.7) becomes understandable against the above background.

Many technical and scientific problems were encountered in the staple industries of Merthyr Tydfil, managers and workmen in the coal-mining, ironstone-mining, limestone quarrying, iron and steel manufacturing industries had a huge practical interest in studying safe and effective working procedures, based on sound scientific principles. Competition was fierce and deaths in these industries from explosions and other causes were all too numerous.

Various Societies were formed, they organised scientific lectures of practical interest to their members. For example, in 1890 Mr. Robert Snape, Merthyr Vale, presided at a meeting of the Merthyr and Aberdare Colliery Officials' Association, when a paper was read and discussed, on shot-firing (*Merthyr Express* 8.2.1890 p.6 col.3).

An essay on "The Martin Family of Dowlais" appeared in *Merthyr Historian*, Volume Six. Henry Stuart Martin, son of Henry William Martin, J.P., Dowlais, was President of the South Wales Colliery Officials' Association in 1907. In an ongoing effort to educate miners in safe working procedures, H. Stuart Martin lectured at several venues on the subject of miners' safety lamps. These lectures were well attended and were reported in the local press, which no doubt led to wide publicity for the topic. (See H. S. Martin at Fochriw, *Merthyr Express* 5.1.1907 p.9 col.4 and H. S. Martin at Oddfellows' Hall, Dowlais, *Merthyr Express* 2.2.1907 p.4 col.4. Martin also lectured at Bedlinog.

Widespread local participation in instrumental music and singing activity led to an interest in the scientific aspects of sound production. Dowlais-born mezzo-soprano Mrs. Watts-Hughes (1842-1907) attained headlines in the *Merthyr Express* with her "Extraordinary Scientific Discovery", pictures were produced by the voice. (*Merthyr Express* 18.1.1890 p.3 col.2.)

Mrs. Watts-Hughes was accorded a Chapter (XX) in *Music and Musicians of Merthyr*, the book published in 1922, written by David Morgans (Cerddwyson). That essay mentions her "Voice Figures" which she experimented with for several years; she exhibited her equipment, called a lidaphone, at an annual Conversazione of the Royal Society held in Burlington House, London. Her equipment is described in David Morgans's book.

Scientific lectures were sometimes organised to raise funds for deserving causes; the following account describes an effort to raise funds following the Morfa Colliery Disaster:

> "On Tuesday evening Mrs. Rogers, the talented head mistress of the Merthyr Advanced Girls' School, lectured on the skeleton as a whole, muscles, tendons and skin and on Thursday evening on digestion and the blood.
>
> "The lectures were illustrated by valuable models sent by the Science and Art Department, and they were well attended and much enjoyed. Etc. A charge of six pence for admission is made, proceeds to Fund."
>
> (*Merthyr Express* 29.3.1890 p.5 col.6.)

The Gilchrist Lectures at Dowlais and Merthyr drew overflow audiences, so short-term success was achieved.

The long-term impact of the Lectures is more difficult to assess. The Gilchrist Trustees encouraged local Committees to harness the immediate excitement and interest generated by the Lectures, to attain some permanent benefit for the community. Three suggested objectives related to Science Classes, Technical Education and Continuation Evening Schools. By 1890 all these objectives had been attained in Merthyr, as related in John Fletcher's book, *A TECHNICAL TRIUMPH, One Hundred Years of Public Further Education in Merthyr Tydfil, 1873-1973.*

At a meeting called to discuss some permanent benefit to aim for in Merthyr (*Merthyr Express* 13.9.1890 p.5 col.6) Dr. Webster stated that there was a sum of £140 left over from the Art Exhibition held in the Drill Hall some time ago (in fact in 1880), and that sum might be utilised for an educational purpose if it took the form of a School of Art. This 1880 Art Exhibition was discussed in *Merthyr Historian*, Volume Seven, in the context of William Menelaus's contributions to it.

This local Committee wished to obtain some action in the sphere of Free Libraries. The history of the Free Library movement in Merthyr was stormy. It was proposed in 1882 that the Free Libraries Acts be adopted for the Parish of Merthyr (*Merthyr Express* 22.4.1882 p.8 col.3+4) There were three Acts, the Public Libraries Act, 1855, the Public Libraries Amendment Act, 1866 and the Amendment Act of 1877.

Editorials and letters appeared in the *Merthyr Express* and a poll of those entitled to vote was demanded. This generated more letters, the poll was eventually held, of those entitled to vote, who bothered to vote, 294 were for, with 531 against. See Declaration of the Free Library Poll, *Merthyr Express* 27.5.1882 p.6 col.4.

The Free Library question proved so thorny and controversial in 1890 that effectively the local Gilchrist Committee had no good cause to promote.

Factors that delayed the erection of Merthyr Central Free Library and peripheral Reading Rooms at Abercanaid, Aberfan, Dowlais, Treharris and Troedyrhiw, even after Mr. Carnegie had pledged money for the actual buildings, included difficulty in acquiring suitable sites, which Carnegie insisted should be donated free, and friction between peripheral rate payers and those in Merthyr. To placate those on the periphery it was agreed as a matter of policy to construct the district Reading Rooms first, leaving Merthyr Central Library till last.

The first Free Library Reading Room was opened at Penydarren by D. A. Thomas, M.P., on 15th September, 1902. See "Foundations", *Merthyr Historian*, Volume Seven.

The Abercanaid Reading Room was opened on 7th January, 1903 by Arthur Daniel, first Chairman of the Libraries Committee. It was erected on the corner of Alexandra-place, opposite the Richards' Arms and although now [1995] disused, still stands (see *Merthyr Express* 17.1.1903 p.8 col.1+2).

Next to open was Troedyrhiw Reading Room, on 26th February, 1903. N. F. Hankey performed the opening ceremony. The site on the Tyntaldwyn-road was generously given gratis by Lord Windsor. N. F. Hankey, colliery owner, confessed that when the library movement was started by the Merthyr Council he feared that the result would be that the larger quantity, or practically the whole benefit would go to Merthyr Town, and the outside districts would be given a very bad second place. Happily such had not been the case, due to the efforts of Arthur Daniel and F. S. Simons. When he [Hankey] found that the outside villages would be catered for he fell in heart and soul with the Free Library movement (see *Merthyr Express* 7.3.1903 p.5 col.8).

Aberfan Reading Room opened on 26th March, 1903.

Dowlais Reading Room was opened on 10th January, 1907 by D. A. Thomas, M.P., on a site presented free by Messrs. Guest, Keen and Nettlefolds (*Merthyr Express* 12.1.1907 p.10 col.4).

Next came Treharris Library, opened on 20th October, 1909 (*Merthyr Express* 23.10.1909 p.5 col.3-5).

These buildings, originally designated Reading Rooms, actually served as Branch Libraries.

Finally, after a lapse of many years, Merthyr Central Library was opened in 1935.

One is forced to the conclusion that the Gilchrist Lectures had little effect on the course of events in the local Library sphere.

The Gilchrist Lectures were interactive. They brought academic gentlemen into contact with practical men engaged in local industries. On 28th October, 1890, A. P. Laurie, M.A., Fellow of King's College, Cambridge, delivered a Lecture at the Temperance Hall, Merthyr, on "Dust, and its bearing on Skycolours, Disease and Colliery Explosions". In the course of his talk, when discussing colliery explosions, Mr. Laurie remarked that he was in a district where he felt that there was probably more for him to learn than he could teach, and he had, by socialising with numerous colliery managers and others, derived an immense store of information.

Mr. Laurie, in the course of his talk, requested details of methods used locally to dampen coal dust in mines and was afforded an opportunity to visit a local colliery by H. W. Martin who, with a Mr. Turnbull, had patented such a method, involving the use of air and water mixed together at high pressures. H. W. Martin had read a paper on "Dust damping in mines" to the South Wales' Institute of Engineers (*Merthyr Express* 22.3.1890 p.3 col.4). The eminent Mr. Laurie was eager and willing to learn, surely the hallmark of an educated person.

Destructive criticism of the Gilchrist Lectures was rare but the following anonymous letter appeared in the *Merthyr Express* following Professor Seeley's Aberdare Lecture:

> "What displeased me was the evident intention of some person or persons at Aberdare to make money out of the fund which, I think it has been made perfectly clear, should be for the benefit of those in

Great Britain who are too poor to pay for the knowledge to be given by such eminent gentlemen as are announced to lecture at Aberdare on alternate Thursdays during this winter.

"TWO THIRDS of the best part of a crowded hall were reserved at a six penny tariff for the use of the elite of the town, and on looking round, to my chagrin I saw folks whom the lecture was meant to benefit herded and packed like sardines in a box, away up in the gallery at the penny tariff.

"As the thought struck me that more money was received at the doors than would clear all expenses, I want to know into whose pocket or pockets did the surplus go?

"If it is intended for the giving of a Christmas dinner to the poor, good; but if it is intended for butterfly catching and cairn tumbling, bad form, say I.

"What say you, butterfly and beetle catchers? GILCHRIST GHOST" (*Merthyr Express* 15.2.1890 p.7 col.5.)

A good humoured and funny reply from J. Finucane, of 19 Clifton-street, Aberdare, Hon. Secretary, Aberdare Naturalists' Society, effectively told GILCHRIST GHOST to mind his own business *(Merthyr Express* 22.2.1890 p.8 col.4+5).

Postscript

The authors are grateful to Mr. Tom Evans of the Cynon Valley Historical Society, for the information that Gilchrist Lectures were delivered at Aberdare in 1926 and 1929 and at Mountain Ash in 1930.

Four Gilchrist Lectures were arranged, by Aberdare Rotary Club, at Trinity Church, Aberdare, and delivered on 25th October, 8th November, 22nd November and 6th December, 1929. (See *Aberdare Leader* 14.9.1929.)

Five Gilchrist Lectures were delivered at New Theatre, Mountain Ash, in 1930. (See *Aberdare Leader* 11.10.1930.)

Gilchrist Lectures were delivered at Aberdare in 1931, again sponsored by Aberdare Rotary Club. (See *Aberdare Leader* 12.9.1931.)

Appendix One
Gilchrist Lectures, Dowlais, 1890

1. 15th January. Sir Robert Ball, LL.D., F.R.S., Astronomer Royal of Ireland.
   "The Sun".
   Chairman, E. P. Martin.
   See *Merthyr Express* 18.1.1890 p.5 col.5.

2. 29th January. H. G. Seeley, F.R.S., F.R.G.S., Professor of Geography, King's College, London.
   "Water and its action in land shaping".
   Chairman, H. W. Martin.
   See *Merthyr Express* 8.2.1890 p.3 col.4.

3. 12th February. Rev. W. H. Dallinger, LLD., F.R.S., ex-President, Royal Microscopical Society.
   "The infinitely great and the infinitely small".
   Chairman, E. P. Martin.
   See *Merthyr Express* 22.2.1890 p.3 col.3+4.

4. 26th February. R. D. Roberts, M.A., D.Sc., Secretary to the London Society for the Extension of Universal Teaching.
   "A geological sketch of the earth's history".
   Chairman, E. P. Martin.
   See *Merthyr Express* 8.3.1890 p.3 col.1.

5. 12th March. A. P. Laurie.
   "Coal dust and colliery explosions".
   Chairman, Dr. Cresswell.
   See *Merthyr Express* 22.3.1890 p.3 col.4.

6. 26th March. Dr. Andrew Wilson, F.R.S.E., lately Lecturer on Zoology and Comparative Anatomy in the Medical School of Edinburgh, and Examiner in the Faculty of Medicine in the University of Glasgow.
   "The heart and its work on the circulation of the blood".
   Chairman, C. Herbert James.
   See *Merthyr Express* 5.4.1890 p.3 col.1.

The same lectures were delivered at Aberdare on the nights preceding or following the above dates. See *Merthyr Express* 4.1.1890.

Appendix Two
Gilchrist Lectures, Merthyr Tydfil, 1890.

1. 30th September. Professor V. B. Lewes, Royal Naval College.
   "The air and its relation to combustion".
   Chairman, W. Morgan, High Constable.
   See *Merthyr Express* 4.10.1890 p.5 col.5.

2. 14th October. Professor C. M. Thompson, M.A., University College, Cardiff.
   "The gases in coal mines and the origins of explosions".
   Chairman, C. Herbert James, J.P.
   See *Merthyr Express* 18.10.1890 p.8 col.5.

3. 28th October. A. P. Laurie, M.A., Fellow of King's College, Cambridge.
   "Dust and colliery explosions".
   Chairman, T. F. Harvey, President of the Merthyr Library.
   See *Merthyr Express* 1.11.1890 p.5 col.4.

4. 11th November. R. D. Roberts, M.A., D.Sc., F.G.S., late University Lecturer in Geology in the University of Cambridge.
   "The building of the earth's crust, with special reference to the deposition of the carboniferous strata".
   Chairman, Thomas Williams, J.P.
   See *Merthyr Express* 22.11.1890 p.3 col.3.

5. 25th November. Professor A. H. Green, M.A., F.G.S., F.R.S., Professor of Geology, University of Oxford.
   "Coal and coalfields, with illustrations from South Wales".
   Chairman, Mr. W. Evans, Cyfarthfa.
   See *Merthyr Express* 6.12.1890 p.8 col.2+3.

6. 9th December. Professor H. G. Seeley, F.G.S., F.R.S., King's College, London.

"The animals and plants of the coal measures".
Chairman, T. H. Bailey, Plymouth (Ironworks).
See *Merthyr Express* 20.12.1890 p.3 col.4.

Appendix Three
Gilchrist Lectures, Dowlais, 1902.

1. 21st January. Rev. Dr. Dallinger, F.R.S.
   "The pond and its minute inhabitants".
   Chairman, Rev. Llewelyn M. Williams, rector.
   See *Merthyr Express* 25.1.1902 p.8 col.4.
   Dr. Dallinger delivered the same lecture at Cwmaman on Wednesday night.

2. 4th February. Dr. R. D. Roberts, M.A.
   "Rivers, their youth and age".
   Chairman, the rector, in place of Mr. W. Morgan, Pant, who was ill.
   See *Merthyr Express* 1.2.1902 p.7 col.6 and *Merthyr Express* 8.2.1902 p.8 col.5.

3. 18th February. Dr. Alex. Hill, Master of Downing College, Cambridge.
   "The brain as the apparatus of mind".
   Chairman, Dr. H. Lewis Hughes, Gwernllwyn House.
   See *Merthyr Express* 15.2.1902 p.7 col.5 and *Merthyr Express* 22.2.1902 p.8 col.4.

4. 4th March. Dr. Andrew Wilson, F.R.S.E.
   "Lungs and air; a lesson in public and personal health".
   Chairman, Colonel Pearson R. Cresswell.
   See *Merthyr Express* 1.3.1902 p.8 col.4.

5. 18th March. Sir Robert Ball.
   "A universe in motion".
   Chairman, Colonel Pearson R. Cresswell, C.B., V.D.
   See *Merthyr Express* 15.3.1902 p.5 col.7 and
   Merthyr Express 22.3.1902 p.8 col.5+6.

Appendix Four
Gilchrist Lectures, Merthyr Tydfil, 1902.

1. 24th January. Dr. W. H. Dallinger, D.Sc., F.R.S.
   "New spider studies".
   Chairman, Mr. W. Griffiths, High Constable.
   See *Merthyr Express* 1.2.1902 p.5 col.7.

2. 7th February. Dr. R. D. Roberts, M.A.
   "Rivers, their youth and age".
   Chairman, Mr. W. Edwards, M.A., H.M.I.
   See *Merthyr Express* 15.2.1902 p.3 col.4.
3. 21st February. Dr. Alex. Hill.
   "The brain as the apparatus of mind".
   Chairman, Col. David Rees Lewis.
   See *Merthyr Express* 1.3.1902 p.4 col.7.

4. 7th March. Dr. Andrew Wilson.
   "Lungs and air, a lesson in public and personal health".
   Chairman, Mr. John Plews, J.P.
   See *Merthyr Express* 15.3.1902 p.4 col.6.

5. 21st March. Professor Sir Robert Ball.
   "A universe in motion".
   See *Merthyr Express* 22.3.1902 p.4 col.5.

Early Libraries at Dowlais, 1907

TRANSCRIBED

"On the occasion of the opening ceremony of the Carnegie Free Library in Dowlais by Mr. D. A. Thomas, M.P., the senior member for Merthyr, in January last, some interesting particulars of the early library movement in the town were recounted in a speech by Mr. David Morgan, Morlais-street, Dowlais, who, with Mr. William Morgan, J.P., Pant, are the sole remaining trustees of the old Cymmrodorion Society, the funds of which are to be devoted to the purchase of a number of standard Welsh books for the new Library.

"A correspondent, who has been to some trouble, now kindly furnishes further details which he has gleaned, and will doubtless find acceptance with our readers.

"The first Library founded in Dowlais, of which there appears to be any record, was that known as the Bute Arms' Library, after the public-house of that name in Horse-street. It was started in 1842 by Mr. David Davies, forge-agent, and others, and was maintained by membership subscriptions.

"The Library was, however, looked upon with a certain amount of suspicion by the general public, as the members were credited with holding what were regarded at that time as somewhat advanced political views. The Library rules prohibited the discussion of either religious or political topics, and a notice to that effect always hung on the walls.

"In consequence of the attitude exhibited by many people towards the institution, Canon Jenkins and the other local ministers were invited to visit the room, inspect the Library, and examine the rules whereby it was governed, but Canon Jenkins alone put in an appearance.

"Another Library was established about 1844, at the corner of Commercial-street and Upper Union-street, in the premises now [1907] occupied by T. Powell, saddler, next to the General Post Office. Sir John Guest was concerned in this movement, and amongst the promoters were Mr. John Evans, the Works manager (grandfather of Councillor F. Sydney Simons, Mayor of Merthyr) and Matthew Truran, J.P., Merthyr, the eminent mining engineer, then [1844] associated with the Dowlais Iron Company's collieries, who acted as treasurer of the Library for many years. The secretary was David James, afterwards secretary of the Dowlais Iron Company.

"Amongst others prominently identified with the Library were William Truran, also a famous engineer, and the author of important works; John Robert Jones, deputy Works manager (father of D. Robert Jones, Middlesborough);

William Morgan, J.P., Pant;
Thomas Hirst, mill manager;
Thomas Edwards, Spring-street (father of Messrs. Edwards Bros.);
Rees E. Lewis;
Rev. Canon Jenkins;
Thomas Jenkins, one of the first schoolmasters;
William Jenkins, Consett, son of aforesaid Thomas Jenkins;
Edward Williams, Middlesborough;
Rev. John Hughes, Bethania; and

Matthew Hirst, who, as headmaster of the Dowlais Boys' School, endeared himself to all his pupils.

"Of the members, it is believed that only two, Matthew Truran and William Morgan, Pant, still live [1907] and it may be mentioned, as a matter of particular interest, that Mr. Morgan, who has now in his possession a copy of the original catalogue of the books in the Library, designed and lettered, free of charge, the sign over the door.

"What must be regarded as the first public reading-room was established and furnished by Lady Charlotte Guest in the old building in High-street, at one time the Swan Inn, Dowlais, opposite the shop of Morgan Evans, grocer. When this place was opened, the subscription library from the Bute Arms was removed thither and accommodated in a part of the premises.

"This institution was chiefly dependent upon the Dowlais Company, and William Menelaus, manager, Edward Williams and other Works officials, actively interested themselves in its welfare.

"There the Library remained until 1863, when it was transferred to what is known as the Guest Memorial, which, until the opening of the Carnegie Library, has been carried on as a Free Library and reading room by the Dowlais Company, and during the long period intervening has proved to be a real boon to the community.

"The foundation stone was laid in 1864 by Mr. John Evans, the intention of the workpeople being to erect a structure to perpetuate the memory of Sir John Guest; hence its name. The money was to be raised by the 'poundage' system on the wage earnings of the men, but the amount realised was nothing like adequate to meet the cost. Owing to a lack of funds, therefore, the work was at a standstill for several years until Lord Wimborne, then Sir Ivor Guest, acquired the building in its half-completed state, and eventually raised the imposing pile as we now [1907] know it.

"Out of the purchase money referred to, the Guest Testimonial Fund was founded, and the accumulated interest was distributed annually at Christmastide in prizes of money and books to the pupils in the upper standards of the local elementary schools, who were most successful in examination.

"Lady Charlotte Guest, whose name will be ever associated with the translation of the beautiful romances of *The Mabinogion* from Welsh into English, was a generous supporter of the institution, and Mr. George T. Clark, resident trustee of the Dowlais Works and Mrs. Clark, largely contributed to the Library in gifts of valuable books and papers, and always manifested a deep personal interest in the concern.

"The first librarian was John Morris, who filled the position for twenty-two years, until his death in 1885, and since that time his widow, Mrs. Morris who, with her niece, Mrs. Davies, resides on the premises, has been in charge." (*Merthyr Express* 25.5.1907 p.9 col.2.)

The Assyrian Bas-relief

by D. W. R. Whicker

Early in May 1993, Dr. John Russell, an Associate Professor at the University of Columbia, on a visit to England to do some research among the Assyrian antiquities in the British Museum, paid a visit to Canford to see the place to which, in 1849, Sir Henry Layard had brought some of the bas-reliefs he had discovered at Nimrud and at Nineveh, the ancient capitals of the Assyrian Empire, in what is now Iraq.

A group of those massive stone carvings, which had lined the walls in Kings' palaces before being dug from the sands and shipped down the Tigris on rafts, had been given a new home in a museum with an appropriately painted ceiling and great bronze doors, designed specially for the purpose by Sir Charles Barry and known to Lady Charlotte Guest, Layard's cousin, as "Nineveh Court". There they stayed for many years until, at the end of the First World War, the Guests decided to leave Canford (they had other houses elsewhere). In 1919, therefore, Sir John's grandson, Lord Wimborne, sold his collection of Assyrian antiquities at Sotheby's, all except some supposed plaster casts cemented into the walls. The purchaser of the collection was John D. Rockefeller, who presented it to the Metropolitan Museum of New York, where it may still be seen.

By the time the School took possession in 1923, it was supposed that what remained, heavily painted over, were merely plaster copies, and "Nineveh" became the school tuck shop. It wasn't until 1958 that some of the supposed copies were discovered bo be originals, to the great delight of a school which, having been founded on borrowed money and totally without

Canford School

endowments, had always depended wholly on fee income to pay its way. The bas-reliefs were sold at Sotheby's in November, 1959, to various purchasers for a total of £14,250 and we were left with nothing but the single "plaster cast", just inside the door on the right, together with some little soapstone maquettes, carved by one of Layard's nieces from original drawings in his book, *Nineveh and its Remains*, written largely at Canford and published in 1849.

During his research, Professor Russell had been reading the notebook of an antiquarian called L. W. King, who had visited Canford in 1908 and had recorded that of the sculpture on the right of the door he thought only the lower part to be a plaster cast, the upper part to be original. Following this clue, Professor Russell, together with Dr. Julian Reade, head of the Department of Middle Eastern Antiquities at the British Museum, visited Canford on 4th May. He was very excited by what he found, for the panel on the right of the door, which corresponded exactly with one of the slabs described by Layard in *Nineveh and its Remains*, although clearly of plaster in its lower half, seemed in its upper part to be of stone. With the Headmaster's permission, he and Dr. Reade returned on 21st May, bringing with them the head of the stone conservation team at the British Museum to attempt to confirm whether or not that upper half was the last remaining example of the Assyrian bas-reliefs sent by Layard to Canford more than one hundred and forty years before.

The rest of the story is now public knowledge. The so-called "plaster cast" proved to be the missing panel from Room C in the North-West Palace of Ashurnasirpal II at Kalhu (Nimrud), which had previously been supposed lost in the Tigris when the magnificent carvings and bas-reliefs had been excavated from the sands where they had been hidden for more than two-and-a-half thousand years were being transported down river. At Layard's urging they had been purchased from the Ottoman Empire (in whose territory the site of Nimrud, and of Nineveh, Layard's next discovery, then lay) by the Trustees of the British Museum. Funds from the Museum were not always swiftly forthcoming and that was why Layard turned for further help to his first cousin, Lady Charlotte Guest, whose husband Sir John was immensely rich. And that was why Canford, founded by the Rev. Percy Warrington in 1923 on borrowed money and still paying off the mortgage for the next fifty years, came to be in possession of such astonishing artifacts.

The Assyrian empire was a militaristic and tyrannical one. Ashurnasirpal II had moved his capital upstream to Kalhu in 879 B.C. and built there a place to his own self-aggrandisement. The bas-reliefs that lined its walls all sought to reinforce the king's power and authority. Our bas-relief is one of these. It shows a royal enuch, bearing weapons to symbolise the military power of the king, being anointed by a winged genie or guardian spirit (apkalle), ritual pine cone in one hand and pail in the other, to show that the king's authority was divinely protected. The carving, once freed of the layers of wash that had blurred its outline, revealed an impressive boldness of line; the fierce eyes, the curling nostrils, the bulge of muscle and flick of feather display the arrogance of a nation that ruled through terror and slavery. The art of Assyria excites in a way more recently associated with Nazi Germany. There is therefore something particularly satisfactory about its providing for the work of a Christian school.

For the governors having decided that the piece should be sold, it was auctioned at Christie's on 6th July, 1994, for the staggering sum of seven million pounds, more than twice the previous record for an antiquity at auction. The atmosphere in the auction room beforehand was thrilling enough, but as the bidding began and quickly rose to three million, a buzz went round the building and people thronged into the hall to witness the mounting competition between a telephone bidder on the auctioneer's right and a Japanese gentleman in a green jacket at the back of the room. When the panel was finally knocked down to the Japanese there was a spontaneous and prolonged cheer from the whole company, born largely of the release of tension and of sheer wonder. The experienced auctioneer was glowing with excitement and I found myself in intense conversation with students of art and archaeology over the artistic character of the piece, while the Headmaster and the Head of School dealt with a press interested only in the hugeness of the price and the oddity of a tuck shop provenance.

As for Layard, he achieved his mention the next day, when Saddam Hussein of Iraq declared his claim to the panel and his opposition to the sale. But Layard's purchase had been entirely legal and the school's title was unshakeable.

So it is that Canford at last has the resources to build a theatre and a sports hall and to make other arrangements in preparation for the arrival of girls from 13 in September, 1995, as well as founding scholarships to make education here available more widely still. We long believed that our bas-relief was made of plaster; there is now a very fine and genuine plaster copy in its old site, just inside the door of the Grubber on the right.

Memories of My Childhood in Dowlais

by ELIZABETH M. DOGGETT

Dowlais, in the constituency of Merthyr Tydfil, is typically old-fashioned and essentially Welsh though it abounds in people of all nationalities from foreign lands. At the turn of the century there was an influx into Merthyr and Dowlais, and other Welsh towns, of people who came to seek a livelihood in the various industries that were springing up. The chief industry in Dowlais was the great Iron and Steel Works owned by the Guest, Keen & Nettlefold Company, and the majority of newcomers were, I think, mainly Spanish and Irish.

In the first decade of the century Dowlais, with the continuous banging and clanging of industry, seemed to be a boom town, a hive of prosperity alive with work. The blast furnaces etc. of the Bessemer-processed steel plant showed off its prowess, as it were, by spitting volumes of firesparks into the air, lighting up the sky at night for a radius of many miles and beaming its importance.

Another feature, too, was the pouring of red-hot molten slag over a tip, which also lit up the sky at night but with a warm, red glow bearing no comparison to the spectacular display of the "Bessemer". By day and night the banging and clanging went on and on – yet it would not have been Dowlais without it! It was the continuous hum of industry.

Coal played its part too, but the mines were all outside of Dowlais itself. They were actually on the fringe of Monmouthshire, at Rhymney, Fochrhiw, Bedlinog, Bargoed, Deri, Tredegar, etc. To get to and from the pits the miners travelled from the Antelope Station in Cwmcanol, Caeharris, near Dowlais Top, then known as the "Klondike".

The road from Caeharris into Dowlais was down a steep hill. To look up that hill from the corner of Market Street, as the men and boys came from work, was indeed a sight to see! It was like a black moving mountain, as they surged homeward.

But despite all this there was extreme poverty and much squalor, for wages were very low and these were the days of large families. Many children went about barefooted and ill-clad and some little girls often went to school wearing little more than a chemise (or vest) and frock – not always their own! Those were the days when fortnightly and monthly pay-days were the usual custom but on alternate Saturday mornings a "draw", or "sub", could be obtained. The womenfolk could go to the offices for this purpose if the men were at work, and I remember going myself many a time with a note, when my mother could not manage to go herself. I could only just reach the height of the counter.

Shops and public houses were open all day with no Acts of Parliament to govern their closing times and on Saturday nights they were open almost to midnight. With the mixed tempers too, there were often brawls and street fighting after the pubs closed. Policemen were always on their toes and very often their whistles could be heard calling for help and reinforcements.

Public houses were numerous and the beverage cheap, with beer at one-and-a-half [old] penny per pint. Children often fetched the supper-beer, or porter, for the home and at one time, however young, could be served with it in jug, jack or bottle. But later, only bottles or jacks could be filled for the purpose and a seal had to be placed over the top of the cork.

Miners paid their "Undeb", union contributions, in a room usually in a public house. The "Clarence" is the one my sister and I remember best, for on occasions we had to take the contributions there.

Markets are always near to children's hearts but none could have given more pleasure than the Dowlais Central Market. It was a great treat to go there with our mother on Saturdays, after the "draw" had been collected from the office. There on the steps at the entrance to the market would be the blind man, a tin mug in his hand and his black dog at his side; nearby, the crippled musician with his rowdy concertina and cap placed to receive any gifts from the kinder-hearted.

But the elderly ladies at the top of the steps, dressed in Welsh flannel apron with shawl over their shoulders, were the favourites – selling their cockles from little tubs, "ha'penny bags" for the children, with pepper and vinegar too. Great fun, really, for all children. There were plenty of other attractions in and around the market, but always it was the scene on the steps that captivated children.

Near the market was another irresistible force – the "Smithy" – called "The Blacksmith's Shop" and owned by Mr. Williams. How true the words of Longfellow's *Village Blacksmith* seemed to be and how well they fitted:

"And children coming home from school
Stared in at the open door.
They loved to see the flaming forge
And hear the bellows roar,
And catch the burning sparks that fly
Like chaff from a threshing floor."

In fancy there is Dad's voice, that rich baritone, singing the *Village Blacksmith* so proudly and with such feeling, for he loved that song – it rang so true! To us, his children, when he sang it we thought it could only be of the Dowlais Smithy.

A stone's throw from there were buildings that stand out in memory. The Stables and Granary, with its archway entrance, beyond which could be seen the little villa in the distance, the great clock above the archway and a weathervane above the tower. Nearby was the police station and the Central Schools. These schools served the children of the area, with all departments – boys, girls and infants – in one huge yard which served as the playground.

A new Infants' School was built during our school days for the old one was gaunt, with a huge hall where most of the classes were held in galleries that seemed to go up and up... It does not give what one could call happy memories to recollect – we fancied there were dungeons behind the galleries!

Our Mum, in her schooldays, paid 2d on Monday mornings for her weekly education in those same schools, whilst Dad paid his two pennies at the Plough School in Penydarren. The Hardie Memorial Institute is now on this site, at the bottom of Dowlais. Somewhere on this "Plough" site too was, at times, the venue of outdoor shows and fairs with their swings and "dandy-horses".

It seems so funny now to think back to those days when women wore long skirts that literally swept the floor as they walked along. If the hands were free the side of the skirt would be picked up as the wearer sauntered daintily. The fashion among some of the elderly ladies was to wear black bonnets and capes, and they often used walking sticks also. Indoors they could be found wearing striped aprons made of Welsh flannel, with small shawls known as "turnovers" around their shoulders. It would be very surprising, too, if they did not possess a red flannel petticoat – a "paish-goch". Nothing could keep them warmer – and red flannel was very popular.

Not so with children – they had cause to loathe it at times for it was traditional with Welsh people that red flannel held medicinal properties so, whatever the ache, the part must first be rubbed with goose grease (sam-gwydd) – or camphorated oil, then covered with *the flannel* which was very prickly. Of course this treatment must be accompanied with the "cure-all" – senna leaves' tea! Any tantrums over this treatment and there was the threat of the "Jinny", always kept hanging by the fireplace.

The "Jinny-fedw" was a bunch of fine twigs, usually birch, tied together, and a flick of this on bare arms or legs gave a nasty sting. Keeping it company around the fireplace could also be seen a pair of bellows to brighten the dying fire and, of course, fastened on the wall a packet with rows and rows of pins. They were almost traditional too.

One could never forget the familiar cries of the street vendors as they brought for sale their daily wares – so appetising! The Italian with his horse and cart, complete with cooking equipment, calling out: "Chips all hot – steaming hot"; the pieman with his pies and bell; and the Irish woman with her kippers and bloaters carried in a clothes-basket. Savoury faggots with gravy in a jack, brought from Penygarnddu; the woman with her tub of cockles on her head, hands on hips, asking at the door: "Rythwn, heddi, Mum?" ("Cockles today, Mum?"); and those others with their bakestone fare, muffins, etc., (Bara-llychwan). Familiar vendors, too, were the women and girls with sand for scouring and for throwing over the flagstone floors. They made this sand by burning and pounding old bricks found in places such as the "Cwm", and carried it in buckets on their heads as they went from door to door, selling a tin-full for ha'penceworth.

Much of the social life was confined to the Churches and Chapels with their denominational features: Penny-readings, Bands of Hope, Christian Endeavour, etc., and Scout and Guide movements too. The older folk had to keep pace with the ysgol-gan (singing schools) and be ready for the annual Gymanfas. Caersalem Chapel stands out in memory for this! Popular festivals of all sorts, drama, concerts, etc., were often held in the Oddfellows Hall, with its numerous steps at the entrance! It was the "Will Stone" movie-picture house too, with its "penny" Saturday matinee for children.

Merthyr offered greater entertainment. Shows of all description were held on the Iron-bridge and the "Fairs" brought people from all neighbouring districts for hilarious fun. Sometimes when a circus was held there, the animals would have a "turn-out", parading the town prior to the show – elephants too! Chief places for indoor entertainment were the Drill Hall, Temperance Hall and Theatre Royal. Merthyr's market was very old-fashioned and quaint, and savoured of Welsh country produce from such places as Brecon, Talybont, Abergavenny and Carmarthen too.

As was the custom in Wales, Dowlais had its own mixed choirs and male voice parties and I can still remember the exciting and triumphant return of Harry Evans from London, after his choir's success. Our Mum had taken us to see the procession, preceded by a band.

For a day's ramble filled with pleasure, beauty spot viewing and education, one could not do better than to make a detour of some of the environs of Dowlais and Merthyr. From Dowlais into Penydarren, through Pontmorlais towards Cyfarthfa Park with its lovely Castle, Museum, gardens and boating-lake; off to Vaynor, through Cefn and thence to Pontsarn, noted for its waterfall and Blue-pool.

Over the woodland, where the Sanatorium has now been built, a little visit must be paid to the historical ruins of Morlais Castle; now to the "Brynna" (Brynniau), and the shooting targets, and the little ponds that had "t'ousands" of tadpoles. Then past the little cottages towards Pant Cemetery where the illustrious of Dowlais lie buried – our Mum, too, who died at the young age of 38. From Pant into Pantyscallog, Caeracca, Penywern, then into Dowlais – a detour that gave such pleasure was made in a short space of time.

Popular rendezvous in summertime were the Works' reservoirs, known as the Penywern ponds. The ponds were flanked by the Twynau mountains, where Dad's ashes were later scattered, and had pleasant walking places around them that were much used by old and young alike, not forgetting Slippery Bridge! Outings and Sunday School treats were usually made to Pontsticyll, Dolygaer, Torpantau, Gilwern, Abergavenny and Talybont.

On festive occasions great fun was had with the traditional "Mari-lwyd", the wooden horse-head on a broom handle. At such times, men and women often dressed up in each other's clothes to add to the spirit of revelry. Particularly so on All Hallows' Eve, which Welsh people called "nos cyn gauaf" (night before the winter), but for children 31st October was "good old ducking-apple night"!

Small mountain ponies with long mane and tail were very much in evidence in and around Dowlais. They roamed roads and mountains, for they were wild, and many children owned one as a pet. It was exciting to watch other horses, all dressed with ribbons and straw hats, on their way to Pantywaun for the Waun fair (fair-y-waun) held annually on the mountain top. There were horses of all descriptions to be seen and it was lovely to hear their hooves clattering up the hill, over Dowlais Top, to the Waun.

From my recollections of the distant past emerges a great political figure, and one of international renown, James Keir Hardie, M.P. He was the first Socialist Member of Parliament in Britain, entering as the member for West Ham in 1891. In 1900 he successfully contested Merthyr Tydfil and represented the constituency until his death at the early age of 59 years in 1915.

Keir Hardie was an inspiration to young and old alike, and was much loved by the ordinary people. He hated tyranny and injustice and spared no one in exposing sordid conditions of life and labour and, for his pains, was often ridiculed and labelled an agitator. Posterity hails him as a benefactor of mankind and at the centenary of his birth on 15th August, 1956, newspapers paid tribute to him as one of the world's greatest social reformers and likened him to "a Hebrew Prophet".

With resolute purpose he preached the ethics of socialism, and inspired people with the need to create a new social order to bring about better conditions of life and social justice for all. He did his best to further the Christian concept: "the poor shall be exalted and shall inherit the earth", and his belief in the brotherhood of man made him apply Christian teachings to the human problems he came up against.

The socialist machinery of that period was confined within the then flourishing Independent Labour Party organisation, the I.L.P. Dad was a founder member, an early pioneer of the Merthyr and Dowlais I.L.P., and a loyal and faithful disciple of his beloved leader, J. Keir Hardie. They were "wheels within wheels" in the movement and nothing was left to chance in giving the people enlightenment and getting them organised.

In summer time, after Chapel, meetings were often held in Thomastown Park, Penydarren, and parents took their children with them. On one such evening, wandering around the park with its lovely fountain and statuettes and, of course, the great attraction for children, its iron drinking cups, Dad and Mam were pointing out to us the various places of interest. We could see a gaunt-looking building and outside were a group of white-capped nurses who were singing hymns – probably a religious break during duty hours. We asked what it was and learned from our parents that it was "the Workhouse", and young though we were the word held a sinister meaning for us – too often we had heard it said with pity: "Poor so-and-so will have to go to the Workhouse".

The institution was hated by the champions of the poor. Keir Hardie and his fellow socialists rebelled against it and it was as a bounden duty that they spread propaganda to awaken the conscience of the nation, to drive away the fearful tyranny of "the Workhouse".

What days they were for election enthusiasm! Men and women, and even the children, all on their toes in the fight to get the candidates representing the poor elected. Women did not have the right to vote at that time and their cause was fiercely championed by the I.L.P. as being a reform long overdue. Women's Suffragette movements were growing in force throughout the country and their members had to run the gauntlet of scorn and criticism in their efforts to focus attention to their cause.

Children felt they were really playing their part in parading with placards, flaunting their candidate's colours, wearing paper hats and singing election words to popular tunes, accompanied by the "toy drum, tin whistle and tomato-tin band"! They did feel important and when celebrations were held later, in the meeting-rooms above local shops, with the partaking of jellies etc. at the "soirees", the children felt they had really earned their reward.

The bigger events were celebrated in the Drill Hall in Merthyr, which was gaily festooned with trimmings and bunting in keeping with the Socialist emblem – "The Red Flag". Children with red ribbon in their hair and collars tied with it, the men and women flaunting the red rosettes they were so proud to wear. Then later, when their beloved leader arrived, the cheering would be tumultuous and only gave way to the singing of the workers' international anthem, "The Red Flag", sung with the fervour of a hymn as a tribute to Hardie and the cause. Nowadays "The Red Flag" anthem is more frequently sung at Communist functions and much less at Labour gatherings.

I well remember an exhibition held in that same Drill Hall. Children were taken there by their teachers to a Tuberculosis Exhibition. Even now, years and years later, I can remember some of the horrible exhibits that were shown, pointing out the ravages of the disease. Great stress was laid on the fact that its ill-health was higher among the working and poorer classes. Dad's ill-health at this particular time had kept him from work for many months. Knowing our poor circumstances, where the only income to the home was a meagre sum of parish relief, made me very worried although I was only ten years old, for I thought that nothing could stop us all having T.B. Kindly help from relatives and friends, augmented by soup-kitchens, kept us together.

When I later told my parents some of the things I had seen at that exhibition they were saddened and indignant to think that children were taken from schools to see such an exhibition. They made a protest.

Somewhere around this time the Iron-Moulders were on strike after a claim for a rise in their measly 3/- a day had been rejected. Their fight was fully supported and championed by the local I.L.P. and by Keir Hardie. During the strike the men would march as a body to the houses of the "black-legs", who had all been given nicknames. Songs with popular tunes were sung outside the houses, and appropriate words substituted with the black-legs' names added. As soon as the marchers were sighted, children from everywhere seemed to gather and, knowing the tunes, sang as lustily as the men. With no knowledge of the serious circumstances, the children found it all great fun.

However, after much bitterness the moulders won their fight. The rise was a very small one, but they had waged a successful campaign to establish their rights. Now came the aftermath – victimisation for all who had taken an active part in the campaign. Dad, who never doubted the truth of "right is might", became a marked man for he had spoken fearlessly on platforms on behalf of the moulders and supported them to the hilt.

The pits and the iron foundries were more or less owned by the same Company so that, although employed in the pits, Dad was told there would be no further work for him under that Company. To further this vicious treatment, they also sacked his only brother, who had taken no active part in the moulders' campaign. While Dad felt very bitter about the treatment he had received at the hands of the owners, when his only crime had been unstinted endeavour to help his fellow men, he determined that his brother should not be made to suffer on his account. After much agitation his brother was eventually reinstated; had this not been the case, greater repercussions would have ensued, for the Miners' Federation had taken up the issue.

Going back in memory to this period of time marks it as one of great economic distress and unrest. It was the time of the Mid-Rhondda Combine strike, 1910-1911, when owners and men were in bitter conflict over the principle of the minimum wage. The struggle lasted for the better part of twelve months and indeed was known as "the twelve-month strike". As can be realised, terrific hardships and material sufferings were endured but the miners made history – they won their rightful claim for a minimum wage!

During those long months of suffering there were many times when the Mid-Rhondda miners came in singing-groups to Dowlais with their collecting boxes. Though poverty was rampant in Dowlais everyone gave what they could, for the workers knew that it was their fight too – the fight for some measure of security in employment.

Social inequalities were noted with much bitterness. Though workers toiled harder with long hours of labour, their material wealth was low for wages were very small; yet the families of the owning class climbed higher up the social ladder and seemed to tread golden ground. Such was the position at the time of a forthcoming Royal visit and I well remember the news was not well received by the I.L.P.

In spite of certain apathy no expense was spared, of course, to make the visit a pompous one. A "bridge and archway" of coal had been built at the entrance to the main offices of the Ironworks. On the bridge was a golden tram, or truck, of coal. Lining the grassy verge of the New Road, at the bottom of Dowlais, were school-children singing their loyal salutations to King George V and Queen Mary. The children, just living for the excitement of the moment, must have made a pleasing picture. The tea and buns waiting for their return to school later, with a pictured mug to take home, made it all seem worthwhile to them.

The policy of the I.L.P., by this time, must have been as a beacon light to those whose political consciousness was awakening. Its members had little leisure time, for working hours were long: ten and twelve hours a day. In winter the miners among them did not see daylight until Sunday, which now seems to hard to believe. Yet even so, they sacrificed the small amount of leisure time they had and gave themselves up to study in order to become well-informed and thus be able to spread their gospel of socialism.

Under the faithful guidance and leadership of their beloved Hardie, they formed themselves into study groups, debating circles, etc. They studied every aspect of social, industrial and political history, local administration, national government and so on, to such effect that they became prolific, well-informed speakers, and many of them brilliant lecturers, fearless in debate. It is true to say that most of them had started work as children of ten years of age, with little or no schooling, therefore to glean and garner more knowledge and further their self-education often meant burning the midnight oil.

My recollections now bring me to the year 1912 when Dad, cruelly victimised, was forced to leave his family in Dowlais for the time being and seek a livelihood elsewhere. Poor Dad, how unhappy he was and how keenly he felt having to leave Mam and the children. So often he had been called "honest John" because of his refusal to bridle his tongue in order to win favour, and now he was obliged to go to Porth, Rhondda, to try his luck.

There he found work in the local pits with lodgings close by, and for a little while felt happier, just living for Saturday nights when he could go home to his family in Dowlais. Saturday nights, then, were nights of rejoicing for us children and we always went part of the way to meet him. Alas, Sunday night would come all too son, with the agony of parting again and the prospect of another week of "Hiraeth" (yearning).

Eventually, with the low wages, it became too great a financial strain to pay the cost of lodgings and at the same time maintain home and family. So, with no prospects of work in Dowlais, in the autumn of 1912 our family were transported to Rhondda – the Rhondda of great tradition in the history of the working classes. Our parents left their dear Dowlais with sad and heavy hearts and many misgivings, for they were leaving home and dear relatives and friends. But to us, the four children, it was a new experience and there was a sense of adventure about it all.

Such, then, was the fate of so many of those early pioneers of social reform, and the price they had to pay for holding steadfastly to their beliefs and principles. It surely behoves us, in this day and age of the Welfare State, to think of those brave men and women of yesterday and remember their sacrifices. We owe them so much, for it was they who laid the foundation stones for a better society; a society that has at long last abolished the dread of the Workhouse and brought a greater measure of social security in its train.

My epitaph to them, in salute, is: "By their deeds shall they be known!"

August, 1975

Book Review

by J. Barry Davies

The Farms and Farmers of Senghenydd Lordship *by T. V. Davies*
Printed on an Amstrad 8256 and bound in two volumes at The Croft, Kibworth, Leics. in a limited edition of 20 copies

It was evidently an awareness of his own ancestors who, for generations had been farmers in the parish, that led a professor of mathematics to undertake the huge task of introducing the "Iron Capital of the World" to its pre-industrial farming heritage. Regrettably I met the author no more than two or three times and always at day schools or lectures organized by this Society, the Valleys Initiative, or the Gelligaer Society. But we corresponded and, from time to time, had long discussions over the telephone which I always found helpful. Our paths were bound to cross as we were engaged on very similar projects in our respective areas. His project has been superbly carried through to a final, though sadly posthumous, conclusion here under review, a conclusion that is an inspiration to us all.

Professor T. V. Davies died on 7th January, 1991, only a few days before completing the typescript of the Gelligaer volume. His plan had been not only to type the whole work, 1220 pages plus introduction, but to bind some 20 copies himself. To the latter end he attended a number of book-binding courses but in the event had time to bind only one copy of the first volume, *Merthyr Parish*. His family completed preparation of the *Gelligaer* volume for publication and members of the book-binding class completed the binding. Thus posterity is left with twenty sets, each an individual work of art.

In the circumstances the lack of an index cannot be put forward as a criticism. Exhaustive contents lists are given to each chapter which are a useful guide but the realization of the author's own expressed hope "that my work will encourage others to study the documentary material which has been presented here" is much more likely if a simple index of placenames and personal names could be provided.

The main source for this micro study of local history in Merthyr Tydfil and Gelligaer is the archive of the Bute Estate preserved in the National Library at Aberystwyth. Historically this large collection of documents is the archive of the lords of Glamorgan from the time of William Herbert, Earl of Pembroke, who was granted the lordship in 1547, right down to the present century.

The Earls of Pembroke and their successors were lords of Glamorgan and Cardiff Castle. This included a number of member lordships, mainly those which had remained in Welsh hands for some two or three hundred years after the initial Norman invasion. Afan, Neath, Glynrhondda, Ruthin, Llanblethian, Meisgyn and Glynrhondda and, of course, Senghenydd. Between them these lordships covered the whole of the Blaenau or mountainous area of Glamorgan and much of the border vale.

Senghenydd is particularly fortunate in the survival of ten accounts of the fifteenth century between 1426 and 1492, a period when the lordship belonged to the earls of Warwick. Eight of these are in the Bute archive, one in the Public Record Office and another in the Plymouth Estate archive in the National Library. T. V. Davies has abstracted and made use of all these, together with Ministers' Accounts for 1540 when the lordship was in the King's hands.

Much of the Bute archive comprises surveys and rentals of the member lordships, beginning with a general survey taken in 1570 which details, firstly, all the demesne lands, wastes and forests then belonging to the Earl of Pembroke in Glamorgan with the names of lessees; and secondly, lists of all the tenants of his manoirs and lordships, with the rents they paid for their land and, in many cases, the names of their particular tenements. These tenements, or messuages, are what Professor Davies has studied as the *Farms of Senghennydd.*

The 1570 Survey was followed by surveys and rentals made at various times during the succeeding three centuries. They have not all survived for all lordships, but generally there are surveys or rentals occurring about once a generation. The surveys are comprehensive accounts of the state of the particular lordship at the time in question, recording all the customs and duties as well as listing the free and unfree tenants. The rentals are no more than lists of the free and unfree tenants with their rents and usually the names of their land. These records can be found clustered in the early seventeenth century and again in 1666. The continuity is broken by a two-generation gap between 1570 and 1630 and between 1666 and 1720 but after that the series continues with frequent rental books from1720 to the late nineteenth century at 10-20 year intervals at first, later more frequently. For Senghenydd, the good fortune of possessing a series of fifteenth-century accounts is countered by not having a rental in 1720. This means that the author was handicapped by a gap between 1666 and 1747, which reduces the extent to which he was able to identify the descent of all the modern farms in his parishes.

There are, not surprisingly, imperfections in the surveys and rentals as a source for deriving the individual history of each farm. In theory it is possible to trace every farm in the upland area of the county from 1570 down to 1840 when it can be plotted and identified on the tithe map. In practice there are a number of reasons why the process is not quite so simple, the most obvious being the generation gaps already referred to. Another shortcoming is the fact that in some cases the name of the tenement is missing and, in any case, usually the name changes over the years. At first the tenements were called by the names of their owners, tenants or leaseholders as, for example, "Tir Thomas Philip Ieuan" or Thomas Philip Ieuan's land. During the sixteenth century the fashion grew of giving the tenements descriptive names like Garth, Llwynyreos, Troedyrhiw, Gurnos, Gwaelodygarth and so forth. Of course some of the "Tir plus personal name" descriptions have survived, but it is those many cases of discontinuity in the name of the land that give the greatest problem of identification.

To overcome this we tend to fall back on the rental paid for the land to identify it, but this again is fraught with difficulty especially as many tenements paid the same rent. Rents ranged from 1d. and 2d. up to six or eight shillings, and another problem with using them to identify properties lies in the fact that tenements were not always stable. They tended to be split up or to be re-amalgamated and the resulting fracture and reuniting of rents did not always add up correctly.

However, these problems are not necessarily insurmountable. Surprisingly often it is possible to trace particular tenements, using only the surveys and rentals, from 1570 to the present day. Where this fails we must turn to other sources and Professor Davies did that with great industry and thoroughness.

For the late medieval period one of the most important and under-used sources for Welsh history is the great corpus of genealogical material which has survived. For over a century we have been fortunate in Glamorgan in having this source readily available in G. T. Clark's *Limbus Patrum*. Clark was, of course, a man of great significance in the history of Merthyr since, in his capacity as a Trustee of the Guest estate, he was for long responsible for the Dowlais Iron Works. It is remarkable that such a man of affairs had leisure to make a large contribution to Glamorgan history in his spare time. A small part of that contribution was the monumental publication of the pedigrees of the gentle and yeoman families of the county.

Too often pedigrees are regarded as simply of use to family historians, but we should not overlook the significance of the close relationship existing between the early pedigrees and territorial rights. This is particularly important for the fourteenth and fifteenth centuries in Glamorgan when documentary sources are so sparce, and Professor Davies has exploited this source fully and effectively, relying not only on Clark but also on the interpretive work of the late Major Francis Jones and the extraordinary industry of Dr. P. C. Bartrum, who has made available a massive *Genealogy of Wales* based on a comparative study of all the earliest sources still extant and covering all the generations born between the years 300 and 1500 A.D.

A third source fully utilized in this work is the wills and inventories that survive either in the Public Record Office in London, where proved in the Court of Arches at Canterbury, or in the National Library, where proved in the Consistory Court of Llandaff. Where the maker of a will can be identified with the owner of land named in the surveys and rentals and also with a gentleman named in one of the pedigrees, we are able to put the ownership of that land in the context of a family that may have exercised territorial rights in the area for many centuries prior to the survey of 1570.

Using all these sources Professor Davies was able to trace the descent of a farm like Pwll y whiaid from the thirteen-century Gwilym Sais of Merthyr, ap Madoc ap Hywel Felyn lord of Senghenydd through the generations: Jevan ap Gwilym Sais – Meiric of Gelligaer ap Jevan – Gwilym ap Meiric of Tir y Gurnos – Morgan ap Gwilym of Tir y Gurnos to Roger ap Gwilym whose daughter Catrin married Madoc ap John ap Gwilym ychan of Aberdare. Their son, Thomas ap Madoc, owned Tir y goetre and Tir Nant y Wenallt, part of which passed to Thomas ap Thomas Madoc, to Jenkin ap Thomas – Thomas ap Jenkin of Tir y goitre and Pwll y Whiaid in 1650

– David Thomas Jenkin of Pwll y whiaid in 1675 – Rees David – Thomas Rees David of Pwll y whiaid in 1750 who died in 1761 – David Rees his son whose two sons died in 1788 and 1797 respectively without issue, but whose daughter, Mary Rees, married David Davies of Garth Farm in 1813 and had issue.

But the author did not limit himself to the basic sources, nor did he ignore the industrial perspective that by the time of the later generations of landowners had become so important. He quotes in full documents whereby John Rees of Merthyr Tydfil gent. leased the minerals under Pwll y whiaid to Jeremiah Homfray, thus linking the long traditional and pastoral past with the dynamic industrial reality of Merthyr Tydfil in the eighteenth century.

The material is organized in chronological order and for the most part the original sources are either quoted in full or in abstract, alongside the narrative historical analysis. Whereas the main value of this work will stand for many years to come as a quarry for later researchers, it contains a number of self-contained essays that would stand alone and the thought occurs that one or two of these might well be published for a wider audience if the author's executors were agreeable.

The first chapter of the Merthyr Volume is an example. This covers the period up to 1400, ranging from pre-history through the Romans, the rulers of Glywyssing from 600-1093, the Llandaff Charters, and concluding with Llywelyn Bren. Based on a wide reading of the modern sources, it attempts to apply the latest thinking on the early history of Glamorgan to the parishes of Merthyr and Gelligaer.

Again, Chapter 5 studies the growth of dissent in the period 1630-1690. Clearly a subject close to Professor Davies's heart, this is written with a sympathetic understanding of the subject and deserves a wider readership than this limited edition is likely to receive.

In conclusion, I should attempt some assessment of the reliability of the work. I am sure that the transcription of documents has been done with meticulous care and Professor Davies took pains to prepare himself to deal with his sources by taking a wide range of advice. He consulted leading scholars in person, as well as reading their work. We have to recognize, though, that such a long span of history presents difficulties of understanding and interpretation, and the medieval period contains many pitfalls for the unwary.

There are one or two errors in the pedigrees and in the attribution of pedigree personages to land – one in particular in the Gelligaer volume, but this stems from relying on Clark's *Limbus Patrum*. In Chapter 7 of Vol. 2, page 630, the author has identified Jevan ap Dafydd ap Grono of Gelligaer with the pedigree given by Clark on p. 134 of *Limbus Patrum*, as Jevan Eos of Gelligaer, descended through Owain Pelldu from Einion ap Gollwyn. Since Clark makes Jevan Eos "of Gelligaer" and since the modern scholar P. C. Bartrum repeats this identification in his *Welsh Genealogies 300-1400*, our author cannot be blamed for this. However, a detailed study of farms in Llanwonno and the Dinas/Cymmer part of Llantrisant in Meisgyn lordship, proves that Jevan Eos owned a tenement in Dinas known early on as Tir Jevan Eos, as well as one in Llanwonno called Gelli Fawr. It is clear that the Gelligaer attribution given by Clark is a transcription error by one of the pedigree copyists for Gelli Fawr and, in fact, Dr. Bartrum amended this in his later publication, *Welsh Genealogies 1400-1500*.

The more general unease which I have is a feeling that the author has not fully understood the complexity of the history of land tenure and ownership, and it is disappointing that he does not appear to have read such recent work as Professor Rhys Davies's *Lordship and Society in the March of Wales 1282-1400*.

It would be pedantic to list the half-dozen or so small points that have struck me as either confusing or misleading, but two examples will suffice. In describing a rental of 1756-7 the author refers to the "annual (ground) rent". Admittedly he puts the word "*ground*" in brackets, but the fact is that the term "ground rent" has a modern meaning which is bound to confuse us when considering rents of medieval origin. The definition of these rents given in the 1570 survey is "rent of Assize", that is to say a rent that has been fixed by the Court of the lordship. Professor Davies knows this and tells us so in another place, so why confuse us by giving this misleading half-definition?

Again, when discussing the early sixteenth-century Ministers' Accounts, reference is made to "Royal Rents" due to the King. But these are the same seigneurial rents that were due to the earls of Gloucester in the fourteenth century, which were paid to Henry VIII in 1540, not in his capacity as King of England, but in his capacity as Lord of Senghenydd. A nit-picking point perhaps, but one which raises the serious question of whether the author has understood the nature of marcher lordship or, if he has, whether his explanations are always as clear and unambiguous as they might be.

Much more important that a few niggling questions of interpretation, however, are the many gems and insights to be found scattered through these two volumes. For instance, Professor Davies has identified in the early rentals some fascinating little quillets of land, now somewhere in the heart of the town, as possibly the remnants of strip cultivation. This merits further close examination and I venture to suggest another possible interpretation, which is that these may be original "burgage plots" laid out for a medieval borough which failed to evolve.

I hope that there will be no shortage of workers to carry this enormous pioneering work forward; there is enough assembled here to keep members of this Society busy for generations to come. Indeed, the best comparison that I can make is with the six-volume *Cardiff Records* compiled by J. Hobson Matthews nearly 100 years ago, which is still being used by local historians as a primary source.

Professor T. V. Davies's Obituary appeared in the *Bulletin of the Institute of Mathematics and its Applications*, October/November, 1991, Volume 27, Numbers 10/11, pp.217-219.

The Dowlais Railway or "Incline"

by LEO DAVIES

So much depends upon your interest in this subject as to whether you refer to it as "The Dowlais Railway" or the "Inky". The matured archaeologist or railway enthusiast wouldn't dream of referring to this most important contribution to the industrial development of the area – indeed, the world of iron and steel – other than the Dowlais Railway. On the other hand, a schoolboy in the mid-twenties would laconically render his account of his latest adventure on the "Inky" – the means of getting to Twynyrodyn School by any other means than walking; on the other hand, such scant regard for the original purpose of the Railway could, providing the lad was brought up "proper" – in the archaeological sense, of course – lead to a wider appreciation of what really went on – apart from finding a moving "buffer" to hang on to.

After the Taff Vale Railway reached its terminus in Merthyr Tydfil in 1842, the rate of growth of its traffic was considerable and soon overtook the other means of communication which had existed hitherto: namely the Merthyr Tramway and the Glamorganshire Canal. It was quite obvious that the increasing activity and output of the Dowlais Iron Company would require access to this new artery of communication.

They "grasped the nettle" and with appropriate Parliamentary Approval proceeded to build the Dowlais Railway, which was opened in 1851.

The northern end of the railway terminated within the confines of the Works and was conveniently situated to The Victoria Inn, The Glove and the Smith and Anvil Public Houses. It has been quoted that the Terminal was called Station Can (Flour Station), but this has to be verified. The south end

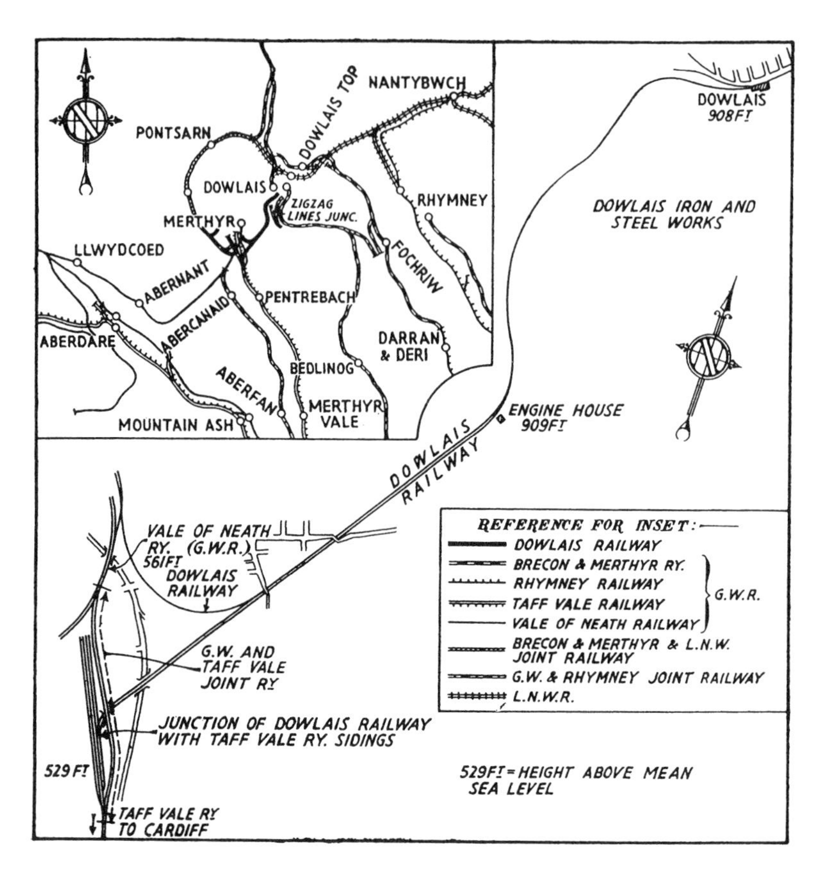

The Dowlais Railway

formed a junction with the Taff Vale Railway, one half-a-mile below their Terminal Station. From this point the railway took a straight line up the Twynyrodyn hillside, passing the Old Ysgubornewydd Farm to Mountain Hare, where the Incline ran out onto a much flatter terrain. This point, quite obviously, became known as Incline Top.

In 1853 the Vale of Neath Railway had, at long last, come through via the Abernant Tunnel, over the Taff Viaduct and then along an elevated railroad supported by no less than 26 arches and two wrought-iron bridges, into the new Vale of Neath Station at Merthyr Tydfil.

Always wishing to take full advantage of deploying wider transport facilities, the Dowlais Iron Company again sought permission from Parliament in 1854 to build a branch line from the Old Ysgubornewydd Farm and swinging westward into the Vale of Neath Station Yard.

In later years, at the point of this junction, there was an irascible old man who pastured his herd of goats. He had an endemic hatred of boys and they, in turn, had that intuitive cruel habit of being able to bait and taunt – safe on the buffers or shackles of 8.30 morning "up"; age and garrulousness together combined to produce both condition of rheumatism and apoplexy that together would not possibly permit chase.

The control cabin which housed the points' control levers for the Vale of Neath Junction was about 100 yards above the Ysgubornewydd Bridge (referred to on some documents as the Occupation Bridge), and on the east side of the line. It could be seen that the points' cabin was only occupied occasionally, so one could presume the traffic down the Branch Line at this late period was intermittent.

Possibly the only technical data that would be of interest both then and now would be the extent of the inclination and that was one foot in twelve.

For those who might read these notes, perhaps the remaining data could be of some interest: "The stationary engine located at Incline Top was built by R. & W. Hawthorn of Newcastle and was installed in August 1851. Two horizontal cylinders of 18" diameter and 24" stroke cycled at 50 strokes per minute: 30 lbs. per sq. inch of steam: two drums 14 feet diameter and 3'3" wide: specified load 33 tons: length of Incline 70 chains 30 links: speed 8 miles per hour."

From experience, I would suggest that the speed specified was very rarely, if ever, attained.

The condition of the rail track in its later years was very rough indeed, and those fishplates could bear a considerable amount of tightening down, judging from the jolts one received as each rail end was passed over – indeed, we began to consider that perhaps the journey was not exactly a worthwhile endeavour.

The rollers mounted between the rails at regular intervals and were there presumably to render less friction and subsequent wear and tear on both hawser and balance engine. An indication of the neglect that had attended the "Incline" for some several years, was the seizure of some of the rollers, with the resultant wearing of a groove in the barrel of the roller. They also contributed further discomfort to the non-paying passengers when the roller well would be full of oily water, which would be thrown up in a spray, some of which was pretty certain to stain the seat of your trousers.

The operation whereby a "lift" was obtained was quite simple. The occupant of the bottom control hut was too far away from the point of entry onto the "Incline" – up the wing wall of the bridge over the Plymouth Railway, through the railings and over to the left side. It wouldn't be long before the hawser would whip and hiss, a forewarning that the four ballast trucks, each half-filled with sand, would pass before you at a nice, sedate trotting pace – adequate to permit grasping the outside rim of the buffer and then to swing both legs up and around the buffer spring housing: if there were prior claimants already possessing places, then the dangling shackle chain was the only prospect open to one. Frequently, this alternative was ignored as the ride it provided was made all the more uncomfortable by the bottom link clanging on those few rollers which were mounted high in their cradles – most decidedly third-class travel – but exciting if that was what you wanted.

It was hardly acceptable, after surviving such experiences, to realise that passenger coaches, with three classes of accommodation, used the line in the early days of its operation. We are informed that in 1852, 755 first-, 1,884 second- and 7,253 third-class passengers used it – it is most doubtful that we third-class qualified but non-paying passengers of 1924/5/6 would match such numbers. It appears that passenger activity stopped after two years.

The right-hand track (always looking up the "Incline") carried all the revenue traffic. At the bottom, this right-hand line swung southward onto the Old Taff Vale Railway and later a bridge was built at this spot to carry the G.W.R. Branch from the Brandy Bridge Junction into Merthyr Station, over the "Incline". The left-hand track terminated at the same point but at a much lower level; there was a fifteen-feet-high revetment wall between the two tracks.

The Mardy Bridge was the spot where single-line operation was committed – there were points shortly before and after the bridge and the control of these points operated from the little hut, already mentioned, at the bottom.

It is unlikely that any railway undertaking can operate for 79 years without incident. In September, 1865, the *Merthyr Telegraph* reported: "At the bottom of the balance incline, which has a siding in the Vale of Neath Station Yard, two wagons laden with pig – after the points draw broke – ran into the pillar and wall at the entrance to the yard. There were no injuries."

The same newspaper, in June, 1868, reported: "Some trucks ran away down the Dowlais Incline onto the Taff Vale Sidings – there was no personal injury."

I remember that in 1928 ten empty wagons were derailed immediately below the Mardy Bridge (no doubt at the points); there was no injury, but a considerable amount of matchwood.

My leaving the Primary School and what appeared at the time the dubious horror of moving into the realms of Grammar School, and the closure of the Dowlais Railway – that is what it had to be in Grammar School parlance – were co-incident. The former of five years' duration, the latter 79 years. I still wonder if my five "Inky" years were the better.

Like most engineering undertakings, at the demise of its active life, it became, in such a very short time, an industrial slum: embankments collapsing, bridges rusting and decaying, dereliction soon prevailed. The "under bridges" were soon demolished, the two remaining "over" road bridges prevailed until the "Inky" was filled in 1946/7.

It was regrettable that acrimony entered into the negotiations between the Local Authority and the G.W.R. concerning the removal of the abutment of the Mardy Bridge. For many years the projection of these abutments onto the main road had been a subject of considerable criticism and they had, in the late twenties, been the means of causing the death of a young lady riding pillion on a motor-cycle. The G.W.R. resisted any claim for their removal for many years after the demolition of the bridging. When they were finally removed, a householder living next to the bridge sought compensation for the cabbages he claimed were damaged during the dismantling of the stonework.

If you care to climb Penylan Hill, you can quite clearly see the straight, green, grassgrown strip of land climbing up Twynyrodyn Hill – still unimpaired by housing development – terminating at Incline Top, under the shadow of the slowly diminishing White Tip of Dowlais – the remnant of great achievements and so much pleasure.

See also:

Serious accident, Dowlais Incline*:*

Cardiff and Merthyr Guardian, 31.12.1853 p.3 col.4.

Inquest:

Cardiff and Merthyr Guardian 7.1.1854 p.3 col.4.
Cardiff and Merthyr Guardian 14.1.1854 p.4 col.4+5.
Cardiff and Merthyr Guardian 14.1.1854 p.3.

Fatal accident on Dowlais Incline:

Merthyr Express 9.8.1890 p.5 col.3.

A Biographical Sketch of Mr. Thomas Williams, J.P., (1823-1903), of Gwaelodygarth House, Chairman of the Merthyr Nonconformist Committee, 1878

Transcribed

His Early Years

"The name of Thomas Williams is inseparably identified with the religious and political history of Merthyr and Aberdare, and with the growth of Welsh Congregationalism during the last thirty years (1848-1878). Possessed of strong and clear scriptural convictions, he has never failed to give earnest practical expression to them, and side by side with men like Mr. Henry Richard, Mr. David Davies, Maesyffynnon, and the Rev. Dr. Price, he has oftentimes fought with undaunted courage the battle of truth against falsehood, of right against wrong. His sterling honesty, transparent truthfulness, admirable simplicity, and entire freedom from selfish notions, have gained him an enviable reputation in the Principality; and his Christian worth and amiable character have endeared him to a very large circle of friends. It is a pleasing task to place on record reminiscences of his exemplary career.

"Mr. Williams was born in Merthyr on the eleventh of November, 1823. His parents, David and Susannah Williams, belonged to the working classes; they were intelligent Christian people, members of the Welsh Congregational Church. Steadfast perseverance enabled them in 1828 to open a grocery business in Hirwaun; this business they conducted with integrity and success.

"Secular educational facilities were then at a premium in Wales; Government officials, for hardly creditable reasons, glossed over the most glaring deficiencies; the clerical autocracy were content to pocket the public revenues, and imbibe public-house beer and, as a subsequent Commission showed, it was left to Nonconformists to ray light into the thick mental fog by means of Sunday-schools. As Thomas Williams was a regular attendant at the Sunday-school it may be fairly assumed that he did not lose very much by non-attendance at the day-schools of the period after he had attained the age of ten.

"When he was sixteen years old [1839] Thomas Williams came back to Merthyr in the capacity of assistant to Mr. David Rosser, grocer. In 1842 he became a member of Zoar Church , and at about the same time he signed the total abstinence pledge; that pledge he has never deviated from.

" 'In 1844,' remarked Mr. Williams at the meeting held for making a presentation to Mr. Rees Lewis, 'my father asked me whether I would like to go and keep a shop for myself or go to the middle-class school of Taliesin Williams (Taliesin ab Iolo). The question was rather a foolish one to ask a boy. I answered, of course, that I would prefer the shop.'

"Thomas Williams opened a grocery business for himself in Hirwaun; there he remained for eight years, following his avocation with diligence and straightforwardness and tact; promoting the Temperance cause and all other ameliorating movements, and doing effective work for his own denomination. It must have been a gratifying circumstance to the father and mother to witness the increasing prosperity of their son, and to see him appointed a deacon at the chapel where they jointly worshipped."

Removal to Aberdare, 1852

"In 1852 Thomas Williams removed to the neighbouring town of Aberdare, where he conducted an extensive grocery business.

"Aberdare was Thomas Williams's home for the next twelve years, and during that period he occupied every local position of eminence; he was elected

a Poor-law Guardian,
a member of the Burial Board and Board of Health,
and High Constable.

"In the three former capacities his sagacity was never at fault, and as High Constable he acquitted himself with very considerable credit. He took part in every public movement of importance, and frequently presided at influential public meetings. He furthered to the utmost of his ability the education of the Welsh people and when their character was defamed by the compilers of the famous Blue-books, he was one of the first to repudiate the disgraceful slanders. Ieuan Gwynedd was deeply attached to him and Ieuan never had a better, truer friend."

Emancipation of slaves

"A memorable meeting in which Thomas Williams took part as Chairman was that held in Aberdare in 1863 with reference to the emancipation of the slaves. In reply to the encouraging resolution forwarded on behalf of the assembly, to the American Legation in London, CHARLES FRANCIS ADAMS, the greatest of American ambassadors, addressed to Mr. T. Williams the subjoined letter:

" 'Legation of the United States, London, May 21st, 1863.

" 'Sir, I am directed by the President of the United States to acknowledge on his behalf the reception of the proceedings of the citizens of Aberdare, which were duly transmitted to him through the medium of this Legation. It gives him pleasure to observe that the proceedings are distinguished by an earnest desire that peace may now and for ever be preserved between the United States and Great Britain; that the union of his own country, which is the bulwark of its safety, may be maintained; and especially that it may not be overthrown so as to give room to a new nation to be founded on the corner-stone of human slavery. I am further instructed to say that the justice of these sentiments, as well as the confidence in the President, which is expressed in the proceedings would entitle the subjects of Great Britain who constituted these meetings to a special, grateful and fervent notice on his part. His sentiments on the subjects involved have, however, been so fully expressed in replies which have been made to the working men of Manchester, to the citizens of London, assembled at Exeter Hall on the evening of the 29th of January last, and to the citizens of Bradford, that instead of repetition he prays that you will consider the spirit expressed in them as equally entertained in the present case.'

"To have elicited such noble sentiments from so noble a man must have been a source of just pride to Mr. Williams."

Brecon Memorial College

"Still more conspicuously did Thomas Williams figure in the bicentenary movement of 1862. That movement had a very deep hold upon the Welsh Congregational Churches. Almost every Church held a special meeting to commemorate the heroic action of the famous 'Two thousand', the fathers of Nonconformity. Lectures were delivered and public meetings were held to recount the history of the ejection, to explain the principles of 'the ejected', to defend them from calumnious mis-representations and to pay a tribute to their self-sacrifice.

"Great efforts were made to build new chapels, and to pay the debts remaining on chapels already built; the extra contributions of Welsh churches for these purposes, from 1862 to 1869, did not fall very far short of £80,000.

"It was the general desire from the outset that some special monument should be raised in which all the Churches could unite; and after repeated and largely attended Conferences which were held in Neath, Denbigh and Carmarthen, it was unanimously decided that the admiration and esteem of the Welsh Churches for the heroes of 1662 should be indicated by the establishment of a MEMORIAL COLLEGE. The annual association of Welsh Congregationalists approved of the scheme, and Thomas Williams was appointed treasurer. Deputations visited the Churches to receive subscriptions, and more than £18,000 was cheerfully promised (to be paid in five annual instalments). But, unfortunately, the decision just then arrived at in England to allow every contributor to devote his money to chapel extension, the extinction of Chapel debts, enlargement of colleges, or the Memorial, affected the promises of the Welsh Churches. The promised £18,000 dwindled down to £1,800, £16,200 being swallowed up in local efforts. These efforts were not condemned, but they necessarily collided with and materially mitigated against the projected Memorial College movement.

"Several gentlemen who had promised large sums to the fund devoted them entirely to home purposes, whilst others paid only a fractional part of their promised College subscriptions, so that the Committee were under the necessity of beginning afresh, and that when the resources of the Churches were nearly exhausted. But Thomas Williams and his helpers were not deterred from carrying out their intention by the altered state of things; after long consideration they selected a site at Brecon for the Memorial College. The situation was one of the most healthy and charming in the Principality, and the plans were drawn so that the front of the building (to which four acres of land were attached) should face the river Usk and the beautiful valley beyond. The cost of the land and building would, it was estimated, amount to at least £10,000.

"In March 1867 a special Conference was held at Neath to consider the financial pros and cons of the movement. £2,500 would be forthcoming, and the remaining £7,500 was divided between the several counties in Wales, according to their number and strength; two of the secretaries were engaged to collect £3,000 in England.

"The foundation stone of the new College was laid on Wednesday, June 13th, 1867, by Mr. Samuel Morley, M.P. There was a magnificent public procession through the town, headed by the mayor and corporation. At the site a number of stirring addresses were delivered by Mr. Henry Richard, the Rev. Robert Thomas, and the venerable Welsh patriarch, the Rev. D. Williams, of Troedrhiwdaler. Mr. Morley, the prince of givers, was presented with a silver trowel by Mr. Thomas Williams. Mr. Morley acknowledged this presentation, and an Address previously presented to him, in terms of much feeling. Mr. Morley presided over a public meeting in the evening.

"From that date Thomas Williams worked night and day on behalf of the College as treasurer. He seemed to regard it as his bounden duty to find every half-penny of the requisite funds. Willing testimony to his splendid efforts was borne by the Rev. Mr. Evans, of Caernarfon and other ministers and laymen at the subsequent opening services.

" 'Our friend Mr. Williams,' remarked the rev. gentleman, 'is always ready with hand, heart and purse to help in every good public movement. I wish our English friends to understand that a treasurer in his case does not mean a man who received and paid the money merely, but one who made himself everything to everybody for the accomplishment of his object. He has travelled from county to county, and he has spoken from chapel to chapel in its favour. He has written thousands of letters; and as for newspaper correspondence, why, his beseeching letters stared the guilty, who had not collected, in the face of every newspaper. There was no quietness to be got except by remitting a collection to Goitre. I am told that there are a few Churches yet who have not collected: I feel sure that they must be either Churches whose deacons never read any Welsh newspapers, or avoid all letters signed "T. Williams", or that previous selfishness has hardened them to such a degree that they are proof against the most pressing appeals and kindest solicitations for help. (Cheers.) I have had the good fortune of receiving several letters from Mr. Williams acknowledging contributions towards the movement, and knowing that he had to write scores of them every week I have been really surprised at their length and tone. They were all kind, friendly letters. It is generally reported, Mr. Chairman, that such was his zeal for the erection of this splendid College, that a letter containing a contribution towards it gave him more pleasure and was always opened and read before another containing the rent of a farm or a house of his own.'

"The Rev. Mr. Thomas, Landore, was the College architect, and Messrs. Thomas, Watkins and Jenkins, of Swansea, the builders. The opening services took place on September 15th and 16th, 1869. Mr. Morley was again present, as well as Mr. Henry Richard, the Rev. Thomas Binney, Mr. Evan Matthew Richards, the Rev. John Kennedy, Gohebydd, and other leading Congregationalists.

"In the report of the Bicentenary Committee, particular eulogy was passed on Mr. Thomas Williams, in the following words:

" 'The Committee desires to express its deep sense of obligation to the Treasurer, not only for his generous donation of £250, but also for his untired exertions and the consecration of his time and labour to obtain the object in view, and believes that to him more than to any other man is due the successful result that is seen this day.'

"On the motion of the Rev. J. Kilsby Jones, the sub-joined proposition was also unanimously passed at a crowded public meeting. 'That the Committee and friends of the Congregational Memorial College beg to express their sincerest thanks to Thomas Williams, Esq., for having in addition to unwearied exertions, presented the institution with a most valuable and varied collection of geological and other specimens, to form the beginning of what is hoped will soon be a noble Museum.'

"Mr. Williams, it will thus be seen, spared neither money, gifts nor labour to make the Memorial College scheme a success, and a success he did make it, and it stands today [1878], a substantial memento of his large-heartedness and sterling merit.

"On September 16th, 1870, Mr. Williams's College accounts were audited and certified by Mr. D. E. Williams, of Hirwaun, and Mr. John Rowlands, stockbroker, of Cardiff. They showed the College expenditure and income to have amounted to £11,651. Mr. Morley had contributed altogether £1,250, of which £200 was promised at the opening services on condition that Mr. T. Williams collected within a specified time another £600. Need we say that the sum was forthcoming?

"The whole of the Treasurer's expenses for eight years were placed at the nominal figure of £21.13s. Well might Thomas Williams's goodness of heart be admired; well might praise be lavished upon his disinterestedness."

(*Merthyr Telegraph* 15.3.1878 p.3 col.1.)

Defence of Mr. Bowstead, Inspector of Schools

"Another important movement in which Thomas Williams took an active part during his residence at Aberdare was the defence of Mr. Bowstead, Her Majesty's then Inspector of Schools for South Wales and Monmouthshire.

"Mr. Bowstead was a man who appreciated merit wherever he found it, and in the report which he presented to the Committee of Council in 1854-55 he stated, with accuracy, the educational position of this section of the Principality, and gave credit to Welsh Dissenters for the work they had accomplished.

"This did not please the more rabid members of the Church of England, and their displeasure was considerably deepened by the circumstance that Mr. Bowstead had not followed the example of his predecessors, and rapturously extolled the National schools and their promoters. He had actually had the daring hardihood to depict things as they were, and not as they might have been; to refrain from throwing the customary sop to the ecclesiastical authorities, to speak the truth, the whole truth, and nothing but the truth.

"Lethargy and incompetence had been meted out censure by Mr. Bowstead, irrespective of persons. The Church clergy were especially aggrieved, for they were almost unexceptionally the National school managers; Mr. Bowstead's outspokenness they regarded as contumacy, and his honesty they deprecated as hostility, a fact which speaks volumes for their penetration, if not for their high-mindedness.

"The clergy's feeble cause found an illustrious advocate, no less a one than the Right Reverend the Lord Bishop of Saint David's.

"The Bishop was no novice in the field of controversy; his pen had in polemics already done the Church and Christianity good service, and it was with an exquisite thrill of anticipative delight that his satellites learnt that he, their intellectual Goliath, was going to do battle on their behalf against the recusant Bowstead.

"For his Lordship's heart waxed wrath at Mr. Bowstead's report, and the services of his Lordship's amanuensis [secretary] were soon in requisition for the purpose of replying to Mr. Bowstead's implications. This reply his Lordship delivered in the form of a diocesan charge. It was characterised by intense bitterness and repudiated Mr. Bowstead's data as untrustworthy, and his inferences as fallacious. It follows in natural sequence that the Church and her National schools were reinstated in their seigneurial position, and the Nonconformists and their schools were relegated to insignificance and semi-contempt. Nonconformists were also credited by his Lordship with virulent antipathy towards National schools.

"The Nonconformists of South Wales, with quiet, impressive dignity, immediately entered their caveat against the Bishop's rancorous manifesto, and crowded meetings were held in all populous centres to discuss the subject fully. At these meetings resolutions were passed exonerating Mr. Bowstead from the Bishop's damaging imputations, and endorsing his report.

"Aberdare, ever careful of the honour of the land of which she is the favoured literary centre, was about the first to protest. Mr. Thomas Williams was appointed Secretary to a Defence Committee and, with spirited patriotism, he promoted the vindicatory procedure in every way he could.

"A public meeting was held at the Temperance Hall on Tuesday evening, 29th January, 1861, under the presidency of the talented Welsh poet and philanthropist, Alaw Goch (David Williams, Ynyscynon).

"In conformity with the sentiment given expression to at this meeting, Mr. Williams addressed the following circular to the various Welsh Members of Parliament:

" 'Mill Street, Aberdare, February 13th, 1861.

" 'Sir

" 'In pursuance of the decision of one of the most crowded, enthusiastic and influential meetings ever held in the town of Aberdare, I have the honour to call your attention to the accompanying resolutions. I sincerely trust, that should the matter in dispute turn up in any form in the House of Commons during the present Session, your voice will be raised in defence of those rights of conscience, which the great bulk of the inhabitants of Wales so warmly cherish, and so highly value; and should any debate on the question result in a division, I hope that your vote will be given in favour, not of schools based upon sectarian principles, but of those which, whilst strictly scriptural in their teaching, are founded upon principles so liberal as to be able to include all Christian denominations.

" 'For the Committee, yours faithfully, Thomas Williams, Hon. Sec.'

"Action of this kind lent weight and dignity to the representations of the Welsh members, and the upshot was the virtual endorsement of every word contained in Mr. Bowstead's report, and the ignominious discomfiture of the Bishop and the lesser Church lights.

"Thus it was that Nonconformity was again freed from unmerited stigma, and the shackles in which a jealous, apathetic, unforbearing priesthood sought to fetter a liberty loving community were once more riven. It redounds to the lasting honour of Thomas Williams that he contributed with such zeal, courage and single-mindedness to this nationally advantageous result."

Political Activity

"At the county and borough Parliamentary elections, Thomas Williams was always an unflinching supporter of the Liberal candidates; and he helped materially to return Mr. Talbot, Mr. Vivian, Sir John Guest and Mr. Bruce. An effective Welsh language speaker, he frequently presided at the election meetings, and his remarks were as acceptable as they were pointed and enlightening. He was one of the guests at the memorable Election Dinner held at Dowlais many years ago.

"There was a healthy robustness about Thomas Williams's Liberalism which evoked admiration even from political opponents. He never paid a Church-rate in his life. The collector once threatened to take away and distrain on his goods in lieu of the amount of the rate. Thomas Williams's reply was that the collector might if he chose take the goods, but he [Williams] would not pay the obnoxious rate. And pay it he did not.

"In local connexional work, Mr. Williams was untiring. He was the secretary of the Trecynon Congregational Church, and the treasurer of many other churches, including the churches at Llwydcoed and Cwmdare. It is a striking testimony to the vigour with which Thomas Williams prosecuted Christian work at Aberdare that, whilst there were only two Congregational Churches in the district when he joined the cause, there were thirteen churches when he took his departure from the town. Mr. Williams was a deacon at Trecynon as well as at Hirwaun.

"In 1859 the Congregational Union held their annual meeting at Aberdare by invitation. The Lord Mayor for that year was a Congregationalist, and he attended the gathering. The proceedings passed off without a hitch. Thomas Williams acted as treasurer to the local fund for defraying the incidental expenses, the necessary £500 was duly forthcoming.

"Mr. Williams was an Aberdare Gas Co. director for many years."

Departure to Merthyr, 1864

"In 1862 Thomas Williams embarked in the iron trade, and in 1864 he removed to Merthyr, his birthplace.

"The severance of Mr. Williams's connection with Aberdare was a subject of deep regret to all who had the privilege of knowing him.

"The Trecynon Temperance Society, of which he was President, presented him with a splendid gold medal as a token of their affectionate esteem, and the Trecynon [Ebenezer] Church, pastor Rev. W. Edwards indicated their gratitude to Mr. Williams for his exertions by presenting him with a handsome gold watch, and a touchingly worded and beautifully illuminated Address.

"The Address is worth preserving were it only for its intrinsic literary merit; there is about it a quaint beauty which recalls to memory the pure idiomatic English of the old Divines.

> " 'Sir,' is remarked in one place, with an abruptness almost startling, 'you owe much to the grace of God for enabling you to throw your heart and soul into everything that is good and deserving.'

"In another paragraph the rising emotional tumult at parting subsides into perfect calm with the soothing words, 'We may confidently leave events in the hands of God.'

> " 'God,' the Address goes on to say, 'has given you a tact and talent for business, and He has not been sparing in giving you an intensely active and enterprising spirit.'

"The Address throughout is pervaded by unaffected, pure spiritual sentiment.

"The members of the Llwydcoed Church presented Mr. Williams with a charming inkstand and pencil case.

"Thomas Williams fully reciprocated the kindliness shown towards him, and he must have felt it a hard task to leave the Church at Trecynon. At times, no doubt, he still reverts with pleasure and maybe with longing feelings, to the very happy years he spent at Aberdare.

"The advent of so consistent and influential an abstainer at Merthyr caused as much gratification amongst local temperance reformers as his departure caused chagrin amongst Aberdarians, and a cordial Address of welcome was presented to him. This Address was signed by Mr. Rees Lewis, the President of the Merthyr Temperance Society; Mr. W. L. Daniel, the Chairman of the Executive Committee, and Mr. Richard Harris, Secretary; and it was pointed out in it that the status to which the Gwent and Morganwg Temperance

Association had attained was to a great extent attributable to Thomas Williams's unceasing endeavours. Mr. Williams was President of the Association in 1861, and Secretary 1860-1878.

"Thomas Williams rejoined Zoar Church, Merthyr, and was immediately elected a deacon. He has been a member of the Congregational diaconal body for twenty-eight years."

Commercial Activity

"Mr. T. Williams and Mr. Davis, of Tynewydd, purchased the Penydarren Works from Mr. Foreman; they carried on the concern for twelve months, then they sold it to Mr. Richard Fothergill, M.P. They then became repossessed of the College Lock Iron Works, near Llandaff, Works which as partners they had before conducted. The partners operated the College Iron Works for years, until the reflux [ebb] in the iron trade set in.

"The Works will again, we believe, be started when times improve, but the proprietary has partly changed; Thomas Williams's present partner is a Cardiff gentleman; Mr. Davis sold out a while ago.

"Thomas Williams owns, besides, other properties, including a colliery at Pontypridd, extensive landed and household property, and he is a Director of the Great Western Colliery Company. Prosperity attends him in nearly every thing he takes in hand.

The Welsh Congregational Union, Undeb yr Annibynwyr Cymreig

"Of immense benefit to Congregationalism in the Principality has been the 'Welsh Congregational Union', Undeb yr Annibynwyr Cymreig, which Thomas Williams, assisted by his friends, Gohebydd (John Griffith, 1821-77), Mr. C. R. Jones, Llanfyllin, and a few ministers, mooted, and after really gigantic exertion, succeeded in establishing. The Union gives strength and cohesion to Welsh Congregationalism, and the annual meetings afford pastors and deacons opportunity of mingling together and interchanging religious ideas which could not be so well obtained at the General Congregational Union gathering. Papers are read and discussed at the meetings, and sermons are preached at night; the former have induced wholesome expansiveness of thought, and the latter greatly popularised Congregationalism.

"The inaugural meeting was held at Carmarthen in 1872, under the Presidency of the Rev. Dr. William Rees (Hiraethog) of Liverpool. The most recent meeting took place at Portmadoc in 1877, the Rev. William Evans,

Aberaeron, was the Chairman. The 1878 meeting will be held at Llandeilo. Thomas Williams was the mainspring of this movement, which did not stand in antagonism to the Congregational Union proper, and he was the treasurer from the commencement. The accounts for 1877 showed a sum in hand, after paying all expenses, of £49.19s.6 1/2d. Every shilling is accounted for in the published report.

"Thomas Williams, in an excellent address which he delivered as Chairman of the Glamorganshire Association in July, 1873, on the "Support of the Ministry" (this address was afterwards published at the request of the Association), remarked that he felt confident that the Welsh Congregational Union would do much towards infusing into Congregational Churches the lay element.

"Time has shown that his confidence has not been misplaced. At the Union Meeting of 1877, Thomas Williams read a masterly paper bearing on Church finance. The matter was so ably treated that the Union recommended the paper to the careful consideration of the connexional churches. Thomas Williams generally represents the Welsh Churches at the United Congregational Union Meetings (no ordinary proof of confidence) and he is a member of the Committee of the Union.

"He is also manager of the Congregational Pastors' Retiring Fund and Pastors' Widows' Fund (the praiseworthy objects of these funds are clear) and he is a Director of the London and Home Missionary Societies. It says something of Congregational energy that the capital of the Pastors' Fund, started at the Aberdare Union Meeting in 1859, amounted to £100,000 in 1878; £5,000 of this was collected in Wales. The £100,000 was invested in the names of Mr. Williams and another gentleman.

"Mr. T. Williams was the treasurer of the " Society for promoting the establishment and support of English Congregational Churches in South Wales and Monmouthshire" since its inception at Cardiff in 1860, and he was Chairman for 1878. When the last report was issued, there were forty flourishing churches in the district, embraced by the Society, which would not have existed but for the Society, and thirty-three churches received grants varying from £8 to £30 to enable them to maintain an efficient ministry. There was a balance in the treasurer's hands of £390. Mr. W. L. Daniel, Merthyr, was one of the auditors. It would be difficult to over-estimate the indebtedness of this Society to Thomas Williams.

"Mr. Williams has been a member of the Burial Board and Local Board of Health for very many years and he has been a Guardian of the Poor, in fact, as well as in name, for a lengthened period; first for the Town, then for Penydarren Ward and in 1878 as an 'ex-officio'."

Temperance Activities

"Thomas Williams was a member of several Temperance Societies, and enroled himself a member of the United Kingdom Alliance as far back as June, 1854. When the Templar Order was introduced into Merthyr, Thomas Williams supported it by becoming one of the charter members of Gwalia Lodge, and an engrossed Address was presented to him by the Lodge in 1874, when he was appointed a Justice of the Peace.

We append a quotation from Thomas Williams's acknowledgement of the presentation:

> " 'He, Thomas Williams, was the son of a working man, was born in Merthyr, became a teetotaller upwards of twenty years ago, when that name was less popular than it is now, and in his business, instead of giving drinks, as was then the custom when shop accounts were squared up, he gave money or articles, a practice followed to this day in Hirwaun and Aberdare. He was told he could not carry on his trade without the drink, but he resolved to do so, and succeeded beyond his anticipation. In this he had only done his duty, and felt that duty deserved no special recognition. However, he could assure them he should look upon this Address as one of his chief treasures, and in response to their kind wishes he would endeavour to live as long as he could.
>
> " 'He had often thought that he ought to curtail much of his public work, for that and his own business usually kept him working when other people were in bed. Yet, when the thought of relaxation was uppermost, a mental whisper seemed to say "You must work, and rest in the grave"; and if so, he hoped he might be spared to help to elevate and benefit his fellowmen. It was not his ability that enabled him to do much, for when he started in life he had not the same educational advantages that young men have now; this had been a great drawback to him; and he hoped those who were now growing up would use well the opportunities that were placed within their reach. To show them some of his private work, he might mention that he was treasurer to about a dozen Societies, and this, besides attending so many committees – for he believed in committee work – absorbed all his time. He had had a great deal to encounter to maintain his principles. On one

> occasion, when in the bread trade, the brewers refused to supply him with barm [yeast] because he was a teetotaller. He then obtained a good recipe for making barm, and not only made better barm, and sufficient for his own purpose, but sold even more than the brewers. After giving other instances Brother Williams said he merely mentioned this to stimulate the young men not to sacrifice principle, but rather seek to overcome the difficulties that might be placed in the way, and to hold fast their integrity to the end.'

"There is a genuine ring of Christian manliness about these observations. 'I shall never forget,' concluded Mr. Williams, 'the leading principles of my life when on the magisterial Bench.'

"Merthyrians of all types and shades will willingly allow that he has not done so, that he has not forsworn his Christianity.

"Thomas Williams was appointed a special Templar Deputy in 1872. He has held Office in his own Lodge, and has been chosen a member of the Finance Committee of the Grand Lodge."

Public Offices held

"He is Chairman of the Merthyr Building Society and Vice-Chairman of the School Board; his business aptitude has borne good fruit at the Society, and his impartiality, judgement and promptitude have fully justified the choice of the School Board. Thomas Williams has never been backward in putting his hand into his pocket for the promotion of educational interests. He was the Chairman of the Committee for erecting the Merthyr British Schools, and in conjunction with Mr. Davis and Mr. Phillips, he gave the site, an acre of the value of £600. Thomas Williams is a thorough going Liberationist, and adherent of the ballot, and is a personal friend of Mr. Morley and, we believe, of Mr. Miall.

"When, on the granting of a second Member for Merthyr, a Nonconformist election Committee was formed at Merthyr and another at Aberdare, Mr. Charles James was elected Chairman of the Merthyr Committee, and Thomas Williams the Treasurer. When in 1872 the School Board election came off, and a difference arose between Mr. James and the Committee, ending in Mr. James's resignation, T. Williams was elected Chairman. That Office he has since held.

"Mr. Fothergill's subsequent misfortunes led Mr. Williams's admirers to form still higher hopes of his political future. It was thought that if he would allow himself to be nominated, Merthyr would get what Merthyr wanted, a member whose political and religious views harmonized broadly with those of the majority of the constituency. These hopes were disappointed; Mr. Williams replied to appeals made to him on the matter that he would not go to Parliament: 'I can better serve my country and my God,' he said, 'by continuing in the course which I have followed so far.' The ultimatum was a disappointment to many, and there are those who still hope Thomas Williams will change his mind on the subject.

"Thomas Williams is a contributor to the Welsh press, and is a staunch friend of the Eisteddfod. He is Secretary to Zoar Church, and issues an annual statistical statement showing all the monies he has received during the twelve months, and all the monies which have been expended.

"The Sunday School he seldom fails to attend; his influence for good there is vast; every encouragement that he can give to the Sunday School scholars to diligence and reverence and careful Biblical study he does give. He has the oversight of one or two classes himself, and there does not exist a more patient Sunday School teacher."

His Christian Character

"Here it is that Thomas Williams's character shines, brightens into beauty. A Christian man, living as well as teaching, and teaching as well as living the pure Gospel faith of his boyhood and manhood and middle age, he has shown the sceptical and the scoffing, the hesitating and the foolishly wise, that Christianity has not lost its virtue, that it is still something more than a name or an exploded tradition.

"There is much, it is true, to admire in Mr. Williams's mental grasp and shrewdness; these have been the means of building up his worldly fortunes. But Thomas Williams is not the only man who, possessed of such distinguished qualities, has out-distanced compeers in the commercial race; men of like 'luck' may be picked out by scores in any town of moderate size.

"It is, we repeat, his practical, glowing, vivifying, heroic and self-sacrificing Christianity which imparts nobleness to his frank (if rugged) nature; which gives him pre-eminence as a public man amongst the public men by whom he is surrounded at home and from home.

" 'The beginning and the end of what is the matter with us in these days,' remarked Carlyle forty years ago, 'is that we have forgotten God.' The truth, savour as it may of cant to the canting, is none the less a truth, and it applies with quite as much force in 1878 as it did in 1838. It is therefore cheering to find men like the subject of our sketch Christianizing society by example and precept, fusing vitality into the spheres in which they move, exemplifying there the moral grandeur of religion, and furthering its extension by little means and by large means; by teaching the child to read as well as by giving successful effect to schemes for training ministers for evangelical work at home, and missionaries for evangelical work abroad.

"We congratulate the Congregational cause upon numbering amongst its members so loyal a gentleman and so earnest a Christian as Thomas Williams, and we trust that the day is far off when his face will be missed from amongst us.

"For him may be claimed the credit of having trod duty's thorny paths faithfully and lovingly, and the generations of Congregationalists who will come after him, in referring to his career, will not improbably speak his eulogy in the pregnant words Longfellow used of Channing, 'Servant of God, well done'. " (*Merthyr Telegraph* 22.3.1878 p.3.)

The Public Life and Image of Lady Charlotte Guest, and the Society in which she lived: 1833-1852

by CLAIRE LOUISE THOMAS

Lady Charlotte Guest not only became a legend after her death but was one in her own lifetime too. Even though she was famous for being the "Guardian Angel" of Dowlais and Merthyr Tydfil, Lady Charlotte was born on 19th May, 1812, and christened Lady Charlotte Elizabeth Bertie, the eldest child of the ninth Earl and Countess of Lindsey. On 30th April, 1833, a short time before her twenty-first birthday, Lady Charlotte left her country home in Lincolnshire to travel to London, where she met her future husband – John Guest. It was Mrs. Wyndham Lewis (later to become Benjamin Disraeli's wife) who was the first to introduce her to John Guest at one of her dinner parties on 17th June, 1833. Within a month John Guest had proposed to Lady Charlotte in Kensington Gardens.[1]

On 29th July, 1833, Lady Charlotte Bertie and John Guest were married, and it is at the end of the week that the first reference to this estimable Lady is to be seen in the newspaper of Merthyr Tydfil in the marriage section.

> "On Monday, the 29th of July, at St. George's Church, Hanover Square, by the Lord Bishop of Gloucestire, Josiah John Guest, Esq., M.P., to the Lady Charlotte Bertie, sister of the Earl of Lindsey."
>
> 3rd August, 1833

Lady Charlotte's new husband was a great industrialist, master of the Dowlais iron works at Merthyr Tydfil, which was situated at the northern rim of the South Wales' coalfield. The home of Lady Charlotte's early years, Uffington, was a great contrast to Dowlais, which was a hub of industrial activity. The picture postcard image of green rolling pastures and sleepy rural communities in Glamorgan had by this time recognisably changed. Industrialisation brought with it a black cloud and a general air of neglect and oppression which settled on the valleys, a cloud of neglect which in some instances still remains today.

The physical contours of the narrow valleys of this industrial area were not suitable for the influx of people who arrived to work in these iron communities. It was a grave misfortune for Wales that industrialisation took place in sparsely inhabited tracts of bleak, open moorland and in steep, narrow valleys. The population exploded and "clearly the almighty had never intended 200,000 to live at these valley heads."[2] Thus, it was a stroke of luck for Dowlais and Merthyr Tydfil that Lady Charlotte was to live in their community. A stroke of luck that was to see her identify herself with the working people of the community, adopt their language as her own, translate their folk tales and, above all, one who was willing and able to alleviate the deplorable social conditions that existed, and who was to perpetuate the cause of moral and educational improvements throughout her lifetime.

The *Cardiff and Merthyr Guardian* was established in 1832, and the paper's first edition was on Saturday, 17th November of that year. It not only contained news of a localised nature, but news of national importance, shipping news, literary news. Its articles were often written by correspondents at the spot so that much of its detail was correct, and it gives a fair and true description of events as they were seen at the time. Lady Charlotte was classed as newsworthy, not only due to the fact that she was married to a great ironmaster, but as an individual, a person in her own right, and she was to feature in this newspaper as much as her husband in the years between 1833-1852.

When John Guest was first elected M.P. for Merthyr Tydfil he declared, "Knowledge is the Power and I wish that power to extend to all ranks of society in order that they may become better and happier men." John Guest kept his promises and Dowlais ironworks prided itself on the schools it provided for its workers at a time when there was no statutory right to education. Coupled with the fact that Lady Charlotte was clearly a well-educated woman of extreme capabilities, it was not extraordinary that she was to become closely involved with the schools of the ironworks. However, her interest may not have been ignited without a visit to these schools shortly after her arrival at Dowlais.

> "Dowlais National School – The boys of this establishment were examined in the last week before Christmas; this examination lasted part of three days, J. J. Guest, Esq., M.P., Lady Charlotte Guest, E. J. Hutchins, the Rev. E. Jenkins &c. were present..."
>
> 4th January, 1834

Lady Charlotte was soon to have her first child, Maria, who was born on 3rd July, 1834 (announced 5th July edition) and nine other children followed afterwards.[3] A complete contrast to most Victorian women, Lady Charlotte accompanied her husband and performed her own duties throughout her pregnancies. Even though Maria was born in London, Lady Charlotte had her second child, Ifor Bertie, at Dowlais House on 29th August, 1835 (announced 5th September edition), showing the depth of feeling for her new home that she would not leave, and the inner strength she possessed to remain when Merthyr Tydfil had no hospitals and no doctors of the experience she would have encountered in London.

While much of the press of the mid-nineteenth century portrays Wales as a dull, drab, neglected and oppressed society, it was simultaneously a rich and vibrant society. Even though it lagged behind the rest of Britain in terms of sub-standard housing, urban overcrowding, health and hospital services, malnutrition and disease, individuals were prepared to help themselves create a better life. The cultural traditions of Wales were kept alive and rose at an unprecedented level, as did the slag heaps on the side of the valleys. Nonconformist chapels were to flourish and become establishments of learning and the social whirl of these places included gatherings such as balls, eisteddfodau and fairs.

Lady Charlotte was to attend the Waun Fair and the newspaper not only comments on this but the attendance and furnishes the reader with accounts of the weather, too. Another paragraph comments on the violence that exists within the community and the report clearly shows that the events that occurred in Merthyr in the summer of 1831 have not been forgotten. It is obvious to see that even though three years have elapsed it cannot be eradicated from people's minds, and that the higher echelons of society are aware of the real danger that exists and that often it merely lies dormant beneath the surface.

> "Waun Fair... among the unbidden though not unwelcome guests we observed J. J. Guest, Esq., and his lovely partner, Lady Charlotte Guest,

> who, we will stake the *Gazette and Guardian* against Dowlais, or any part thereof, were never better pleased amid the gayest, proudest throng of a Court day... There were, we are happy to say, fewer martial displays than usual, for we only witnessed one fight, although some of our war like friends from Dowlais attended decently begrimed from the collieries."
>
> 27th September, 1834

The social whirl of Merthyr Tydfil also consisted of a theatre which Lady Charlotte was to visit. Although almost certainly not to the standard of any London theatre she had been used to, Lady Charlotte is gracious in her praise and inspires others by her comments. It must be remembered that the article gives us a greater insight into Merthyr society in showing us that the theatre was not just for the elite but for all individuals. The new industrialisation had led to a greater affluence in the area, an affluence that demanded more outlets for people's wealth than the public houses that littered the town.

> "Merthyr Theatre... Lady Charlotte Guest patronised this theatre... Lady Charlotte, we understand, spoke in high terms of the exertion of Mr. Glover and his company, and expressed herself highly pleased with the performances of the evening – her ladyship in thus patronising the theatre has revived their drooping spirits..."
>
> 3rd January, 1835

It is evident with the visit of Lady Charlotte to the Merthyr theatre that Welsh society was not always as backward as some may have portrayed it. John Guest also held election balls to help his political campaign, which is not unlike politicians of today. We are also able to observe that industrialisation was certainly having an effect on the politicisation of a nation. More important is the toast that Lady Charlotte received from Mr. Taliesin Williams[4] at this election ball.

> "... I have seen during my many years' residence in this friendly town, several English families settled among us, who, not withstanding their various grades of respectable intellect, still could not surmount their national prejudices and unjust animosities; ... they have viewed our national habits and our indefeasible attachment to our ancient language with jealous unkindness... a distinguished Lady, from the noble House

of Lindsey, now resides among us; – her lofty mind is, from exalted sympathy, attached to our towering hills; she has adopted our costumes – and our language, and from the first day that she honoured Merthyr with her residence... she has visited the widow and the fatherless and fed the poor and the needy... 'the health of Lady Charlotte Guest.' "

24th January, 1835

It is obvious that Lady Charlotte was held in high esteem and that the Welsh people were touched by the fact that she has learned their language. Also the benevolence she displayed to the poor is noteworthy. Contrasted to the acquired wealth Lady Charlotte possessed, she not only gave of her money but, more importantly, of her time, which was unusual in the Victorian era.

The *Morning Chronicle*'s observation that the "lower orders speak a language unknown to the educated classes," is untrue in this instance. Lady Charlotte was certainly well-educated, but the difference between her and her contemporaries was that she took the time to look at her surroundings and recognised the need to learn Welsh. She knew that the Welsh language was the key to open many doors, and would enable her to push for social improvements at a time when there was no Welfare State or sign of one for years. Lady Charlotte also possessed the character and determination to persevere at her studies so that she learned Welsh, and she learned it well.

Lady Charlotte did not remain in Merthyr continuously all through the year; she took part in a number of social events which took her away from the area she had grown to love. There are references to Lady Charlotte attending the Cowbridge Hunt on Thursday, 19th November, 1835, and attending Her Majesty's Drawing Room in early March, 1836. It was not unusual for her to give parties in London, though this was to be expected when you consider that her husband, John, would have had to visit the City on Parliamentary business. What was astonishing was her ability to integrate two societies together and become adept at composing herself in either – two societies that were so totally opposite.

Lady Charlotte was continually interested in promoting education and learning amongst all classes of society. There are continual references throughout the years 1833-1852 to this end. There are also many references to her association with the Abergavenny Cymreigyddion Society, that range from her attendance at meetings to her donating the prize money for the best essay entitled "The History of Merthyr Tydfil".

It is also possible to trace the development of improvements in transportation by following the social life of Lady Charlotte. Transportation was a fundamental issue in the nineteenth century, especially where industry was concerned and this had an effect on Lady Charlotte through her husband. Due to her position in society, Lady Charlotte was often invited to perform the honours of opening a fete, etc., but on 16th August, 1837:

> "The first stone of the Taff Vale Railway was laid by Lady Charlotte Guest, ... 'it gives me great pleasure to perform the duties I have just completed. I hope that this great undertaking will be the means of doing much good...'."
>
> 19th August, 1837

Lady Charlotte would often accompany her husband to such railway functions as it was usually iron from the Dowlais works that had constructed the rail track. Four years' later, on 24th April, 1841, Lady Charlotte is reported as feeding the gentlemen who had arrived from Cardiff due to the opening of the entire main line of the Taff Vale Railway. However, she was to wait a further ten years to see the extension of the railway to Dowlais. It was reported on 30th August, 1851, that Lady Charlotte was entertaining at Dowlais House due to the opening of the Dowlais branch of the Taff Vale Railway. It is not only the advancement of rail travel that is evident while following Lady Charlotte's public life, but the opening of the Bute Ship Canal in October, 1839. Industrialisation had led to a greater commercial awareness of the importance of the reduction of transportation costs, and thus there was a continual need to advance methods of transporting coal and iron from the valley heads to Cardiff.

Lady Charlotte was always a great ambassador for her adopted country and took every opportunity to promote Wales and its people. On 16th June, 1838, she attended the Grand Cambrian Ball dressed in a Welsh costume.

> "... Lady Charlotte Guest, appeared in the Welsh character as Makkwt Merthyr, and Mrs. Hall, as Gwenny Gwent. Never did two Saxon ladies adopt the Bwmbast a gwlain, and black hat more successfully. Had they been natives, or brought up in the Principality, they could not have succeeded better."
>
> 16th June, 1838

Not content merely with her own achievements, Lady Charlotte endeavoured to enlist the help of others in her cause of promoting Wales and instigating moral and social reforms.

Probably the most memorable of all this Lady's achievements was the translation of the Welsh romantic folk tales collectively known as the Mabinogion into English. Lady Charlotte would have earned the respect of the Welsh by learning their language alone, but to translate the old folk tales that were in danger of being lost to the nineteenth century was to endear her to their hearts for ever. She was not the first person to undertake the translation of these tales; the significance of her achievement lay in the fact that she was the first person to succeed.

> "The accomplished Lady Charlotte Guest has done good service to Welsh literature by her labours, more especially by the publication of this splendid work, which will long remain as a trophy of her genius. Too many of adequate talents and blessed with rank and station, are content to rest in unlettered ease; not so the fair authoress of the work before us, and she is well-deserving the gratitude of Welshmen..."
>
> 16th April, 1842

Lady Charlotte was a character who could not lie idle and, coupled with her wealth and independent spirit, it allowed her to do more than most of her contemporaries for Merthyr society.

While trade was buoyant, wages were high and there was a friendly atmosphere which characterised the area. It was a place where a full, rounded life could be experienced, but also a place where an individual had to be prepared to take the bad with the good. The hinge of many communities was the friendly society which became an integral part of the area and the era. They were clubs which people subscribed to which would administer funds to its members in harsh times. In the absence of a welfare state and the severe social conditions and hardships experienced by many, it was often these societies that kept death at bay.

The dangerous conditions and long hours of work made the cry for such benevolence institutions louder. It was not a rare occurrence for a man to lose a limb while at work, or even his life. When this occurred, his family often had no means of support. The squalid conditions and overcrowding did little to prevent the spread of disease, and individuals were just as likely to die of disease as they were of an industrial injury.

"... The beginning of the year was marked with much sickness, fevers were prevalent, and small-pox, measles, scarlet fever, with other diseases, made great havoc among both adults and children; hence the distress of some families at that time was very great..."

9th February, 1839

However, Lady Charlotte would not be kept isolated from the community, at Dowlais House. She had visited the iron works and was aware of its dangers, so it is no surprise to discover that she became involved with the "Dowlais Benevolent Institution for the Relief of Sudden Accidents and Rare Infirmities."

"... The Committee feel gratified in acknowledging their obligation to Lady Charlotte Guest, for the attention she continues to bestow in watching the progress of the Society; and for her readiness to meet cases of emergency, whensoever presented to her notice..."

9th February, 1839

Lady Charlotte epitomised the goodness in society, and was prepared to help those who were unable to help themselves. Her efforts to relieve the poor, sick and needy did not go unnoticed.

"... A meeting was held at the Kings Head Inn, in Dowlais... which was called by workmen engaged in extensive ironworks of Sir John Guest, to acknowledge in the most expressive manner the great benefit they have received from the Honourable Baronet and his most amiable Lady, by their formation of a benevolent institution..."

9th April, 1842

Lady Charlotte's attention to the conditions of the lower orders of society was a lengthy one, in fact she continued to take an interest in their welfare throughout her entire lifetime. It was her passion and interest that compelled others to become involved, such as Mrs. R. T. Crawshay.

"... To Assist the Fatherless and Widows in their Affliction. Under the patronage of Lady Charlotte and Mrs. R. T. Crawshay... members of the lodges in Merthyr and Dowlais to join together for procession and tea party to raise funds for the above..."

22nd September, 1849

There was not only a need within the community to alleviate sickness but there were problems that faced a family when a death occurred which needed to be addressed as well. Within the community there would be a correct procedure to deal with funerals and burials, but this often meant a great deal of money – money that a family would not possess. On 12th April, 1851, Lady Charlotte is noted as giving the Odd Fellows money because their funeral fund was overdrawn due to the recent outbreak of cholera. It is obvious that Lady Charlotte's need to help individuals less fortunate than herself was not a one-off occurrence. It is even possible to trace when trade has slumped and times were hard by the calls for such benevolent institutions and the appeals for subscriptions that would appear in the newspapers. In the months previous to April, 1851, one can ascertain by the reports on death in the newspaper that cholera was a worrying epidemic and that the Public Health Act of 1848 had had no immediate effect on the town of Merthyr Tydfil.

This kind of club is not the only one Lady Charlotte was connected to. In a community where hardships were continually experienced, clubs were a release from the harsh realities of normal life. One such club that helped individuals forget about their surroundings and worries of work was the excursion club. An excursion club was formed at Dowlais under the patronage of Lady Charlotte on 22nd February, 1851. Lady Charlotte not only gave her name but her money and time, too. On 26th July, 1851, the *Cardiff and Merthyr Guardian* reported that Sir John Guest paid for 200 of his workers to travel to London and stay there a week in order to visit the Great Exhibition and other places of interest.

> "... they were met upon their arrival at the station by Lady Charlotte and Miss Guest, who accompanied the party to the extensive and convenient lodgings provided for them by Sir John at Pimlico. From this place they started every morning, according to the arrangements previously made for each day's amusement by Lady Charlotte Guest... the party were accompanied by Mr. Barry and Lady Charlotte and the Misses Guest..."
>
> 26th July, 1851

When studying the *Cardiff and Merthyr Guardian* it is always advisable to remember that there may be an element of bias present. However, the newspaper is keen to report and leave the individual to judge and the fact that it is written by correspondents at the time means it is an extremely valuable source of information. It is definitely probable that Sir John would have paid for his workers and that Lady Charlotte would have accompanied them on their travels. If it was untrue, undoubtedly some individual would have written to the Editor and corrected him, as this was not unusual.

We can learn a lot concerning what ordinary individuals thought of the Guests and Lady Charlotte in particular by what we read in the newspaper. Many social events in Dowlais and Merthyr Tydfil were not concluded without a toast, or a cry of three cheers for Sir John and Lady Charlotte Guest. Perhaps this shows how important they were as individuals, to the community in which they lived.

Lady Charlotte was not merely concerned with the social welfare of the community but the moral aspect too. Her name was often connected with the temperance movements in the area, bringing to our attention that alcohol abuse was prevalent in the community and often the only way some individuals could escape from the realities of everyday life. In May, 1840, the Third Temperance Festival of Gwent and Glamorgan was held in Dowlais, which meant the movement was not a new phenomenon. Lady Charlotte was reported as requesting that the hard, dusty road that the procession was to walk on be changed to a "fine, circular, gravel walk." Often if Lady Charlotte was involved in an event, certain things would be changed, i.e., the road in the above instance. The road remained after the festival had ended so that Lady Charlotte helped to alleviate conditions merely by her name being connected to events.

At this time there were a great many patriots and promoters of Wales outside the country. It was often the London Welsh who would be effusive in their love of their country and paint a romanticised picture to the outside world. Lady Charlotte tended to romanticise the country but this is hardly surprising when she was drawn to the classical Welsh of the middle ages and the folklore of King Arthur. Lady Charlotte was also concerned about Wales while in London and attended meetings and was toasted at the London Cymreigyddion Society.

> "... they had enlisted the four daughters of Cambria on their side. First and foremost in their rank stood the Ladies Hall and Guest – and if exalted virtues – extensive learning – pure patriotism – added to loveliness in form and feature, could command their respect..."
>
> 2nd January, 1841

Lady Charlotte's resurrection of the *Mabinogion* from extinction is not allowed to be forgotten. From the time she started translating the works there are continued references to the fact, showing how great is the appreciation of her labours. It set her apart from the majority of the English who had settled in industrial South Wales. Also the fact that it was a woman who undertook the task was amazing to most, at a time when it was usually only the male gender who were educated to the degree needed to do this. Lady Charlotte never conformed to the idea of an idle, genteel Victorian lady of leisure. To ensure her involvement in a cause, one would only have had to infer that the task could not be achieved.

> "... King Arthur yet lives, 'although dead for so many weary an age'... and who has achieved his resurrection? why a Lady, who till the other day had probably never seen Wales. And with mighty Arthur our ancient romances, the premature grave of shameless neglect..."[5]
>
> 17th June, 1843

From her introduction to the schools of Dowlais in the early months after her marriage, Lady Charlotte's interest in these institutions grew. Lady Charlotte was highly pleased by the number of individuals who had gathered in the procession to Dowlais House from the Sunday School Movement. The process was noted in the 24th June, 1843, edition and the reason why Lady Charlotte did not follow the procession was probably due to the fact that it was a week before she gave birth. If this was not the case, undoubtedly Lady Charlotte would have followed their progress to the end.

It was in the later years that Lady Charlotte directed her attention to the schools of Dowlais. This may have been due to the fact that at this time she had to deal with the prospect of her own children's education. Lady Charlotte was particularly drawn and concerned with the ends of the educational scale, the infants and the adults, and it was not unusual to find her present in the evening classes. Lady Charlotte did not merely go to observe but to assist in whatever way was necessary.

> "Night Schools – ... the teachers attend regularly to discharge their most praiseworthy engagements; and, in common with other ladies, that most estimable woman Lady Charlotte Guest, is frequently in attendance, and encouraging by her presence and assistance both pupils and teachers..."
>
> 20th January, 1849

Lady Charlotte and Sir John set themselves apart from most of the upper class in Welsh society by being actively involved in the community in which they lived. And by having the foresight to realise that the encouragement of education in any shape or form could only be beneficial in the future. Perhaps there were more pressing needs for the community in the shape of adequate housing and sanitation, but if an educated working class could be achieved they could help themselves. The *Cardiff and Merthyr Guardian* was not exaggerating when it printed:

> "EDUCATION has in her one of its great promoters."
>
> 30th March, 1850

Lady Charlotte was selfless in her promotion of education for all. She was particularly attached to the Girls' School at Dowlais. Perhaps through her own studies she could appreciate what the female mind could achieve if given the chance. Whenever Lady Charlotte was in residence at Dowlais House, time would be found to visit these institutions of learning, and she provided a great stimulus to other philanthropic projects. In November, 1847, her generosity lent itself towards the Dowlais Tradesmen and Workmen's Library.

> "... increased to 900 volumes, comprising of works in English and Welsh language, several of which in the latter language have been presented by Lady Charlotte Guest..."
>
> 27th November, 1847

It was in 1890 that she last visited the Dowlais Schools at the age of 78, and in all her years away from them she had not forgotten them. It was a "farewell visit to dear old Dowlais!",[6] by a remarkable Lady who had helped the education of a community on to a path which would not have been possible without her.

Lady Charlotte was not only concerned with the education within the community of Merthyr but Wales as a whole.

> "... Lady Charlotte has consented to lay the foundation stone for the Normal College of Wales, to be erected near Uplands, Swansea."
>
> 12th May, 1849

There is no doubt that the community had a great deal of respect for Lady Charlotte and her husband, Sir John, but it was a respect that they had rightly earned and deserved. In July, 1848, on arrival at Merthyr, crowds of people came to greet them, there was "great public rejoicing" at their presence and the news that the Dowlais lease had once again been secured.

It is without a doubt that throughout her entire lifetime Lady Charlotte did not conform to the ideal of a Victorian lady, if she did not want to. When her brother Lindsey died in 1877, she followed the funeral cortege as no woman had before her. In Merthyr society she followed the same course of action, scrambling around the ironworks and increasingly taking on the burdens of high finance and big business when Sir John became ill.

Lady Charlotte had an affinity with the poorer people of society and sought to devote her free time to improving their social conditions. When Sir John bought the Canford Estate near Wimborne in Dorset in 1846, there was a change in the frequency in which the Guests visited Dowlais and stayed there. Lady Charlotte's drive for continuous improvement in whatever field did not diminish in her absence, in fact it was as if her batteries were recharged so that when she returned she was able to fuel everyone with the great enthusiasm that existed within her.

> "... I am taking an unusual course, but I wish very much to propose to you a toast which lies near to my heart – The prosperity of the labouring classes..."
>
> 9th November, 1849

Although these words were spoken at the Canford Estate Agricultural Show, they could just as easily have been uttered outside the Kings Head Inn, Dowlais, or the Castle Hotel in Merthyr. It was a cause that Lady Charlotte identified herself with throughout her entire lifetime.

The darkest days of Lady Charlotte were to arrive in 1852 with the illness of her husband and his subsequent death. Increasingly the burden of the ironworks fell on her shoulders and the worry over his illness and the question of the Dowlais lease enveloped her. In her own words she wrote that the future loomed "as one chaos of darkness". On 26th November, 1852, Sir Josiah John Guest, her partner of adult life, her husband, died at the age of sixty-five, and Lady Charlotte became:

> "... the hope of Dowlais – whose service to the literature of the

> Principality is widely known and profoundly appreciated, and whose whole life and commanding talents are devoted to one object – that of doing good..."
>
> 4th December, 1852

With the passing of this great man the community virtually came to a standstill and the passing of an era was signified. Lady Charlotte Guest was never again to spend the time in Merthyr Tydfil that she had in earlier years. Without a doubt, Lady Charlotte was an achiever in her own right and many philanthropic causes in Dowlais and Merthyr Tydfil would not have succeeded without her help. She was a great asset to the community and her arrival in 1833 was a blessing in disguise.

The *Cardiff and Merthyr Guardian* charts the public life of Lady Charlotte from her arrival through to her departure, and is an extremely valuable source of primary evidence in portraying her public life and image. It sheds great light on the causes she promoted and those close to her heart. It allows us to build up a picture of conditions of life and how unusual was the path Lady Charlotte had embarked upon.

When studying individuals, the thoughts of others are crucial to our understanding and the *Cardiff and Merthyr Guardian* has allowed us to see how others viewed Lady Charlotte. The thoughts and impressions of the people of Dowlais and Merthyr Tydfil are clearly conveyed in this newspaper. Impressions of love and gratitude for the kindness and thoughtfulness of a Lady, who stood apart from her contemporaries by her willingness to help, to act. A willingness to help that she did not materially gain by.

Perhaps nobody else can sum of her character better than herself:

"I am iron now – and my life is altered into one of action not sentiment."

Notes

1. John Guest proposed to Lady Charlotte on 12th July, 1833, in Kensington Gardens.
2. Gwyn A. Williams, *The Merthyr Rising*, 2 ed. pub. University of Wales Press, Cardiff, 1988, page 22.
3. Lady Charlotte had ten children in thirteen years, a list of which follows:

1.Charlotte Maria Guest	July 3	1834
2.Ivor Bertie Guest	August 29	1835
3.Katharine Gwladys Guest	January 29	1837
4.Thomas Merthyr Guest	January 18	1838
5.Montague John Guest	February 28	1839
6.Augustus Frederick Guest	August 12	1840
7.Arthur Edward Guest	August 17	1841
8.Mary Enid Evelyn Guest	July 11	1843
9.Constance Rhiannon Guest	October 17	1844
10.Blanche Vere Guest	August 25	1847.

4. Mr. Taliesin Williams was the son of the famous Bard Iolo Morganwg, and a schoolteacher at Merthyr.
5. This speech was recorded at the housewarming of Iolo Mynwy.
6. Angela V. John and Revel Guest, *Lady Charlotte: a biography of the nineteenth century*, pub. George Weidenfeld and Nicholson Ltd., 1989, page 73.

Correspondence

The following interesting letter, dated 9th November, 1994, has been received from Mr. Walter W. Rees of 5, Dare Villas, Gadlys, Aberdare:

"Dear Mr. Holley,

"I have just read Mr. Huw Williams' interesting article in Volume 6 of the *Merthyr Historian*, in our local reference library, dealing with the life of Jonathan Reynolds (Nathan Dyfed), and wondered if Mr. Williams was aware that here in Aberdare (at Cwmbach, to be exact) is the last resting place of Dafydd Reynolds, the father of Nathan Dyfed. There was no mention of this fact in the article, and I thought that the author might well be interested if he was not already aware of it. The gravestone itself is quite an interesting one by virtue of the inscription on it, being headed by the name Nathan Dyfed, in the old coelbren script, followed by the description of the person interred (in 1845) and is in very good condition. I became aware of its existence last summer, when our local Council placed a notice in the local paper to the effect that the chapel (which had been demolished last year) and graveyard site was to be turned into a lawned area or such, with trees planted and benches set among them for the elderly, and that anyone interested in the proposals could see the particulars and a list of the gravestones still legible, the last burial there having taken place over 100 years ago. Being interested in local history, I had a look at the details, and was told about this gravestone being both the oldest and the most interesting because of the coelbren script, and that being in such good condition, they were proposing to scrap the other stones and make a feature of this particular headstone. Later, I made a visit to the site with a friend who provided a translation of the Welsh inscription for me, which was also quite interesting, and he explained that Nathan Dyfed was a very famous Eisteddfodwr in his lifetime. It was not until this week, however, that I was able to discover much about him, when quite by chance, looking for something else in our reference library, I happened on Vol. 6 of the *Merthyr Historian*, and discovered Mr. Williams' article...etc..."

Merthyr Tydfil during the War Years. Some Recollections from 1939 to 1952

by H. Watkins – Secretary, Merthyr Tydfil Historical Society

1995 saw the nation celebrating, firstly, the 50th anniversary of V.E. Day in May and on 19th August, 1995, V.J. Day. A day of pageantry with the Queen, ELIZABETH II, leading the celebrations outside Buckingham Palace. The Veterans' parade led by four Gurkhas from Nepal bearing the VICTORIA CROSS, the highest award for valour which they won in the Far East campaign; the arrival of a Lancaster bomber which signalled the start of two minutes' silence; when it returned the bomb bays opened to release thousands of poppies, a fitting memory to all those who made the supreme sacrifice in World War II.

The Queen's water-borne procession from Westminster Pier to the Pool of London accompanied by the famous little ships of DUNKIRK; the aerial display followed by a massive firework display on the River Thames.

The remembrance service from Carlisle Cathedral, followed by the timely screening of David Lean's *Bridge on the River Kwai*; the anniversary of the dropping of the ATOMIC BOMB on HIROSHIMA and NAGASAKI; the final ceremony to celebrate the 50th anniversary of the end of World War II, namely, the Gurkha band piping a lament from the roof of Buckingham Palace before the Queen, massed bands, choirs and one thousand children, for the Beating of Retreat.

Members of my generation can stand on the bridge near the modern confines of the new shopping precinct in the centre of Merthyr Tydfil and watch the red doors of the local fire station fold abruptly, in answer to the siren. The siren, yes, now it tells of the danger to one unfortunate family. In the early 1940s, a different sounding siren, which was then housed on the roof of the old Boots Chemist, Merthyr, had two functions: one was a warning of imminent danger, causing fear to all the inhabitants of our town – not only to one family – and the second function was the All-Clear, bringing instant relief to all the people.

This was the beginning of the War Years. Great Britain had declared war on Hitler's Nazi Germany on 3rd September, 1939, over Germany's invasion of Poland, whom we were obliged to assist. However, events proved disastrous with Germany victorious over most of Europe. In 1940, from the 27th May to 4th June, hosts of pleasure steamers, launches and motor-boats, many of them manned by owner-volunteers, had rescued 338,226 men of the Allied Armies from the beaches of Dunkirk in France; we were alone. Then came what we thought was imminent invasion. This German invasion was, however, checked by the Battle of Britain, fought between 10th July and 31st October, 1940. Wave after wave of German bombers were attacked by British fighters, Spitfires and Hurricanes; individual combats were often at heights of 15,000 to 20,000 feet. It resulted in large losses for the German Luftwaffe and the Germans abandoned their invasion plans.

In Merthyr Tydfil during the early 1940s, sirens "wailed" out both day and night. A day-time siren meant (to a school boy) being systematically herded into the dark, forbidding confines of the air-raid shelter, not a purpose-built shelter but the unused cellars of the school building. There everyone sat around singing King George VI's action song – *Underneath the Spreading Chestnut Tree* (this song we had seen on the Pathé & Movitone News in the cinema when the King had sung it when visiting the Boy Scouts' Jamboree), and *Ten Green Bottles*, with both teachers and pupils anxiously awaiting the All-Clear. When it arrived it was back to school as normal, or as near normal could be in wartime. The preponderance of women teachers did not come to my notice at that age of my life. Now, I realise it was because they were filling in for the men in the Armed Forces.

My school, at the time, in the 1940s, was lit by gas; some fittings had mantles, other bare jets. To light them was a major feat: the teachers had to climb, first on to a chair, then on to a table, to pull these down from the ceiling to a reasonable height, which enabled us to see fairly adequately. This procedure had to be repeated for every pair of gas lights in the room.

(It must have been heavy on matches.) I remember the open-coal fires in each classroom, and how we lined up in winter to warm ourselves. The cold, blue-weathered knees of the boys were noticeable during the winter months; no-one under a certain age wore long trousers and the winters seemed to be much colder in the late thirties and early forties.

Lessons went on as well as they could under the circumstances: English and Arithmetic, Reading and Spelling. Writing with those nibbed pens and highly-polished brass inkwells – no-one wanted to be ink monitor as he had the messiest job.

I began to believe that my right shoulder was one inch shorter than my left, owing to the fact that it constantly provided a fairly safe anchorage for my gas mask, which was carried in a reinforced cardboard box with my name and address written in large capital letters on the front. The real fear at this time was from German gas attacks. Weather permitting or not, we stood in rows, class by class in the school playground for gas mask inspection and practice drill by the Headmaster (the *Planet of The Apes* had nothing on us). I would like to know, even to this day, why as soon as I put mine on, my nose started to itch. We looked at each other through a fog of condensation. The highlight of the week, if one could call it that, was the visit to the Headmaster's study, class by class, to receive our tablespoonful of Scott's Emulsion and a sweet. What was a sweet? They were on ration. Things we now take for granted seemed during the early 1940s to be "food of the gods". Where had all the sweets, oranges, bananas, fruits, gone? At the time I didn't realise that the convoys had great difficulty in getting through the U-boat packs, bringing only the essential foods to sustain fairly healthy life. To help the food rationing situation and to enable the mothers of my generation to work for the War Effort replacing the men serving in His Majesty's Armed Forces, the Government decreed that dinners were to be served in schools. Milk was provided at a cost of 2 1/2d per week for a morning session, or 5d a week if we had milk in the afternoon; the cost of a school bottle of milk was 1/2d.

One day we were told to bring a one-pound jam pot to school; this we did without knowing what it was for. We lined up and our teacher filled everyone's jam jar to the brim with a brown, very fine powder, quite unknown to us. We licked our fingers – sticking them into this strange concoction – and then, after licking our fingers we discovered with great delight that it was – *Chocolate*. It was drinking chocolate really, from the United States, but we preferred to eat it in the dry state.

Soon our homes were inundated with dry foods, by courtesy of "Uncle Sam" (U.S.A.): dried egg powder, dried powdered potatoes, dried milk, dried beans, etc. Merthyr, like everywhere else, was now in the throes of rationing.

Rationing began in January, 1940. I remember a set of strange books my mother kept, with little coupons: 2 ozs of meat; 2 ozs of tea; 2 ozs of butter; 2 ozs of lard; one egg (if you could get one); and 1/4 lb of sweets to last a whole month. Along with the ration book went "Food Facts" in the press, "On the Kitchen Front" on the radio, "Food Flashes" at the cinema and helpful dietary talks from the radio doctor. Soon, as well as the food ration books, there were coupons for clothing, dockets for new furniture available only to the newly-married or people who were bombed out.

Soon, a bartering system circulated the neighbourhoods of Merthyr Tydfil, when neighbours and friends exchanged goods: rice for margarine, tea for sugar. I can remember my mother and aunts giving up their needlework classes and joining a "Make-do-and-Mend". This was a system when besides making socks and scarves and balaclava hats for the troops, clothes of all descriptions were recirculated for junior members of the family, cut down to size. Not only did the convoys have to bring vital foods and ammunition, they also had to carry raw material for cloth, the latter the least important. Therefore, it was not – "Did you have the money to buy clothes?" but "Did you have the coupons?" This system affected both rich and poor alike. It wasn't until years later that I learned of an illegal thing called the "Black Market".

One of the posters seen in the press and on the billboards of the town was "Dig for Victory". This was to encourage men to grow their own vegetables on every piece of available ground, in allotments, etc. Common sights came into existence – wartime queues; 5 o'clock in the morning queuing outside the Home & Colonial for a luxury called – jam. Another thing my deprived taste-buds had not encountered was ice-cream. On the rare occasion that our local Italian café owner made his own delicious ice-cream, the queue spread way out of the café and half-way along the High Street. I stood at the back of the queue hoping, if not praying, that the supply would not run out before it was my turn.

I remember sitting at home listening to the family's accumulator wireless set, the batteries of which I had to take to be re-charged frequently. Listening to "Lord Haw-Haw", the German propagandist, telling us on one occasion that the situation in the British Isles was so desperate that they were even ripping up the tram-lines in Merthyr Tydfil for use with the "war machine".

Little did he know that our town was not in imminent danger; it was in the process of re-development. We were having a more adequate transport system, turning over from trams to omnibuses. The last tram had run on Wednesday, 23rd August, 1939, a few days before Hither marched into Poland. I also remember two songs of the famous Vera Lynn – the soldiers' sweetheart. One was *There'll be Blue Birds Over The White Cliffs of Dover*; the second song meant very little to me at the time: it was *When the Lights go on again, All Over the World*. I, at that time, failed to imagine a world full of lights, because to show the slightest gleam of light through a chink in the blackout would have an Air Raid Warden banging on one's front door and bellowing "Put That Light Out". This was total blackout, for any light, however dim, would give an adequate target for German bombers who, perhaps, had not dispensed their full load of bombs on their return journey to the "Fatherland", after an attack on their industrial targets. Therefore blackout was the order of the day, and I mean *blackout*. If I went out at night, I carried a small pocket-torch which had, been covered over with plaster, leaving a tiny crack giving just sufficient light to see curbs and lamp-posts. It was a common thing in the 1940s, saying "Sorry" to lamp-posts! Later on, kerbs were painted white. Cars and public transport had their headlights covered with a shade roughly resembling half-closed Venetian blinds.

We were now in the throes of a real war: air raids, namely the Blitz. In every part of the country men turned out to be trained to defend their own localities in the Home Guard, and every citizen became accustomed to seeing barriers on the roads near their homes and pill-boxes at local crossroads. A barrier could be found under the Cefn Bridge; a barrier and pill-box at Cwm Taff; tank traps at Abercanaid, and in many other areas. Men and women now joined the Civil Defence, Air Raid Precaution Wardens (A.R.P.), Auxiliary Firemen and Policemen and Women's Land Army. Then came the air attacks by hundreds of planes on our cities: first London, then Coventry, Birmingham, Liverpool, Sheffield, Manchester, Bristol and Avonmouth. People now built Anderson shelters, many of them in their back gardens, or improvised ones under the stairs, pantry or cupboard. We could on many nights hear the drone of the German bombers passing over Merthyr and see the flares dropped by enemy planes looking for targets.

On the nights of 19th, 20th and 21st February, 1941, the War came nearer home. My father said, "Come and see the light in the sky. Swansea is on fire." The Luftwaffe had sent 250 aircraft to bomb the City, resulting in the deaths of 352 Welsh civilians. The whole civilian centre of the town was levelled to the ground by bomb and fire, thousands of damaged homes, a burnt-out shopping centre, market and 200 food shops and stalls put out of action. Alternative food shops were arranged and the emergency food services did not fail. Communal feeding centres were set up; mobile canteens took hot food to the people. The third and last raid took place on a Friday night. The rate of Swansea's mental recovery can be measured by the fact that in the Blitzed streets, still filthy with the litter of the blast, one of the most normal of all Welsh sights was seen on Sunday afternoon: group after group of children in clean frocks and well-brushed suits set off to Sunday School. The sight of them brightened the desolate suburbs. Parents took for granted, with good reason, that though churches and halls had suffered, arrangements would have been improvised so that Sunday Schools could carry on.

In January, 1941, the Luftwaffe's New Year gift was an attack on Cardiff. There were thirty raids on the city, the worst on 2nd January, 1941, when the Cathedral of Llandaff suffered greatly, also the docks, and some heavy bombs were dropped at random in residential areas on the outskirts. One rescue party set to work to see who might be buried in the debris of a demolished house; they were warned of life to be saved and guided to their mark by the notes of *God Save The King*, sung at the top of his voice by a little boy of six. It turned out that he was trapped under the staircase, where he had to stay for six hours until rescued. He was singing most of the time. His rescuers asked him why. He told them – "My father was a collier, and he always said that when the men were caught and buried underground they would keep singing and singing and they were always got out in time." In Merthyr, windows of public transport and principal buildings were now taped in a criss-cross design with brown adhesive tape to try to minimise the damage that would be caused by flying glass in the event of an explosion. The billboards of the town had different kinds of advertisements in 1941, such as "Careless Words Cost Lives", "Talk Can Kill, "Mum's the Word", "Keep It Dark" and "Walls Have Ears". Merthyr was fortunate in having very few bombs. I can remember going to see a crater at the bottom of the now newly-built Gurnos Estate. A stray German bomber followed a train coming from Nantyffin Drifts and bombed it near Cwmbargoed.

On the way to school one day, I wondered why the people had taken down their iron gates and railings and when I went home, I asked about this and was told all cast-iron was needed to be melted down for the War Effort. Gradually people replaced these railings with large stones from the mountain area near Morlais Castle.

On my way to the newsagent, one day in 1942, I saw some policemen clearing the road. I wondered what was going on, so I stood around to find out. It was one of the American convoys passing through Merthyr Tydfil. Where they came from or where they were going to, no one knew at the time. One of the children shouted out, “Any Gum, Chum?” Soon dozens of packets of American P.K. and bars of chocolate were thrown out of the trucks by the passing American servicemen. They soon became our friends and convoys were looked forward to eagerly on every occasion. With pockets stuffed with chewing gum and chocolate, I lost all interest in my day’s reading of *Flash Gordon*, the *Beano*, *Dandy* and *Knockout*. America had entered the War, after the surprise attack on Sunday, 7th December, 1941, at Pearl Harbour in the Hawaiian Islands.

Saturday’s treat in those austere years was never-the-less still a treat. With parents or grandparents, I was taken armed with sufficient coupons to enable me to purchase my bag of boiled sweets: red, yellow, green and white, made in the shape of fish. These were purchased in what I thought a most exciting place, with its myriad of stalls of all descriptions in a large, dimly-lit, girded-roof building, lit by gas lamps, known as the “Merthyr Market”, the site of which is now a block of shops in the new precinct.

After the shopping expedition in the market, we usually went to the British Restaurant for faggots and peas (the site of The Nationwide Building Society). These establishments were set up to supplement the food rationing of the people, which I did not know at the time; one could eat without coupons. The murals around the walls of this establishment were painted by the war-time students of Cyfarthfa Grammar School.

In 1944, the Government decided that too many children were missing secondary education because their parents did not care enough about education to pay fees and house, clothe and feed them, or because parents were too poor to do so. A new Education Act was therefore brought into force. The most important change was the abolition of fees in all State Grammar, Modern and Technical Schools. Cheap meals and some free clothing were also provided, so that no parent should have any reason for not keeping his children at school until they were fifteen. (The pre-War school leaving age was fourteen.)

When I was eleven, I knew a big day was coming up which would have an effect on the rest of my life. It was a day when teachers from other schools would come to my school to supervise an examination called the

"Scholarship" (11+). This examination consisted of an Intelligence Test, Arithmetic Test and an English Test. On the result of this examination my future academic life would be judged. On the day of the results, the teacher called out our names in alphabetical order, usually two children to Cyfarthfa Grammar School, one to the Merthyr County Grammar School, because one school was bigger than the other. The children whose names were not called out were told they would be going to a Secondary Modern School.

I entered the Grammar School and things for me and for the rest of the world took on a happier turn. People started talking about something called V.E. (Victory in Europe) and signs painted on walls began to appear, a few at first and then gradually more frequently V ...–, the Morse code for "Victory".

6th June, 1944, was also a momentous day: D-Day, when the Allies landed in Normandy. I remember on that Summer evening, with hundreds of others, watching hundreds of planes and gliders crossing the sky.

When victory occurred in Europe, people were so overjoyed and relieved that the imminent danger had passed and that Hither was dead, that they all wanted to celebrate. The first street parties that I can remember were organised: trestle tables were erected down the centre of each street, owing to the fact that very few people had cars, so that they were not causing any obstruction. Bunting was strewn from window to window across the street, dusty Union Jacks and Red Dragons hung side-by-side. Pictures of King George VI and Queen Elizabeth were displayed in windows, together with the famous portrait of the War-time Prime Minister, Sir Winston Churchill (then Mr.), giving his famous victory sign and smoking his large Havana cigar. People brought gramophones (record players with handles to wind up), the grown-ups danced and we children played games and sang songs such as *You're in the Army, Mr. Jones*, *The Quartermaster's Stores*, *We'll Hang out the Washing on the Seigfried Line*, *Over There*, *The Yanks are Coming* and *Lili Marlene*. Neighbours and friends all made sandwiches and cakes, tea and lemonade, and jelly made with gelatine. In a street party in Penydarren, two American soldiers arrived in a Jeep and were given good food and a grateful welcome by the people. To repay the hospitality they went off, but soon returned with a pair of distress signal guns, which they fired into the air, thus giving the children of Penydarren their first glimpse of what future firework displays would be like.

The War had still not come to an end, although the situation eased a little. I will always remember writing in my Chemistry book in 1945, "An Atom, the smallest particle in the Universe, cannot be split". A few months later on 6th August, 1945 – *Bang* – the Americans exploded an atom bomb in the air over Hiroshima in Japan, and another – Bang – when a second bomb over Nagasaki was exploded on 9th August, 1945. They had split the atom in spite of my declaration that an atom could not be split. The result was the end of War when the Japanese surrendered in Tokyo Bay on 2nd September, 1945. It was a marvellous excuse for another street party.

On 8th June, 1946, Victory Day was celebrated throughout the country. In London a great parade of 21,000 men and women of the British and Allied Forces with detachments of civilian workers took place. It was a proud day in school for us, for we each received a personal message from H.M. King George VI, thanking the boys and girls of my generation for the hardships and dangers we had gone through.

The austere years were to be with us for some time, but in 1947, as well as rationing, we had another frustration to cope with – namely, the inclement weather. The 1947 winter was to be the worst on record, with Arctic conditions spread over South Wales as well as the rest of Britain. Our schools closed for five weeks. We had the worst blizzards in memory: drifts up to 20 feet in depth. I remember food was a problem. I struggled with my father through drifts down from Penydarren to Merthyr looking for food. Snowdrifts were up to roof height. My father was buried by snowdrifts in the Abernant Tunnel for two days until dug out.

During the late forties, I used to look at the speaker of the wireless longingly, wishing it could receive pictures. We were just starting to read about a new gadget that was being adopted in many American homes – a thing called "Television". However, in those days we were still thrilled to the Wireless. Valentine Dyall's *The Man in Black*, *Stories of Mystery and Imagination*, *Dick Barton, Special Agent*, *Jungle Jim*, *The Adventures of Paul Temple*. We laughed at the *ITMA Show* and *Much Binding in the Marsh*.

The Pop Scene was a far cry from what it is today, as Donald Peers stole the scene with *Put another nickel in – in the nickelodeon*. One artist who is still "modern" with his Latin American Band is Edmundo Ross. Our Sunday night culture was Max Jaffa and the Palm Court Orchestra.

The cinema was our main form of entertainment. Queues were a familiar sight outside all the main cinemas of Merthyr, namely the Theatre Royal (now a Bingo Hall), The Palace Cinema (now the disused "Sands"), The Electric Cinema ("Do It Yourself Centre), the A.B.C. Castle Cinema (Studios

I and II) and the famous Temperance Hall (The Scala); The Cosy Cinema (Penydarren); The Victoria Cinema and Oddfellows' Hall (Dowlais). It was the era of the great film-stars and John Wayne's first generation of film fans. The Castle Cinema in the late forties and early fifties ran a club called the "ABC Minors", which showed children's films every Saturday morning: *Flash Gordon, Dick Tracy, The Bowery Boys.* At one time a technicolour film was an occasion, the majority being made in black-and-white; gradually these were replaced by colour films.

Chapels and Churches on a Sunday were much fuller than they are today. It was a regular thing to attend a place of worship in one's "Sunday Best", twice or sometimes three times, with the traditional Sunday lunch and tea in between. After the Sunday evening service in the local Welsh Baptist Chapel, the only entertainment meant either visiting friends or going on the "promenade" or "monkey walk". This was a ritual of walking up and down the main High Street and Promenade of Merthyr Tydfil, meeting friends and talking, or going for a coffee in an Italian Café. The town was as full then as it is now on a busy Saturday. During the week nights one attended the Band of Hope, or the Y.P.S. (Young People's Society), the Gymanfa Ganu on Easter Monday or Tuesday. Square Dancing was held in Dowlais. Church halls were used for dances, Old Time and Modern (no Rock and Roll). Every Thursday and Saturday night, a dance was held at the Kirk House. Drinks could be obtained, but not the alcoholic type, which no-one worried about in those days.

After the austere years of saving clothing material, fashion suddenly went mad and brought in a new style called "the new look", with long, full, flowing skirts that looked like a ballerina's dress, and so long that they reached right down to the mid-calf. This was in direct contrast with what women wore during the War years. People were once again earning sufficient money to go on holidays; some very adventurous people even went abroad, 1949 being the first year this was permitted, with a £25 allowance. The Chapel annual outing was still the event to look forward to: Barry Island without Butlin's; Porthcawl without the expanse of Trecco Bay.

1947 saw the wedding of Princess Elizabeth to Philip, Duke of Edinburgh, on 20th November. The United Nations' Organisation had been formed on 10th January, 1946, replacing the old League of Nations, its first meeting being held at the Central Hall, Westminster.

In 1946, John Strachey, then Minister of Food, announced that from 21st July the Government would introduce bread rationing. Normal customers were to receive 9 ozs per day. It lasted until 25th July, 1948.

In 1947 the coal mines were nationalised; in 1946 the railways of Britain became nationalised. The old names of the separate railways, G.W.R., L.M.S., L.N.E.R., gradually disappeared. 1948 saw the Fourteenth Olympiad held at Wembley and, on the 5th July, 1948, the National Health Scheme came into being due to the famous Minister of Health, the late Aneurin Bevan. March, 1949, saw the lights go up in London after a ten-year ban of total blackout.

Christmas time in the late forties was just as enjoyable, if not more so, than it is today. The type of Christmas presents we received and gave were far less sophisticated. (Have you ever had a sugar pig in your stocking?) Money was still fairly short, so parents made their own toys: dolls' houses for the girls, forts with lead soldiers for boys; sewing and knitting sets. Reading was the order of the day. Books, writing books, sets of coloured pencils made in plain wood, all seemed to be the predominant type of gift. Television had not yet robbed us of the arts of reading and conversation.

Christmas was a busy time at home, as to buy Christmas cakes and puddings was virtually unknown. I remember my grandmother and mother mixing in a large earthenware pan, the ingredients for making Christmas cakes and puddings. Although some people had gas cookers, in my home we relied on the oven by the side of the fire – the heat of which could not be controlled adequately so, rather than risk the cakes burning, it was the task of my brothers and I to take the cakes in their tins to the local bakehouse, where the baker would cook them in the oven in which he normally made bread. Hours later we collected the brown, well-cooked cakes from Hurd's Bakehouse in Dowlais.

With the ending of the War and the beginning of the fifties, a lot of changes took place. Coloured motor cars appeared on the roads. Up until then they had been black. There was a saying then, "You can't take a coloured car to a funeral". The revolutionary shape of the Morris Minor appeared and the SS Jaguar, with its beautiful, streamlined rear, elegantly long front bonnet; wings were still called mudguards. The whole country was still on strict rationing: food, clothing and petrol. Rationing did not end until 1954. The Commonwealth was splitting up and countries were gaining their independence.

In School we were now coming across new phrases, such as: displaced persons, refugees, the Marshall Plan, the Berlin Airlift and, the most famous, the "iron curtain". As a result of World War II, Communism spread westwards into Europe to embrace eight new countries, with a population approaching 100 million. Stalin was unwilling to share control of the countries his forces dominated.

Devastated by the war, Russia needed Eastern Europe as a source of economic aid and a defensive belt against Germany. The Western Powers, busy with their own internal post-War problems, made little effort to resist the expansion of Russian influence in Europe. This was the origin of the division of the world into "East" and "West", in which the East looked to Russia for leadership and the West to America. Contact with the outside world from the communist countries was reduced to a minimum at this time.

1951 for us in Merthyr was a momentous year, with the "Festival of Britain" on the South Bank of the Thames. King George VI, on 3rd May, broadcasting from the steps of St. Paul's Cathedral, declared the Festival open. Two thousand bonfires were lit all over the country to unite symbolically the young people of the nation. Merthyr also held a week of events and activities as a new step forward into the fifties.

War once again reared its ugly head; Communism was now the fear. Communism spread to the east to Outer Mongolia, North Korea and North Vietnam. In 1949, a Communist government came to power in China under the late Mao Tse-Tung. These were the years of conscription – "National Service". Once one had reached the age of eighteen, exemption was not permissible unless on medical grounds, so my "Generation" were called "to arms". Having gained my Central Welsh Board Examination (G.C.E. had not yet come into being), I left School to enter the Army. A new and terrible war had begun between the forces of the United Nations and that of the Communist World, – namely, the Korean War, 1950-53.

The last sad event I recall when in the VIth Form, was the Headmaster announcing the sudden death of King George VI and the accession to the throne of Elizabeth II. This was to be the commencement of a new age, namely the "Elizabethan Age" of the sixties and seventies and all that it would bring.

The Rt. Hon. Mr. Atlee, Deputy Prime Minister,
meets the 9th Battalion's V.C., Sgt. Major J. Collins, V.C., D.C.M.

Sergeant James and his team of despatch riders, Merthyr Home Guard.

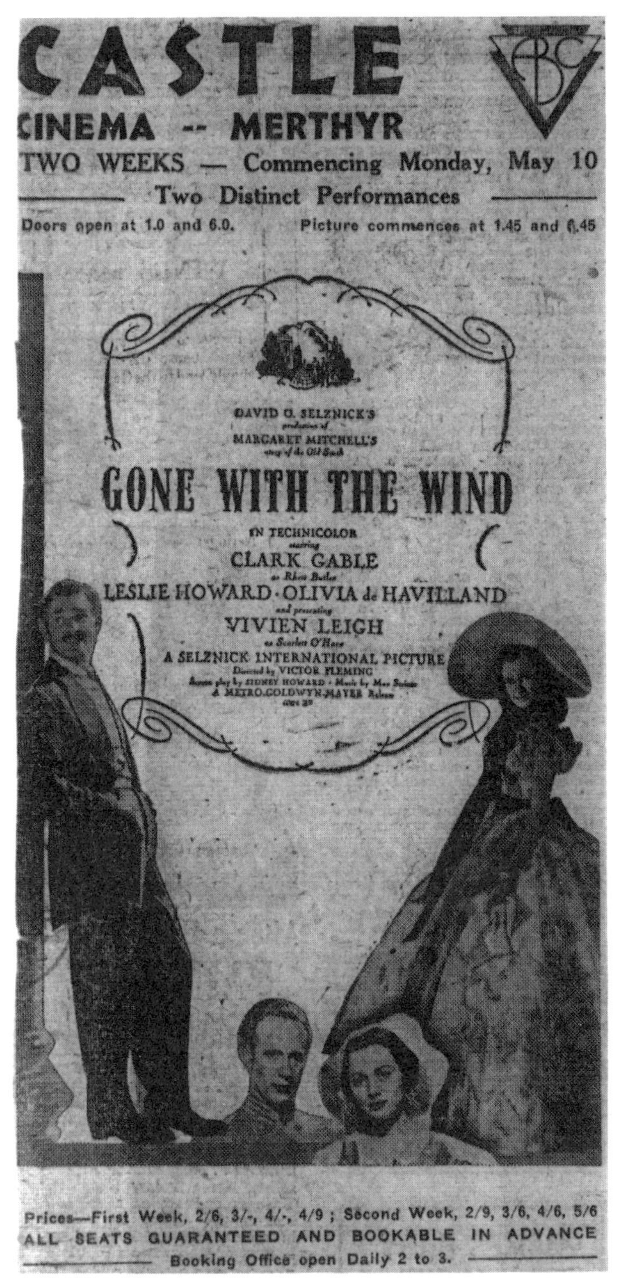

Wartime Cinema, Merthyr Tydfil.

GELLIGAER AREA

TARGET £100,000

The cost of twenty Spitfires

SHORTAGE OF GIRL LABOUR

Local Factory Shows Concern

TAKE WARNING!

We are asked by the police authorities to make a strong appeal to all citizens to take their gas masks with them at all times. This warning is regarded as essential.

"Wings" Queen and Her Attendants

The Merthyr Wings for Victory Queen, Miss Betty Leigh, of Treharris, is seen above with her attendants. From left to right: Kathleen Griffiths, Beryl Caswell, June Morgan (Deputy-Queen), Sheila Reed, the Queen, Margt. Thomas, Betty Richards and Marjorie Pearce.

A START FOR "WINGS FOR VICTORY"

"WINGS FOR VICTORY"

GALA

Whist and Bridge Drive

MINERS' HALL, MERTHYR

On THURSDAY, MAY 13th

at 7 p.m. prompt.

Trump *All Hitler's* Tricks

Why Wait ?

'Home' Saving

SAVE TO SAVE **THIS**

in the Borough of Merthyr Tydfil.

Towns that are Bombed have the best record for STREET SAVINGS GROUPS.

HAS YOUR STREET A GROUP ?

We want and must have a Savings Group in every Street in the Borough. Call To-day at the War Savings Centre (next to G.P.O., Merthyr) and volunteer as a Street Group Secretary.

Issued by Merthyr Tydfil Local Savings Committee.

TEMPERANCE HALL

Twice Nightly 5.20 & 8.0

Tel. 77. — Matinees Monday, Thursday and Saturday at 2.15.

MONDAY, JAN. 17th. ALL THE WEEK

LAUGHS • THRILLS • DRAMA

WALT DISNEY'S

Victory through Air Power

in TECHNICOLOR

"...Calculated to keep your laughter glands working at full pressure."

News of the World

"Extremely entertaining."

Empire News

From the Book by MAJOR ALEXANDER P. De SEVERSKY

Work and play in wartime Merthyr Tydfil.

ANOTHER 318 EVACUEES COME TO MERTHYR

The Merthyr Railway Station platform was thronged with officials waiting to greet another 318 evacuees who arrived at Merthyr on Tuesday.

There were present members of the Civil Defence Volunteers under Mr. John Williams (A.R.P. officer), Merthyr Police under Inspector W. Griffiths, Glamorgan Red Cross under Mr. T. Thomas (health department), together with Mr. Evan Evans (Ministry of Health), Mr. David J. Owen (chief billeting officer), Mr. W. T. Owen, M.A. (director of education), Mr. R. Protheroe (billeting officer), Mr. T. S. Evans (deputy town clerk), Dr. T. H. Stephens (medical officer of health), Coun. C. J. Griffiths, J.P., Mrs. Gwyneth Williams (evacuation welfare officer), and Mrs. N. Francis-Williams (W.V.S. organiser).

Tired and weary, the party arrived just after 5 p.m.—an hour late—and the civil defence workers took charge of the luggage while the evacuees went to the British Restaurant, where they were provided with a satisfying meal. The party consisted of about 318 persons from the Maidstone district—93 mothers, nine escorts, and the remainder children. Mrs. E. A. Mottram was in charge of activities.

Several mothers told a representative of the *Express* that they were very grateful for the reception they had received.

The Mayor-consort (Mr. B. M. Thomas) was at the British Restaurant to welcome them, and after they had finished their meal the evacuees boarded two double-decker buses provided by the Corporation and were taken to Cyfarthfa Castle, where they were temporarily billeted. The Mayor (Mrs. Mary Thomas, J.P.) and the Town Clerk (Mr. Edward Roberts) were at the Castle to welcome them.

While the evacuees were getting into the buses, Merthyr workmen, returning home after a hard day's work, stopped to help by putting cases, prams, etc., on to the bus.

Several of the evacuee mothers paid high compliments to these men for this exhibition of practical kindness. Several of the men accompanied the buses to the Castle and helped to unload the baggage.

Victory street party, George Street, Merthyr.

V.J. Day Celebration, Garden City, Merthyr.

8th June, 1946

TO-DAY, AS WE CELEBRATE VICTORY, I send this personal message to you and all other boys and girls at school. For you have shared in the hardships and dangers of a total war and you have shared no less in the triumph of the Allied Nations.

I know you will always feel proud to belong to a country which was capable of such supreme effort; proud, too, of parents and elder brothers and sisters who by their courage, endurance and enterprise brought victory. May these qualities be yours as you grow up and join in the common effort to establish among the nations of the world unity and peace.

An Old Merthyr Theatre, 1861

TRANSCRIBED

"A few yards within the narrow street leading from Pond-street into Caedraw, there is an interesting relic of old Merthyr, in the form of a building, fashioned as buildings were in past days, after primitive models, and in a queer manner. The stones are built up just as they were taken from the river, and would amaze a geologist with their varieties: here all red, there grit, here a bit of limestone and garden padding stone. The building, though, possesses another characteristic of old days, and in this respect excels modern erections. It is strongly built, and though nearly a century old, promises to weather another if not pulled down.

"THIS WAS THE FIRST THEATRE EVER BUILT IN MERTHYR, and in its day, was well patronised. The old playhouse, for by this name it figures, dates from the period when the iron works began to have a name in the country, and from every Shire in the principality, large numbers of men and their families came to settle here. The playhouse was open only at certain seasons, and then by a band of strolling players, who played well, reaped great harvests and delighted the playgoers. Outside the building a large flight of stone steps led to the theatre, and the ground floor was formed into small tenements, in 1800 principally occupied by paupers. Thus, above, monarchs, queens and nobles strutted their one brief hour, underneath poverty lived and starved always.

"Something like fifty years ago, a contributor tells me, he went to the playhouse, mounted the large flight of steps and stood for the first and the last time in his life amidst a large number of men, women, and children, within the walls of a theatre. He recollects that there were three divisions, gallery, pit, and a few boxes. The play, from what he remembers, appeared much about the same as now, there was a drama to begin with, in which officers and noblemen flitted before the scenes, talking grandly, and astounding the rude workmen with their jewels, fine clothes and speeches. Then followed a song by a Merthyr amateur, a carpenter, known as Bosha, which of course met with hearty applause, and lastly came the farce. This finale, from what I can glean, was intended to show how Dame Fortune sometimes showers her benefits on poverty, and how poverty, represented by a digger of the fields, behaves under the circumstances.

"The curtain drew up and showed a fine big fellow hard at work with his spade, but in order to do his work thoroughly he put the spade down and threw off his coat, then he threw off another, and another, but still no shirt sleeves came in sight, and thus he continued until a little mountain of coats was by his side. This caused immense roars of applause.

"The scene changed, and our ex-labourer is transformed into a fine gentleman, scattering his cash about everywhere, ordering everything, having dumplings brought him as luxuries, and kicking the said luxuries about the stage to the delight of his admirers.

"The whole performance terminated with an interesting row between a cobbler and his wife, ended by a grand scrimmage, in which the good lady shows a wonderful restraint in not using her tongue but instead throws the shoe at him with vigour.

"Skilful fellows these players. See how admirably they catered to the peculiar taste of the people; serving up all sorts of finery, and grand speeches, that the humble men and women below might be astonished, then appealing to their nationality by producing a Welshman, and a villager too, in order to sing them a good song, and ending with hearty rude wit, lots of fighting, scolding all fashions, and arranged around the shadowy and remote possibility of fortune, pushing aside the clean and jewelled hands so earnestly outstretched towards her, and taking instead the dirty living palm of a hedger and ditcher!

"Year after year the players continued to make their periodical visits to Merthyr Tydfil, without let or hindrance until it came to pass, as old historians word it, that, the season opened at a time when the zealous efforts of the Methodists of Merthyr had caused a strong religious feeling to spring up in the town and neighbourhood.

"The players came, but instead of warm greetings of past time, they had unmistakable cold shoulders turned to them, and it was with some difficulty that even lodgings could be had. At length the company were housed and things went on as usual, when, without warning or the assignment of any reason, they found themselves turned out of their warm quarters into the street again.

"The cause of this untoward event is soon told. David Williams, the energetic Calvinistic Methodist, and afterwards founder of Adulam Chapel, but at this time only a leading member, happened to learn that the players boarded at the houses of men and women who were members of his chapel.

"He at once in his usual zealous manner laid the case before the church, and the offenders were duly and severely admonished. These in turn, feeling that they had not acted consistently by harbouring men who ridiculed their faith, ejected the players, and thus sought to atone for their misdeeds and win back again their place among the members.

"THESE EVENTS CAUSED A GREAT STIR IN THE VILLAGE, and being noised about and talked about, the true reason of their ejectment came to the ears of the players.

"The manager, a determined man, very loath to leave the wealthy village, took counsel with his men and brought the case before Samuel Homfray, Esq., Justice of the Peace, who summoned David Williams to appear before him, and account for such strange and harsh conduct. David came, and rarely had such a gathering been seen before. There were the members of the chapel, sober faced men and women of the true Welsh type, and, besides them, a little gathering of the strangers, the poor players, shaven and shorn for the stage exigencies of flowing beards and wigs, and in front the great man Homfray, great in position and name, but a plain homely man withal. David Williams stood near him and then the case was opened.

"Mr. Homfray listened to the complaint stated in a few words, and to the effect, that they (the players) had been turned out of their lodgings and unable to get others from the opposition of Mr. David Williams, who had punished those who had boarded them, and that as licensed players they were entitled to accommodation from the people, and to the protection of the law. Well, said Homfray, that's fair speaking. I don't think you have acted well, Williams, these players, you see, are under the protection of government, and besides they are entitled to our sympathy and kindness. True, they are players, but see how much good advice is given, what warnings to the young, see how vice is exposed and virtue honoured. Don't think you have done well, Williams.

"Your worship, said Williams, I maintain that the tendency of plays is for evil, and that these play-actors corrupt youth instead of improving the mind, and fitting them to become good men and women. Look at the theatres, what class frequents them other than the very worst. You may see it thronged every night by the lowest in the village, a very strong proof that these seek only stimulants and food for their bad and depraved appetite. And I maintain, your worship, with all due respect to the Bench, that if these inhabitants, who refused to lodge them, choose to do so they are perfectly at liberty, and it is quite in keeping with the liberty of the British subject, whose house is indeed his castle. Much more David Williams said to the same purpose, all spoken in a bold uncompromising manner, and at the close Samuel Homfray, completely won over by Williams's fire and arguments, DISMISSED the case and slapping David Williams on the back with his hands familiarly, which justices and magistrates would now a days shudder even to think of, cried out, 'Well done, David Williams, preacher!'

"The remark, I may add, was prophetic. David soon became a minister."

Mrs. Clark of Dowlais

by EIRA M. SMITH

Sir Josiah John Guest died on the 26th November, 1852. He willed the Dowlais Iron Company to his widow, Lady Charlotte, during her widowhood, in trust for their children.

After negotiations with Lord Bute, one of her first duties was to sign the new lease, which had awaited her husband's signature during his long illness. Trustees and executors were appointed to assist Lady Charlotte. They were Edward Divett, a confidential adviser at Sir John's London Office, and George Thomas Clark, a close friend and adviser.

George Thomas Clark was a consultant engineer. He worked with Isambard Kingdom Brunel on the Great Western Railway. He left England on the 14th February, 1853, as he was involved with sanitary and water projects in India.

Problems arose in Dowlais in July, 1853, when the first major strike took place. A 10% reduction in wages had become necessary as the Dowlais Iron Company had recently lost over £19,000 in profits. During Sir John's lifetime monies had been used to purchase outright the shares in the company, together with property and lands. Money was now needed for further investment to improve the works, although trade was in a decline, as iron was down 20/- per ton.

Lady Charlotte met Robert Crawshay and Anthony Hill, two local ironmasters, in London to discuss the problems. However, she was compelled to leave her home in Spring Gardens, London, and return to Dowlais to try and resolve the problems. By the 31st August, 1853, the strike was over. Dowlais still demanded all the attention, energy and experience she was able to give, especially on new schemes for the welfare of the workers and their families.

Gradually over the coming months she attempted "to let" the Dowlais Works as she contemplated remarrying and felt her management of them was an obstacle. She had become enamoured with Charles Schreiber, tutor to her son Ivor Bertie Guest.

On the 10th April, 1855, less than three years after her husband's death, Charlotte married by licence Charles Schreiber, at 12 noon in St. Martin's Church, London. Soon they embarked on a period of travel, especially to the continent where they collected china, fans and playing cards. Charlotte became an authority on these forms of art.

Henry Bruce, later Lord Aberdare, had succeeded Sir Josiah John Guest as Member of Parliament for Merthyr Tydfil, became a trustee for certain purposes, e.g., contracts. George Thomas Clark became resident trustee and brought to Dowlais House his wife Anne. She was no stranger to the Dowlais Company. Her great-grandfather, Thomas Lewis of Newhouse, Llanishen, had been an original partner, owning three of the shares out of sixteen in the Dowlais Furnace. Her brother, Wyndham William Lewis, inherited these shares and acquired two more. He sold his five shares to Sir Josiah John Guest for £200,000 in 1850.

This was a significant year for Anne Price Lewis because, on the 3rd April, 1850, she married at St. John's Church, Cardiff, George Thomas Clark, a bachelor and gentleman of Essex Street, Strand, London. Nothing is known of how and where they met. When George called on the Guests at their London home and announced his engagement and forthcoming marriage to Anne, they were not surprised. When in London, both Anne and George had moved amongst the notable people of that time.

Anne's uncle, Wyndham Lewis, had been a Member of Parliament prior to his death. His widow remarried Benjamin Disraeli in August, 1839. Another of Anne's uncles, the Rev. William Price Lewis, died in 1848 and left her half of his estates in the counties of Glamorgan and Monmouth. These properties brought rents of over £200 per annum and were used as her marriage settlement. Two children were born to the Clarks. A girl, Blanche Lancaster, on the 2nd January, 1851, and their son Godfrey Lewis on the 30th November, 1855. The birth registration of these children does not exist in the records at St. Catherine's House, London, neither were the births announced in the local newspapers. The 1872 Census for Dowlais said Blanche was born in London and the 1881 Census for Talygarn, Llantrisant,

Mrs. Anne Clark. (Photo courtesy of Glamorgan Record Office.)

that Godfrey was born in Dowlais.

George Thomas Clark came to Dowlais in 1855 as resident manager and trustee. He had great difficulty in asserting and maintaining his authority when John Evans, the previous manager, retired due to ill-health. Later a process by Henry Bessemer was secured for the Dowlais Works and a new era embarked under the managership of William Menelaus, and the administration of G. T. Clark.

As the wife of the latest Dowlais ironmaster, Anne was now the hostess and ensconced at Dowlais House. Over the coming years, as her husband became chairman of the Board of Health and Board of Guardians, etc., she fulfilled other duties expected of her.

In October, 1862, she operated the valve to commence the flow of water from the Taf Fechan reservoir to Dowlais and Merthyr. Previously water had been used in the houses from springs, wells and the river, causing health hazards over the years. It was many years before the Board of Health was able to supply the flow of water as we know it today.

The Dowlais Company supplied Welsh iron used to build the first iron steam-ship upon the banks of the River Taff, by the Bute Iron Works. Anne was asked to launch this iron paddle steamer called the *Mallorca*, built for trade between the Island of Majorca and Barcelona, for the Spanish Mail Company. On the 16th November, 1864, Anne Price Clark launched the vessel with "a flower wreathed bottle of champagne with a well directed aim".

In September, 1866, cholera returned to the Merthyr area. Dowlais needed to prepare as an infirmary, a cottage hospital for its patients. An untenanted house was found in Ivor Street, Dowlais, belonging to the Dowlais Iron Company. Labourers were sent to clean up the garden and house, whitewash the walls and make it suitable for patients. On the 5th September, 1866, a public meeting was held, and the Dowlais workmen passed the following resolutions:

1. That we object to taking a sick man or woman or child to the infirmary if circumstances will permit the proper attendance on them at their own dwelling.

2. That we object to taking a dead body to be buried but to a grave chosen by the relatives of the deceased.

3. That we object to having our bed clothes burned without proper compensation given for the same.

4. That we object to Mr. Cresswell being our medical man.

G. T. Clark considered the system of deducting monies from the men's wages to pay for medical treatment etc., and decided to abolish the system. He defended the choice of Dr. Pearson Robert Cresswell as the Chief Medical Officer for the Dowlais Works, since no Welsh doctor was available. He assured the men that Dr. Cresswell was the best trained English doctor who was also prepared to learn Welsh. Pearson Robert Cresswell was the first doctor in Wales to use antiseptic treatment for surgical wounds, pioneering the use of Lister's Carbolic spray. Two more generations were to follow him as doctors to the Dowlais Works.

By March, 1869, the Board of Health urgently needed to build a Fever Hospital costing nearly £1,000 at Pant. Epidemics of typhoid and typhus prevailed in Dowlais at that time. Cottages were over-crowded, the air and water were impure as there were no water-closets or privies, and the water was still not suitable. When the epidemics subsided, half the hospital was offered to Anne Price Clark, as it was no longer required. She was permitted to use it for eight male and female patients who chose to apply for admission of their own free will. A nurse was employed and Dr. P. R. Cresswell superintended the medical treatment. Previously, staff from the hospital had been dismissed as they had been seen frequenting a local inn, near the hospital. They had been accused of spreading the disease.

When an outbreak of smallpox occurred in Dowlais in December, 1871, Mrs. Clark offered to vacate the accommodation she had been allowed in the hospital by the Board of Health. It was gratefully accepted to house the Board's new patients.

In March, 1872, the Dowlais Iron Company organised for Mrs. Clark, cottages Nos. 130 to 139 inclusive, in High Street, Dowlais. These premises to be used to nurse accident and surgical cases back to health. Here patients as well as a nurse and doctors resided. It became known as Mrs. Clark's hospital, as she personally supervised and managed it. She was assisted by Mrs. Jane Cresswell, wife of the Chief Medical Officer of the Dowlais Works. The 1881 Census for this property shows iron workers and coal miners were patients in the hospital. These two ladies saw to the needs and welfare of the Dowlais families, and dealt with the problems personally.

Whilst Chairman of the Board of Guardians, G. T. Clark made it possible for the inmates of the Workhouse to have a substantial meal on Christmas and New Year's Day. Some years he visited on New Year's Day, accompanied by Anne and they distributed gifts to the poor. Their visits were always appreciated with votes of thanks and cheering as they left. Banners were sometimes hung to greet the Clark family on the festival occasion.

As an engineer, historian, author, capitalist, philanthropist, etc., George Thomas Clark is well documented. His wealth increased and by February, 1865, he had purchased Talygarn House, near Llantrisant, which became their country home. This would be a retreat from the noise and smoke surrounding Dowlais House. They also had a home in London at 44 Berkeley Square, yet Anne found an interest in the care and welfare she personally bestowed on the Dowlais people, and was well loved by them for it.

Her friend and helper Jane Cresswell died in Dowlais on the 22nd June, 1884, aged 48 years, after a short illness. Anne's health deteriorated and she died after a winter's illness at their London home on the 6th April, 1885, aged 66 years. Their hospital had closed sometime previously. Anne's body was conveyed to a churchyard near Talygarn House.

George built the church of St. Anne in 1887 in the same churchyard, as a memorial to his wife, and in 1898 he was buried next to her. Talygarn was inherited by their son, Godfrey, and their grandson, Wyndham Damer Clark. He sold it to the South Wales Miners' Welfare Committee. It later became a Miners' Rehabilitation Centre to restore miners to fitness and health, as Anne had succeeded in doing at Dowlais.

Today Talygarn continues under the National Health Service. Here people are sent from East Glamorgan Hospital for physiotherapy, to encourage them to overcome their severe injuries, and so the work of Anne Price Clark continues. Talygarn House and gardens are still monuments to a lady whose tender heart overcame the distrust and prejudice of people ignorant of the health hazards of their time. Dowlais House and her hospital, in the High Street, Dowlais, have long disappeared.

Abercanaid, Some Remembered Yesterdays. (3)

by EDWARD RHYS-PRICE

New York

New York is the chief city and port of the United States and lies on the Atlantic coast at the mouth of the Hudson River. The heart of the City is the Borough of Manhattan, a long pointed island where the water in the harbour is deep enough for the largest ocean liners to moor at the Hudson River piers. Manhattan Island is bounded on the west by the broad Hudson River, on the north by the narrow Harlem River and on the east by the Long Island Sound, which is often called East River. Modern New York has spread out beyond Manhattan to cover four other boroughs, the Bronx to the north, Queens and Brooklyn on Long Island and Richmond on Staten Island. Every traveller entering or leaving the harbour sees the great Statue of Liberty on Liberty Island as a landmark and a sign of the United States. This statue, made by F. A. Bartholdy, was given to the United States by France in 1886. Henry Hudson, an English navigator employed by the Dutch, explored the water around New York in 1609. In 1615 the Dutch built a fort at the southern tip of Manhattan and this area is still called The Battery. In 1624 a few settlers came to live there and the colony was named New Amsterdam, the land being bought from the American Indians with cloth and beads worth about $36. The English considered that all this region was part of their colony of Virginia in the south and sought to drive out the Dutch. In 1664 King Charles II gave New Amsterdam to his brother the Duke of York, who sent an English fleet to enforce his claim. The Dutch did not resist and New Amsterdam was renamed New York.

New York is an easy city in which to find one's way about. The streets are either west or east of 5th Avenue and arranged on a grid system. There are fifty houses on each block, with even numbers on one side of the street and odd numbers on the other. Broadway runs diagonally across Manhattan through the heart of the business and amusement centres. I found it difficult to adjust to life in New York at first. I had come from Philadelphia, where all places of entertainment were closed on Sunday, and at first I would not go to the cinema on that day. But boredom soon made me change. I endeavoured to get to the cinema at 10am, as that was when prices were cheapest. As the day went on the prices rose. Sometimes I went to the Welsh Language Church, but it was way up town so I didn't go very often. Some years later when I went to look for it again, I found it had been sold to another denomination for there were no longer enough Welsh-speaking immigrants to keep it going. It was the strict use of the Welsh language in several of the churches which killed them off. The children born of Welsh parents in America were not taught to speak Welsh so they couldn't understand it.

Transportation was very cheap in New York City. The standard fare was 5 cents for unlimited travel in any direction on the subway. The elevated railway was still in existence in some areas, but it was being replaced by the subway. This was run by the Irish, and the Irish mayors of New York would get themselves elected by promising not to increase the fares. Eventually, however, it ground to a halt as there was not enough money to replace rolling stock and then it was taken over by the State.

Corruption was rife in some City Departments. If someone committed a minor crime the first thing the family did was to consult the alderman of the district, who would get in touch with the judge and expect him to give a reduced sentence in exchange for the votes of the family and their friends.

One of the first things that impressed me in New York was the fact that Jimmy Walker, who was running for mayor, put on his posters not "Vote for Walker" but "Win with Walker". He was Irish, so the New York Irish voted for him, come what may. It was the same with the other ethnic groups: they all liked to vote for someone with whom they could identify. Eventually Walker had to leave office because he was so corrupt. His wife was in a wheelchair and he took up with an English chorus-girl. He embezzled money to spend on her and had to leave the country when he was found out. In my day there used to be a popular saying, "New York City – owned by the Jews, governed by the Irish, and the native Americans pay the taxes"!

I soon found that the standard rate of pay for men without a trade was 50

Mr. Edward Rhys-Price. (Photo courtesy of Mrs. I. Stevens.)

cents an hour. A good suit cost $24, so I didn't buy many of those! But meals were very reasonable. A good breakfast could be had for 25c, consisting of toast, ham and egg, and a cup of coffee. A good dinner cost $1. Most restaurants were run by Italians and Jews and they gave good value. Many of the Italian restaurants were called "The Coffee Pot".

During my stay at John Morgan's hotel, I had struck up a friendship with a man called Edmund Roberts, Nem for short, who persuaded me to go with him to a small town in New Jersey where we both worked as labourers on a housing complex for a few months. A change of job was very stimulating and the fresh air was wonderful after being in New York. New Jersey is a state about the size of Wales, adjoining New York State. The trip by ferry cost 5c each way. After buying a beer in Hoboken at a saloon, you could help yourself for nothing to a buffet lunch, but it was not wise to eat too much of the meat because it was deliberately made very salty so that you would buy more beer. This was during Prohibition, of course, but beer could be bought at Hoboken because the officials in charge at that end had been bribed. So the round trip on the ferry cost a quarter, which is 25c. Beer could also be bought in the speak-easies. Everyone knew these existed but officials were bribed to keep their eyes shut. However, you could only be admitted to one if you could say that your friend Joe (or whoever it was) was already in there drinking.

Being anxious to visit my family again, I signed aboard a ship from New York to Southampton, although I still had no entry visa to the United States. Once on English soil, the thing to do was to skip ship and get home as quickly as possible by train. I spent a few days with the family at Abercanaid and then went back to Southampton. Of course I was not the only one doing it. The Chief Mate would threaten to leave us behind but we knew he was forced by law to take us back to New York, so we just stood with bowed heads while the storm swept over us, impatient for it all to be over. Our pay was stopped for those few days but we didn't mind. It was worth it to see our families again.

We are not a family to show our feelings easily, but when I first went to Canada my mother had cried because she had thought she would never see me again, so it was always a real tonic to her when I walked through the back door. I wouldn't even walk down the street because I didn't want anyone to run and tell her I was coming. Instead, I walked along the side of the river and through the back garden.

On one occasion some years later, I got to 54 Nightingale Street, only to find the family had moved. The new people sent me to 21 and when I knocked the door, an upstairs window was opened and, as it was dark, it was only my voice that was recognised.

Back to Sea

With so little work available on shore, it was inevitable that I should go back to sea again. As I waited to sign-on I recognised many of the same old faces. I was standing behind one man when I heard the Shipping Commissioner, who was a representative of the U.S. Government, say to him, "I've been signing you on for ten years and you were thirty-five then and you've given me your age this time as thirty-five. Either you go younger or older, but no more thirty-fives." These signing-on sessions were rather nerve-racking for me, because one reason why they were conducted by a representative of the Government was to catch illegal immigrants but, fortunately, I was never asked for any means of identification. Then someone told me that by registering at Colon in Panama I could get a visa sent to me, thus making me a legal immigrant. This I did and received it eventually in 1929 after I had been in America for several years. It was about this time also that I changed my name from Price to Rhys-Price. There were so many Welshmen and so many Prices that it caused some confusion, but once I had changed my name it was alright.

Only the officers on the ships were Americans, the rest of the crew were immigrants of one sort or another. We were the only ones who would take the jobs because the hours were so long and the pay was so low. A lot of us were illegal ones and every so often immigration officials would try to get rid of us. They would come to where the men were waiting to sign on and shout – "Anyone here with Cooks' discharge papers?", or stewards, or whatever it might be. Lots of arms would go up and these men were taken away to find work, as they thought, but in fact they were put in jail if they didn't have a visa and then deported back to their homeland. But a few weeks later they would be back again.

Discipline was very slack on American ships. We had lifeboat drill on the way out and on the way back. We had to look at the noticeboard to see which lifeboat we were assigned to and assemble at the appropriate place to be counted. This was only the crew: the passengers simply had a notice in their cabins to say which lifeboat there were assigned to. As for fire drill, I only remember that happening on a few occasions. It was very different from the British ships, where fire drill was practised regularly. In fact, on the American ships it was possible for a seaman to buy a certificate for $1 from a federal government office in Florida to say he was proficient in fire drill, without having to do anything to prove it. Fortunately we never had a fire on any of the ships I was on, but I heard about one on an American ship where the passengers had gone up on deck and then jumped overboard hoping to be rescued, leaving their shoes on deck. Some were rescued but others were not so fortunate.

In boat drill the lifeboats were let down into the water and we had to climb down a rope ladder and sit in our places before going back up again. Climbing the ladder, I used to look up at the ship, never down, otherwise I felt giddy because it was a long fall into the sea and if it was choppy the lifeboat would be bobbing about like a cork.

I started off as a Silver King, then became a pantryman, a waiter and a store keeper, each time bettering myself and earning more money. There was no question about setting my sights on anything ambitious, survival was essential. I was three thousand miles from home with no trade, there was no social security, so it was a question of work or starve. I would have done any work I was offered, provided it was legal. It is not surprising that most of the stewards took refuge in drink, especially the older ones, but I never drank on board ship. My relaxation was reading anything that came my way.

On shore I liked to go sightseeing. In Jamaica I tried to find the grave of Henry Morgan of Cardiff, the former pirate who became Governor of Jamaica. What an amazing life he had. He was born in 1635 into a prominent family in the little Welsh village of Llanrumney, which is now a suburb of Cardiff. As the eldest son he enjoyed a privileged life-style. He was very adventurous and while roaming around Bristol Docks he was kidnapped and taken to Barbados, where he was sold as a slave to a plantation owner. In 1654 Admiral Penn came in search of recruits and the nineteen-year-old Henry joined him. Admiral Penn captured Jamaica and Henry married and settled on the Island at Port Royal, where he became the leader of the buccaneers who used it as their base.

He led an assault on Panama City, either not knowing or not caring that Charles II had signed a peace treaty with the Spaniards. To appease his new allies, the King had Henry arrested and taken to England, where two years later he knighted him and sent him back to Jamaica as Governor-General. He died aged fifty-three and was buried on 26th August, 1688.

While searching for his grave I learned that in 1692 an earthquake had destroyed Port Royal and two thousand people died. However, in 1971, archaeologists began digging on the site. On Jamaica's north coast is the village of Llanrumney, named after Henry Morgan's birth-place and each Sunday in St. Peter's Church, Port Royal, his favourite silver tankard, said to have been plundered from a church somewhere in the old Spanish Americas, is still used as the communion chalice. At his burial all the ships in the harbour fired a twenty-two-gun salute. Not bad for a former pirate!

The passengers also liked sightseeing ashore and we had to be ready to look after then, even if they returned in the small hours of the morning, but we got no extra pay for this.

Each ship had a doctor and a barber. In the barber's shop was sold an assortment of goods bought in New York and other places where they could be obtained duty-free. When in each port the barber would grease the palm of the *Commandante* or man in charge, and was then given permission to open his shop for anyone living in the port. They could go on board and buy things which were not available on shore. The barber could charge what he liked and make a handsome profit.

One unpleasant job for the doctor was to examine the crew when they returned after shore leave, to see if they had picked up any sexual infection. Another job was to treat any members of the crew who had sunbathed too enthusiastically. We might be only five days out from New York, near Jamaica, but the sun was very hot and, being used to a temperate climate, they would sunbathe for too long and get sunstroke.

One day I was summoned by bell to the cabin of one of the passengers and found she was very agitated and calling for a doctor. Later, when I asked him how she was, he said her only trouble was that she had run out of drugs. She stayed in bed for the rest of the voyage. On another occasion we had to take a body in a coffin from New York to Santa Marta. Sailors always say that sharks know what is in a ship's hold; certainly they swarmed around us on this occasion and the butcher got a rope with a hook on one end with some meat on it and caught one. We cut the head off and he gave us all one tooth each, as we had all helped to pull it up. I had mine for a long time, but can't remember what happened to it.

At every port below the Panama Canal the custom officers would come aboard. Some of the stewards' department had to stay behind and feed them, although we were longing to go ashore. They all had big appetites. We used to take menus in, hiding them behind our backs and ask in Spanish, or at least our own broken versions, "Would you like some cold cuts?" When they said "Yes," we were delighted because we thought we could get ashore early. Not so. After the first course they asked for a menu and never left the table until they had eaten enough to feed two normal men, so of course we didn't get ashore until it was late.

I remember particularly that when we went ashore in Santa Marta no matter what time it was, or what time we returned to the ship, the band was always playing one certain tune. After a rest they would play the same tune again, so I presume it was the only one they knew. It was at Santa Marta that we took on our cargo of green bananas, around 60,000 stems, a large load for a small ship such as the *Zacapa*.

Once or twice we lost a member of crew who was murdered when he went ashore, so members of the stewards' department made a collection and handed it over to an agent of the company in that port, so that a headstone could be purchased. Of course any of us who went ashore in the dark in a foreign port, unable to speak the language, were laying ourselves open to trouble, so we always went ashore in groups. The *cantinas*, or drinking places, were simply shacks run by Chinamen and rum, which was made from the local sugar-cane, was very cheap – about 10c a glass. We used to mix this with Coca Cola and it made a very pleasant drink.

When we turned out after a few drinks to go back to the ship, we used to link arms across the street and make fun of the local policemen, who all seemed to be very small men. They wore denim trousers with a red stripe down the side and a cotton jacket, and they were always on the look-out for trouble-makers, so that they could take them to court and get them fined, because these fines augmented their very low wages. I don't think they ever caught any of us because we used to run like hell for the ship.

I had one very unpleasant experience aboard ship. I was helping one of the Spanish kitchen boys carry a very heavy dustbin to the leeward side of the ship to empty it. We had to lift it to the rails before tipping the contents out, but his hand must have slipped down between the handle and the dustbin and got trapped, so that he was pulled right over the rail and fell over the side with the dustbin. The ship stopped at once and a lifeboat was lowered, but his body was never recovered. All we could see was his hat floating on the surface of the sea. The incident had to be entered in the ship's log, but as to whether the company ever paid any compensation to the boy's family, I have my doubts.

A Landsman Again

On one of my times ashore in New York, my old friend Nem Roberts, of John Morgan's bar, suggested I should go to Wilkesbarre, Pennsylvania, to look for work. He gave me a note to a friend of his who was also called Roberts, and that man found me lodgings with a family named Evans. After three or four weeks I found work in a drift mine in the area as helper to a Polish miner, loading the coal into cars as he cut it. I was there about twelve months and got into the habit of going to the Second Welsh Congregational Church at Wilkesbarre, where the service was in English. On occasions I would take a Sunday School class.

As the demand for coal fell off, the mine was working only two or three days per week, so I went back to New York. A friend I had met in the Church asked me to take something back for one of his relations there, so I agreed, and he said, "Ask him if he can find you a job." The relative found me a labouring job on the new subway being built on 8th Avenue, and Columbia Circle, and this lasted six months. Then I went back to sea again.

On one occasion when the ship docked in New York, I decided to revisit Canada. I went back to the people I had stayed with before in Toronto. A friend I had known in those early days was now living in Bridgeburg, which is now called Fort Erie. He invited me to stay with him and I found a job with the Hamburg Floral Company, Fort Erie, Ontario, eighteen miles from the Niagara Falls, making artificial flowers. I felt this was woman's work and when someone said that workers were needed at the Erie Downs Golf Club, I walked up there and asked for a job. I was told I could start in two weeks as a barman, although in all the time I was there I never sold a drink. This was because Prohibition was in force in America so the members, 90% of whom were Americans, used to bring in the bottles of liquor they had bought at the licensed Government liquor store and then I would mix the drinks for them behind the bar and they would sign a chit to say what they had had. Their bottles were kept in their own lockers, to which they had a key. One man used to smuggle bottles of drink across the border to America in a secret compartment of his car. The buyer would pay for the bottle plus commission and, as far as I know, the man was never caught. The traffic across the Peace Bridge was very heavy and the police didn't have time to make a thorough search of every vehicle, so I suppose that is how he got away with it.

Another thing the Americans used to enjoy at the golf club, as well as the drinks, was the ham and eggs that we served. There is something about Canadian bacon which makes it to me the best in the world, and I am not the only one to think so.

My hours were long: 9am to 11pm, with one half-day off per week. On my half-day I would go to Buffalo, New York State, have lunch and then go to the cinema, as there was no entertainment in Bridgeburg.

When the golf course was closed for the winter by snow, I was out of a job until the spring. The club house was still open for members to come and play cards or have a drink, but they didn't need me there, so I went back to Philadelphia to stay with my aunt and look for work. My uncle was also looking for a job so, with no money coming into the house, my savings soon went. To make things worse, I had earlier bought shares amounting to $1,000 in the New York Edison Company. Then I was advised by one of the golf club members, who was President of a small bank, to invest my money in a company he was interested in instead. Unfortunately the company went bust and I knew I wouldn't see that money again.

After a month I went to New York to find work on a ship but there was nothing available. I only had a few dollars left so I went back to Philadelphia to find that a telegram was waiting for me at my aunt's house. It was from the Erie Downs Golf Club and read, "Job awaits you come at once." I went to the Western Union Telegraph Company to inquire what was the cheapest way to send a letter. I was told it was 60c to send a night letter, so I wrote to the golf club asking if the job was still open. The following day I received a telegram which read, "Job still open, come at once."

Now I was faced with a dilemma. I had a job to go to but no way of getting there. I had already pawned my watch and chain and had no money whatsoever. When I came down next morning my aunt told me that two letters had come for me. I certainly didn't feel like reading the letters, but I opened them eventually and found that one of them contained a cheque for $10, the interest due on my investment with the New York Edison Company before I had sold my shares. I went down to the Greyhound Bus Company and asked, "What is the price of a one-way ticket to Buffalo, New York?" I can still see that man adjusting his glasses and thumbing through the book. I held my breath and said a silent prayer. At last he said, "Nine dollars." "I'll have one," I said, "when does the bus leave?" "At eleven tonight." "I will be there," I promised.

At a stop on the journey I spent 25c on a cup of coffee and a piece of cake. When I reached Buffalo I made a telephone call to the golf club and caught the next bus to Canada across the Peace Bridge. This cost me another 25c, so of my $10 I had just 25c left. Then I walked the rest of the way to the golf club. Charlie Remus, the manager, told me I was looking rather rough. When I explained that I had travelled all night and not eaten since the previous day, he told me to have a meal and report for work next day. Almost as an afterthought he asked me, "Where are you staying?" When I told him I had nowhere to stay, as I was down to my last 25c, he told me to sleep on a couch in the lounge until I received my first week's pay. Then I would be able to find a room somewhere. So there I was, back at the golf club with a meal inside me, a place to sleep and a job, after all those weeks without work and no prospect of getting any. Even when I was offered the job at the golf club I had no way of getting there until that unexpected cheque dropped through the letter-box. If I read this in a book I would hardly believe it, but it is all true.

In three months I saved a hundred pounds, mainly because I had nowhere to spend money. A contributory factor was that I also received tips from the members who liked to stay late playing cards, and always gave me something to stay behind the bar, especially if there was a big "pot" on the table. I had been told there was a British Consul in Buffalo but, although I searched everywhere, I could not find it. Then I was directed to his office, which was down an alleyway. I went there to see if my passport was in order so that I would be able to travel freely between America and England. This way it would be easier for me to visit my family in Abercanaid. Each time I said goodbye to my mother after one of my visits, she would cry because she thought she would never see me again. I was determined that she would because she had always been such a wonderful mother to me, so the easier it was to travel, the more chance I would have of seeing her. When I found the Consul he was able to confirm at once that my passport was in order, so as soon as the golf club closed for the winter I booked a passage to England.

After visiting my family on this occasion I travelled to Monmouth to meet my friend, Lionel Ward, at Wheatfield Estate, Watery Lane, because of course I no longer had to hurry back to join a ship, which I had been forced to do on other occasions. There I met a friend of his sister Dorothy, a teacher from Newport, who had come to visit her, and he showed me a brochure about a rather unusual college in the United States. It was called Commonwealth College and it was on the outskirts of Mena in Arkansas, nearly on the State border with Texas. The college consisted of fairly primitive wooden buildings and was built from a grant given by the Garland Foundation. Students attended lectures in the morning and then in the afternoon worked on the land to produce their own food. Tuition had to be paid for so, as I had some savings, I applied to join and was accepted. Then I went back to Abercanaid to see my family before taking a ship for New York. Really I would have preferred to stay in England, but I had no training and there were so many unemployed that the only jobs available were very menial ones, apart from coal mining, of course. But I had sworn never to go back down the mine. There was no social security for those out of work, and it was a matter of taking any job simply to survive.

From New York I went by Greyhound Bus to Mena and signed on at the college, ready for the new term. Words can't express how excited and happy I was at the thought that at last I would be continuing my education. The huts we lived in were made of wood and very cold, but we collected wood to burn in the stove and kept warm that way. We also dug up peanuts and roasted them in a bucket on the top of the stove. But after a few months some of the students in the hut I was in called a strike. To this day I don't know what the strike was about but, coming from South Wales where a blackleg was just about the lowest form of life, I felt I had to go along with them. So we were all expelled from the college. I had no money left to get back to New York so a group of us rode the trains the thousands of miles to get there. We went down to the Depot and in the dark got aboard an empty box-car. At the end of each section, which was 110 miles, we would get out and look around in the yard for another train going in the direction we wanted.

Sometimes we would see whole families on the train, not travelling for pleasure but simply looking for work. Father, mother and children, all shabbily dressed but clean. The conductors were supposed to throw them off, because of course they had no tickets, but they turned a blind eye. As one of them said to me, "It may be me tomorrow".

On the outskirts of cities, shanty towns sprang up, made of kerosene cans, cardboard, or anything else. Unemployed people lived there. They were called Hoovervilles, after President Hoover, who was always promising that things would get better. But they never did while he was in office. At that time there were fourteen million unemployed in America.

We padded our clothes with newspapers to keep warm and on one occasion when we couldn't find an empty box-car, some of us hung on to the outside, hooking our arms through stanchions and anything else that we could find to keep from being flung off. This was in the depth of winter and when we reached Chicago we were so cold we just fell off into the snow like so may stiff corpses, until we thawed out. Looking up we saw a sign, "spare ribs and mashed potatoes 15c". Although it was midnight we went into the cafe and had a hot meal with gravy and gradually thawed out in the warmth. On this occasion we had an address to go to, but usually we slept in the town jails. I don't suppose there are many Welshmen who can boast of having slept in jails right across America. In one town the Town Marshal stopped us in the railway yard; he was an imposing looking man of about seventy, with a heavy walking stick and a large brass star on his coat. "Are you boys staying the night in the town?" he asked us. When we said we were he warned us to hurry because the town jail was nearly full. It was cheaper to let us sleep in the jails than to bury us next morning, for we would have died overnight in the cold. The jail was a new building and he was very proud of it, but the plumbing was not very good, because when someone flushed the toilet in the night the cells were flooded. There were no beds, we had simply made ourselves comfortable on the floor, wearing all our clothes and covering ourselves with newspapers. When the water came in as a tidal wave across the floor, we all had to scramble to our feet and sit or stand where we could until the warmth of the big stove dried the floor again.

We learned a lot from the people we met in the jails. One man had a wooden leg and he used to take this off, wrap it in his jacket and use it as a pillow. Another man went out first thing in the morning, telling us he was going to get his breakfast; he came back with a stale roll, an egg, a slice of bacon and a potato. While we washed he took a big, long-handled coal shovel, put his food on it and held it inside the fire-box to get it cooked. He told us never to beg, but to go to the baker's and ask if there were any stale rolls for sale. That way he usually got one given to him, and the same with the rest of the food.

One evening we entered the jail of the town we were in and saw an extraordinary sight. A man had taken off his outer clothes and was wearing an old-fashioned, striped bathing suit as underwear. He told us he was going to Florida as he wanted to be warm in the winter. He was certainly well prepared and we met him several times after that. Another man told us which town served the best food in their jail. These were ones where the jailor's wife did the cooking, but these were the exception. In most of the jails we were expected to serve our own food or go hungry.

One night we arrived at a small town in Kansas and as it was night-time we were anxious to find a place to sleep. We enquired of a man we met in the street and he said, "The Salvation Army runs a place down there, but hurry because it is filling up quickly." They had taken an empty shop and had filled it with bunks to accommodate the homeless. We slept in our underwear and we caught the biggest dose of lice we ever had. They bothered us the rest of the way to Philadelphia, and we had to keep scratching all the time. When we got to Harry Fisher's sister's place in Philadelphia we took our underwear off and boiled all the garments, as the lice were in the seams. All the time we were hopping box-cars we had tried to keep ourselves clean, as we found that it paid. We would shave in the station waiting rooms before anyone else was about.

One of the best meals we had on our travels was a breakfast we had in Kansas. It was advertised as "all you can eat for 25c". It was cornflakes and milk, ham and egg, toast with marmalade and coffee. One of our gang who was Jewish went to the rabbi and was given a dollar. Out of this he bought two breakfasts, both for himself, but the shunting of the box-car made him bring it all up again.

New York Life

Once we got to New York we had to find somewhere to live. We got a flat no-one else wanted because it was up six flights of stairs, so it was very cheap. The toilet was on the outside landing and was apt to flood when the chain was pulled, giving a cascade of water down the stairs. There was no bed but we found one dumped in the street and gave some boys a few cents to help us carry it up. We all four shared the bed until we found another one, and got that upstairs as well. Meals were a problem as, apart from being short of money, there was nowhere to keep the food fresh. After we had tried unsuccessfully to eat the remains of a chicken which stank to high Heaven, we held a conference in desperation, and I was elected cook. None of us was working. At that time there were fourteen million unemployed in America and no social security. So how did we live? Simply because the Jewish boys I was with had some good friends who worked in restaurants and hotels. They brought food with them whenever they came to see us, and not only food but bottles of sauce, cutlery and cruets, producing it all out of their pockets for us. One man who was working in one of the best nightclubs one day brought us some caviar. Caviar? We would rather have had roast beef! But he said, "Eat it. If those b...s can have it, why shouldn't you?"

Two of our gang took me to the Jewish Welfare Association which provided second-hand clothes. One of them wore a good overcoat he had been given by the Rabbi of one of the towns we had stayed in on our way to New York. My friends taught me a few words of Yiddish and with these I tried to pretend I was one of them. But I don't think the man in charge was deceived for a moment. He smiled and handed me some underwear which I should think dated from the early years of the century, but it was beautiful quality and very warm.

There was no gas connected when we first moved in, but one of the boys' friends fixed that for us. He came with a bag of tools but by-passed the meter by using a piece of rubber hose which looked as if it was the real gas pipe. When the gas man came to read the meter we had to keep him outside the door for a few minutes while we quickly connected the pipe to the meter again. When he came in he wrote something in his book, but I don't think he was fooled.

Any time we had an unwelcome visitor we went through the same procedure to make them think someone was taking a bath. This bath was in the kitchen and had an enamel top on it which we used as a table. We would quickly slide the top to one side and swish the water about with our hands, at the same time calling out, "Wait a minute, the wife is in the bath." Then we would slam the bedroom door and let the visitor in. Our friends always knocked in a certain way so they could be admitted at once.

Because of the unemployment there was a large pool of skilled and professional people who were glad to give their services free or for a small fee, simply so that they had something to do. They gathered on street corners and people who needed advice, or who needed a job done, simply went to them.

As we had no heating in the apartment, I used to go to the cinema in the morning when it opened at ten and sit at the back near a radiator, where I could sleep through two performances before going home in the evening. It cost 10c to get in and if I had a few cents left over I would ask at the pay desk for a candy bar to be split in half for me. That is how poor some of us were. I used to collect milk bottles from the streets, wash them carefully and take them to the grocery store, where I got 3c each for them.

Some of the owners of the big apartment blocks in Manhattan, such as the one we lived in, tried to save money by not turning on the heating in October, as they were supposed to by law. Then some of the residents would complain to the City Hall. If they could say the magic words, "There are children here," that soon brought someone to inspect the building. The owner would eventually be traced and be presented with a long list of defects, which would have to be put right otherwise the building would be condemned. When he reckoned up the cost, the owner usually decided it would be cheaper to turn on the heating, which is what the official from City Hall had intended all along.

We heard later that there had been a gruesome murder in one of these apartments we were living in. A mother objected to her daughter's boyfriend, so the two young people murdered her and put her body in the bath under the enamel cover. It was some weeks before the smell caused the neighbours to tell the police and the body was discovered.

When Fiorello H. La Guardia was elected Mayor of New York, he imposed a small purchase tax on everything bought in New York shops. He used this money to give a small allowance to the unemployed in the City and a small sum towards the cost of the rent. He was one of the best mayors New York ever had. He swept away corruption and did everything he could to restore the good name of the City.

The average wage for an unskilled man like myself was $4 a day or 50c an hour. Breakfast at a restaurant cost 25c, lunch 50c and a slap-up dinner $1. Newspapers printed menus for feeding a family of five on 50c a day. Tailors would turn a man's well-worn suit for $45, a process which involved restitching lapels, pockets and buttonholes so that the suit looked new. Cheap shirts from the laundry, whose owners had neglected to claim them, cost 50c.

When the term of office for President Hoover came to an end, Franklin D. Roosevelt was elected in his place, and then things really began to turn for the better for the whole of America.

President Roosevelt's favourite saying was, "The only thing we have to fear is fear itself". He made it possible for several states to obtain a grant from the Federal Government to carry out essential repairs in any part of the countryside. This was called the National Industrial Recovery Act, or NIRA. Thus, many people who had been too poor to buy proper food, clothes or shoes, were now able to do so. He passed a bill that anyone with savings of $5,000 in any bank could not lose the money if the bank failed, because the savings had to be insured by the bank with the Federal Government.

Another thing which began to raise the standard of living and provide more jobs for people, was the fact that Roosevelt was suspicious of Hither and began building up the country's arms and forces. He felt that strong armed forces would ensure peace for America if war did come.

Knowing boredom to be one of the dangers of mass unemployment, he also engaged out of work musicians to give concerts, and I went to many of these.

In the evenings I worked voluntarily at the Reading Room of the Socialist Party and could read the books and newspapers there. On one occasion Sir Stafford Cripps came from England to pay a visit to the Socialist Party of America and I met him in the Reading Room. One of the leading lights of the Socialist Party in New York was Norman Thomas, an ex-clergyman.

Sometimes a march would be organised by the Socialist Party, protesting at unemployment and the low standard of living of the unemployed. We would march along Fifth Avenue and the burly Irish cops would swing their police clubs as if daring us to step out of line and warning what would happen if we did. The majority of the New York police seemed to be Irish, but there were also Jews and Italians, and these seemed more sympathetic towards us. It was on one of these marches that I met a former student from Commonwealth College, a German boy called Hugo Fischer. He had been riding box-cars with us but we had become separated before we reached Philadelphia. He used to get a few nights' free board and lodging by committing some small offence and being put in jail. After the war I helped his son.

Farmers had ploughed too much of their land to grow corn, with the result that the fertile top soil blew away and nothing would grow there. Cattle were starving for lack of grass, due to a drought, so the Federal Government stepped in and had the cattle shot, and turned into tinned meat, such as corned beef and bully beef, to be distributed free to the unemployed. Pork and bacon were treated in the same way.

The Jewish boys I lived with had many Jewish friends who were unemployed and, of course, they were not allowed by their parents to eat this pork and bacon at home. So they used to bring it to us and we cooked it for them and they ate it with us, bringing us other things from their home in exchange.

When any relative of the Jewish boys came to visit, they always brought cakes or other food, which they shared with all of us. On Fridays I used to light the candles at the home of my Jewish friend, Harry Fischer. Apparently it was part of the ritual of preparation for the Jewish Sabbath to get a non-Jew to light the candles. I didn't enquire too closely into that aspect of it. In those days I would have lit anyone's candles in exchange for a square meal, which is what Harry used to give me. I didn't want to give the impression that we were wasting away due to starvation. We always had tea and coffee and bread and butter in the place and had a plain meal once a day, made from the cheapest ingredients I could find in the open-air markets. But square meals were few and far between.

Since I was the oldest member of the four of us by about ten years, the Government cheque towards the rent came in my name. If there was any delay in the rent cheques, the owner of the building, who was Jewish, would come and appeal for his money. Immediately the two Jewish members of our group would go to the window and start upbraiding him in Yiddish, which I could not understand. I later learned that they asked him how he could bring himself to ask for rent for a place such as we were living in and wasn't he ashamed to do so. It always ended up with him saying, "I speak only to the Englishman, not to you. Bring him here." Then the girlfriend of one of our gang found him a job. So he moved in with her but he sent us a few dollars each week to help those of us who were left and he kept this up for several months.

There was a lighter side to life. Every once in a while friends who were working would take us to a late show at the Paramount Theatre, Times Square. This was where the new shows were tried out. The performance began at midnight and we came out at about 3am. We would have a cup of coffee in an all-night restaurant and, if it was a nice evening, stroll home to bed. Even at that hour the streets were safe. There were no muggings or robberies, despite the desperate situation many people found themselves in.

I remember that when the mother of one woman died, the woman was too poor to pay a minister to take the burial service, so a friend of mine was asked to go and read some portions of the Bible over the body. Funerals were very expensive in New York. In the north, embalming was the general thing, but in the south people were too poor, but they were sometimes persuaded to buy new clothes for the corpse to be buried in. When someone died at home, the body would be taken to the funeral parlour and the face would be made up so that it looked as though the person was sleeping. If the relatives could not afford all this, they would see the minister and ask him to intervene and then the funeral parlour would usually lower its prices, otherwise they knew the minister would not send people to them again.

A family staying at John Morgan's hotel decided to go back to England after failing to find work in New York. During the night before, their child died, so John Morgan suggested that as they had no money for the funeral, the mother should clasp the child to her and say it was asleep. Then it could be buried at sea.

However poor they were, people did all they could to ensure that a relation had a decent burial. When a pauper died in New York and the body was not claimed, the City Council took charge of the burial. If there was anything of value on the body, such as false teeth, these were sold to anyone who wanted them. I have an idea that paupers were buried somewhere outside Manhattan. A trench was dug and the bodies were laid in this side by side, with a shuttering to keep the earth from falling into the still vacant part of the trench after each body had been covered over.

One of the saddest places in New York City is Skid Row, on the Bowery. This word Bowery comes from the Dutch and is the place where they had their gardens. But there is nothing garden-like about it now. I have seen men sitting on the pavements drinking meths, and all kinds of horrible concoctions. They spent what little money they had on this drink rather than food, so of course they did not last long. I remember seeing one man with a pair of pince-nez with the lenses coloured blue and a chain looped around one ear, and I wondered how he had got into that state. But it was a mistake to take too close an interest in them, otherwise they would become abusive and follow you along the road, thinking that you had come to take delight in their misery. It is said that when one of these men died there was a wreath with no name on it sent by the Vice-President, who had discovered that the man was a former mayor and that they had been at college together.

During my time in America I found that the rich were very rich, much more so than in England, and the poor were much poorer than any I had seen elsewhere.

Although I could have taken part in any of the Government schemes for the unemployed, I never did, because I was hoping all the time to get back to sea. However, in 1934 I did sign on as an emergency snow labourer with hundreds of other unemployed men. We were given a card which I have still got today. This had to bear our photograph and, according to the instructions on the back, we had to report at the first sign of snow, or at the time designated by the foreman. I did about two days' work shovelling snow off the side walks into lorries, then I had to make way for other unemployed to take my place. On one occasion I even got work as a butler in Buffalo, New York State, but I didn't like it, so I didn't stay. I just took what jobs I could. One was for two hours every lunch time, working at a lunch counter. This paid me 50c for the two hours. But what I wanted most was the free meal I was given. In those days survival was the name of the game.

I had a good friend, Robert Churchill, with whom I had sailed on many occasions, and thanks to him I was sometimes able to find work on board ships. He was Chief Steward on a small ship and when the ship docked we would often go out for a meal together.

On one occasion I took him to Harlem, the coloured area of New York. Although it was safe to walk the streets of the City in the small hours of the morning, Harlem was a different matter. If Joe Louis, World Heavyweight Champion, was fouled in a fight, or had a decision given against him, there would be a minor riot and white people were advised to stay away. On this occasion, Robert Churchill picked up a girl there and she took him to her room. She told him where to leave his clothes and when he went back to them, he found his pockets had been emptied. Outside he met a hefty Irish cop and told him what had happened. The cop told us angrily, "You shouldn't come to Harlem picking up high-yaller girls." This was the term used for anyone of mixed race. After going on at us for some minutes, he came back with us to the girl's apartment, pulled all the drawers out and put his foot through them, smashing them to pieces. Then he said to us, "Let that be a lesson to you," and told us to go.

I was always homesick for Wales. If Robert Churchill couldn't find me a job, I would go to New Jersey to see if I could get work on board a cargo ship going to England. If I couldn't get work as a steward, I would take anything. Sometimes, if a captain didn't have a full complement of crew, to be legal he would take me on anyway. I got no pay and the food and accommodation were poor, but at least I got a passage to England for nothing. Sometimes I would be sent up on deck at midnight to check that the ship's navigation lights were working. The officer on the bridge would call "Are the lights shining?" "Lights are bright, sir," I would call, whether I could see them or not. All I wanted was to get back down below and into my bunk again. In England I always tried to get a permanent job but often all I would be offered was work in a public house in exchange for my board and lodging. I always refused, as I wanted a proper job, as long it was not coal mining.

The Erie Downs Golf Club

It was always pleasant to get back to the golf club in the spring if I had spent the winter away. As soon as the golf club opened again in the spring I would go back there, because I knew I was always sure of a job. Occasionally I spent the winter there, looking after the locker room so that the men could come in and drink and play cards. Altogether I spent five or six seasons at the Erie Downs Golf Club. There was never any shortage of food, for one thing. The chef had a large ice box, what we would call in England a refrigerator, and he used to keep it carefully locked at all times. But a small piece was missing from the glass-fronted door, so in fact it was quite easy for anyone to help themselves to a piece of chicken or to what else they fancied, whenever they were hungry.

It was at the golf club that I had the most frightening experience of my life. One Christmas Eve a dinner-dance was being held at the main restaurant. I was in the locker room in case anyone came over to fetch anything from their locker and I was half asleep. At 3am, I suddenly found a gun being held against my forehead and a man demanding the master key for the lockers. I am not going to pretend I was a hero. I remember my uncle telling me once that if a man's eyes sparkled he was either drunk or on drugs. So I looked at this man's eyes and promptly handed over the key. I thought it was better to be a live coward than a dead hero. He collected up all the bottles of drink he could carry, while my hair stood on end, and I wondered what he was going to do to me. When he was ready he told me to walk out with him to his car and get in. He drove me to Bridgeburg and then pushed me out. I walked back to the club and reported what had happened. Next day a police car came up and drove me down to Bridgeburg again and I was told to see if I could identify the man anywhere. I couldn't, and that was the last I heard of the matter.

When working at the golf club I had a very good friend, Milfred, who had a twin sister, Mildred. He worked at the Hamburg Floral Company. When I was out of a job in the winter months, he often took me out to his parents' farm in Western New York State at a place called Springville. I used to stay there for weeks at a time and they were very good to me. At the onset of winter, stakes would be sunk in the ground about three feet from the house walls and straw would be packed behind them to insulate the house and save fuel. It was very effective. Heat in the house came from a pot-bellied wood burning stove, for which I helped to saw the wood with a two-man cross-cut saw. On one occasion I found embedded in the wood a flint arrow-head, no doubt shot by an Indian many years previously. I wish now I'd kept it.

Not far from the farm was a small, wood-built school house. We used to take a load of wood down there from time to time and it had to be measured by a committee of farmers before we were paid for it. While I was there the school was closed, and after that the children from the scattered farms were taken by bus to a central school.

Most of the farmers had an old "tin Lizzy" motor car to run around in, often second- or third-hand. I remember when a part was needed for one of the wheels it could be purchased in Woolworths in the local town for 10c. Of course, when snow was on the ground the horse would be harnessed to a sleigh for going shopping. Before setting out, bricks would be warmed in the oven or on top of the stove and these were then wrapped in an old sack and placed in the straw on the bottom of the sleigh. they were a great comfort on the way to town for our cold feet, as of course the horse took its time. By the time the shopping was finished the bricks were no longer hot, so we were glad to get home.

At other times Milfred and I would stay in some other town and then we would always share a room to save money. I will tell you an amusing story about shared rooms. A Jewish friend of mine in Bridgeburg asked me if I knew of a country place where his wife, in her twenties, could go to recuperate for a few weeks after an operation. I made enquiries and found a farm where she could stay for one dollar a day. She slept in an upstairs room and the old couple slept downstairs. Also sleeping upstairs was their son, Curtis, and it seemed that the girl got tired of sleeping alone and shared his room each night. In the mornings the son was so tired he used to fall asleep while he was ploughing and the horse used to stand still until he woke up again.

On one occasion I was offered a job in Bridgeburg for the winter months and I asked the man what it was. He said I must not tell anyone else, but it was smuggling whisky across the Peace Bridge into America. "What happened to the last man?" I asked. "He was buried yesterday," the man told me, and I said "No thanks."

Another man who offered me a job was a cripple who ran a hamburger stall. He had only one arm so, feeling sorry for him, I took the job, although I got no pay, only commission. He had a large sign above the stall, A loaf of bread, a pound of meat and all the mustard you can eat, 10 cents." Well, only the part about the mustard was true and as for the so-called commission, I made barely enough to pay my room rent, but I did get a free meal, so that was something. I stayed there only a few months until something better turned up.

Most of the jobs I took on in the winter were only for a day, but at least I did eat on that day. In the winter when the Erie Downs Golf Club was closed, I usually went back to Philadelphia to my aunt. On one occasion when I was staying with her, she told me about her Catholic woman friend with whom she often went to the cinema, when they both lived in Wilkesbarre. The woman told her, "You will have to wait for a few minutes, I am just going to get some holy water from the priest." "Give me the bottle," said my aunt, "and you get dressed." My aunt didn't go to the priest, she told me she filled the bottle at the first stream she came to and they were none the wiser. To my aunt, one bottle was just as good as another.

Being interested in history, I paid several visits each time I was in Philadelphia to the room where the American Declaration of Independence had been signed. This was in Carpenters' Hall, now known as Independence Hall, and a shrine to all Americans. The chairs in the room were still in the positions that they were in at the signing. At the signing of the American

Declaration of Independence on the 4th July, 1776, eighteen of the fifty-six delegates were of Welsh descent, that is 32% out of those present. This so enraged the English King, George III, that he branded it "that damned Welsh document". The declaration was written by Thomas Jefferson, the third President, whose ancestors had emigrated to America. He wrote once, "the tradition of my father's family was that we came from Capel Curig at the foot of Snowdon, the highest mountain in Wales." His father was Peter Jefferson, and Thomas married a widow, Martha Wayles Skelton, on 1st January, 1772, when he was aged twenty-nine. When Peter divided his estate into two parts he called one Shadwell, because that is where his wife was born in London, and the other he called Snowdon, because his father's ancestors came from there. Thomas Jefferson was born in 1743 and died in 1826. One of his favourite sayings was "Rebellion against tyrants is obedience to God." When I see today how the Israeli soldiers threaten the unarmed Arabs with the help of money given by the U.S.A., I think that if Thomas Jefferson could see it, he would turn in his grave.

In the museum in Independence Hall I saw George Washington's teeth, made of wood by a carpenter. On the dollar bills you will see that his lips go in where he has no front teeth of his own. I think George Washington was never a happy man. In his younger days he was in love with an English girl, Sally Fairfax, and when she returned to England something went out of his life. He wanted to leave the presidency after his first term of four years, but Thomas Jefferson persuaded him to seek re-election. He was a military man rather than a politician, very fair and just, but somewhat contemptuous of the ordinary people. No-one was allowed to stand nearer than six feet to him and he never went out except in a carriage and pair. Some Americans said, "We have got rid of one king, only go get another."

George Washington's ancestors lived in the Warton area of England for hundreds of years and helped to build the fifteenth-century church there. Their arms were three stars and two stripes, and these were displayed in the tower and they are part of the American flag which was first made by Betsy Ross in Philadelphia.

Charles II repaid many of his friends and courtiers by granting them land in America. Being interested in history, I went sightseeing whenever I could. At the top of Wall Street in New York City is Holy Trinity Church and I went there one day, but was rather put out to see an open coffin near the altar with the body of a soldier in it. I believe is buried in this church General Montgomery, who was either killed or died of wounds during fighting in Canada after the American Declaration of Independence. The woman he had intended marrying refused to go out of her house until she herself died twenty-one years later.

I remember once I was walking in the woods near Arkansas on the borders of Texas with some friends and, as it was a hot day, we approached a log cabin to ask for a drink of water. The roof was falling in and it looked so derelict that we decided to keep well away because it looked unsafe. At the next cabin we came to there was a bucket of water by the door with a dipper. We knocked and asked the woman if we could have a drink. She told us to help ourselves. We said we had gone first to the other cabin where the roof was falling in and she told us the family was going to repair it. Her daughter was going to live there when she got married. I have never seen women work harder than those women in the south, white and coloured, in the cotton fields under the hot sun. The skin on their faces seemed to shrivel because of the heat.

I thought Washington was a beautiful city when I went there, but around it were some of the worst slums in America where the black people lived. I remember being in Maryland once and hearing beautiful singing when I was sitting outside the hotel. When I asked where the singing was coming from, the proprietor said it was coloured people in their own part of the town. they didn't dare come to the white man's part of town, they were not allowed to use the same toilets as the whites and if they got on a bus they had to go to the back. Now, there are black politicians and things have changed for the better, but in those days in some parts of the south the coloured people didn't even have a vote.

In about 1935 or early 1936, Hugo Fischer, whom I had met again on the unemployed march in New York, decided to go back to Germany, his homeland, and I went back to Wales. After visiting my family I went to see him in Essen. Everywhere people seemed to be marching, even elderly people, often up till 2am at night. I used to go down to the station for the English edition of the *Daily Telegraph*, but it was only there on about three days a week. I couldn't speak German, but when the woman at the newspaper kiosk told me it was censored, I understood that. Everyone gave "Heil Hitler" salutes. I was going into the public toilets one say when a man saluted and said, "Heil Hitler," and without thinking I said it back to him, but when I realised what I had done, I swore under my breath.

Hugo was working with his brother and told me he was keeping the tank of his car filled with petrol so that at the first sign of any trouble he could rush me across the border into Holland. He took me to see his brother's wife on several occasions. The first time we went there she kept staring at me, so in the end I said to Hugo, "What's wrong?" He assured me it was nothing, simply that she expected me to be wearing a monocle. I laughed at that and told him to tell her I came from Wales, and it was only the Englishmen who wear a monocle. She was very good to me and gave me cigars to take away with me.

Every night at eight o'clock we listened to the latest news on the radio in English. I don't know where the broadcast came from but it was loud and clear. Occasionally Hugo would take me out. When we travelled on the *autobahn* I thought how efficient but featureless these motorways were. They induced in me a great desire to sleep. If only some trees or grass had been planted to break the monotony!

I was in Essen for about a week or ten days before I decided to go back to England. When people knew I had been in Germany they would ask if a war was coming and I would tell them, "It is not *if* a war is coming, it is *when*!" because I had seen Germany's unmistakeable military preparations.

After the war I got in touch with Hugo again when I wrote to his old home in Essen. Some years later when I had my health-food shop in Chiswick, his son came to stay in London. He was in his teens but was tall and looked much older. I found a nice room for him with full board. He had learned to speak English in school but needed practice in speaking it, so his holiday in London gave him a chance to do this. I never saw Hugo again after the war and when my later letters went unanswered I presumed he was dead.

Ynysfach Murder

by EIRA M. SMITH

On the 30th September, 1908, the Merthyr Tydfil Borough Police Force was formed, and James Wilson was appointed the first Chief Constable. He started clearing up the town of the drunks and prostitutes, many of them sleeping rough, as they had no fixed abode.

Here are a few examples:

Eliza Hursely and *Alice Gough*, women of ill repute, were charged with sleeping out at the Coke Ovens, and were sent to prison for seven days.

David Walters and *Thomas Richards* were also sent to prison for twenty-one days, and seven days respectively, for sleeping in a stable at the rear of Bethesda Street.

Gough was one of the women for whom *James Andrew Scot* awaited trial at the Assizes. He attempted to drown her by throwing her into the Canal. Merthyr had a Magistrates' Court at that time, but no Quarter Sessions. Jurors and witnesses had to travel, either to Cardiff or Swansea, when cases were referred to a higher court. Petitions were arranged to have Quarter Sessions in Merthyr, which eventually happened.

Let us go back to the 23rd December, 1908, when Mary Greening, a local prostitute, was released from Swansea Prison. She was married to Daniel Greening, but they lived apart, she being of no fixed above. When Mary Greening arrived at Merthyr railway station, she was met by her friend, a fellow-prostitute named Mary Ann Rees, known as "Sloppy". She was 33 years of age, of no fixed abode. Her family lived in Ynysgau, but she had not lived with them for fifteen years, i.e., since she was eighteen years of age.

The two women left the railway station and went to The Wheatsheaf Inn in Glebeland Street, where they had two-pennyworth of rum each. (The Wheatsheaf Inn would be where the Job Centre now stands. Two more pubs in the story are The Rainbow Inn – later a common lodging house, where we now have the entrance to the bus station in Castle Street, and The Red Lion, also in Castle Street. The Income Tax office now stands on this site, formerly the site of B. Harris Jones.)

From The Wheatsheaf Inn, two ladies of the street went to The Rainbow Inn, where they each had half a pint of beer. Mary Ann Rees bought some food and they both went to the Ynysfach Ovens, where they met two men with whom they shared their breakfast. One of the men was John Edward Bassett, a labourer of no fixed abode and the other, William Joseph Foy, ex-truant school-boy and ex-soldier, aged 25 years, who had family living in Penyard. So we have the four characters in our story.

After eating their breakfast, all four went to the Mardy ash tip. We already know the police were active in arresting both male and females as vagabonds. The four probably went there to escape the notice of the police. They stayed there until 3 p.m., then returned to the Ynysfach ovens where Mary Ann Rees, alias "Sloppy", cooked a meal for them in a bucket of ashes. She also washed and dried the apron she was wearing, outwardly making herself more presentable.

She and Mary Greening went to the Iron Bridge area, notorious at that time for the rogues, vagabonds and prostitutes who frequented this area. Prostitutes were known to wear white aprons, and stand between the two bridges, i.e., the Iron Bridge and the Traffic Bridge. They charged each customer 6d per time. The two women had a shilling each, probably four customers between them, and took Bassett and Foy to The Rainbow Inn, and "Sloppy" bought each man a pint of beer. The women then went into town.

Later, all four met at The Red Lion Inn, where the men drank a pint of beer each and the women half a pint. At 10.30 p.m. they went back to the Ynysfach ovens. The landlady of The Red Lion confirmed they were all sober. The four characters went to the last but one oven, and they had to cross a plank or beam 33 feet long and 15 inches wide, with a drop of 39 feet 6 inches to the bottom of the furnace. There was no light for them to see. Both women took off their shoes and lay down. Sometime later, "Sloppy" was heard to say, "You don't want me. It's Polly Gough you want." Obviously, Foy did not mind Mary Ann Rees buying his food and beer, but he did not fancy her sexually. She put on her shoes and left the oven. Foy followed her, intending bringing her back to her friend, Bassett. She threatened to expose him for living on her immoral earnings. In the argument that followed, she fell down the furnace. No-one heard her scream and Foy returned to Greening and Bassett, saying, "I have shot Mary down the hole." Bassett went to see if there was a body and struck some matches, but could see nothing.

Foy left the furnaces and met Sgt. Hunter and P.C. Richard Henry Lewis in the High Street at about 2 a.m. He asked to be locked up, because he had thrown "Sloppy" down a hole in the old works, as she was going to tell he was living on her immoral earnings. Sgt. Hunter, P.C. Lewis and Foy met Detective Edward Jones on their way to the site. At the site, Det. Jones found an apron and corsets belonging to the deceased.

Foy told them how he had caught hold of "Sloppy", swung her round, dragged her to the hole and dropped her in, and even showed them the marks where it had happened. Bassett did not believe Foy had done this, but when he realised what may have happened he said, "You ought to swing for it." Foy hit him on the jaw. Foy insisted he was telling the truth, and pointed to the shawl he had thrown in after "Sloppy". The body could not be seen and so they tried calling her, but there was no response.

Foy was locked up at the Police Station and the police returned with a long rope and a lamp. They could now see the body. Mary Ann Rees was lying on her right side, her head resting on a piece of iron, face downwards. There was a cut on her cheek and top lip. She was dead, but not quite cold. The body was taken to Dr. Ward's surgery at 5 a.m. Dr. J. Chisholm performed the post-mortem examination. No limbs were broken and the body was well-nourished, but dirty. The face was swollen and bruised and there were several cuts inside and outside the right cheek. The right upper jaw was broken, and the cause of death was "shock".

Mary Ann Rees was buried at the Ffrwd Cemetery, Cefn, on Sunday, 27th December, 1908, from her parents' home in Ynysgau. There were four mourning coaches following the glass-pannelled hearse, and about 50 people on foot. To this day her remains are alone in the grave at Cefn.

Foy was found guilty of wilful murder at the Glamorgan Assizes on the 31st March, 1909. He had pleaded "Not Guilty". He was conveyed by train to Swansea to await his hanging, if there was no reprieve. Whilst there, he wrote to his sisters and friends and, during his stay at the prison, was comforted by the assistant Chaplain, who carried out the condemned man's wishes. At 8 o'clock on Saturday, 8th May, 1909, Foy was given a cigarette and Albert Pierrepont, the hangman, dragged the white cap over Foy's face – cigarette and all. Ellis, his assistant, pulled the lever, the trap-doors parted, and all was over.

It seems Ynsfach had, apart from one accidental murder of Mary Ann Rees, also the lawful murder of William Joseph Foy.

The Lifeguards

by DAVID LEWIS JONES

The, name the "LIFEGUARDS" conjures up a variety of different meanings to many individuals in many communities throughout the world. The picture of a "Lifeguard" in a sentry box outside Buckingham Palace, the "Lifeguard" on horseback, plumes flying doing duty at Horse Guards Parade. The "Lifeguard" saving lives around our coastal resorts and, more recently, the impact on T.V. viewers of *Bay Watch* on sun-drenched beaches of California. The picture of bronzed "he-men" and curvacious lifeguards like Pamela Anderson, all come to mind when the word "LIFEGUARD" is used.

To the people of Merthyr Tydfil, the South Wales Valley and in parts of the world such as the U.S.A., France, Bahrain, Ireland, Scotland and England, the word lifeguard has a totally different meaning. Eighteen years ago a new breed of lifeguards came on the scene, nothing to do with military, swimming, etc., but indirectly their enthusiasm for their hobby is surely saving lives by their act of charity toward the community.

A group of local men with a talent and a love for singing decided to put their talent to good use. They were unique in that they did not require any musical instruments, for theirs is basically a four-part, close-harmony group, not to be confused with "Barber Shop" or "Acepelo" singing methods. The only instrument used by the group to commence singing is an inexpensive pitch pipe.

On hearing this the group pitch their songs accordingly and have done so successfully for the last eighteen years.

Their popularity is infectious, again being recalled by many who have heard them time and time again. It is for this reason, and the fact that they sing for charity, that the "Lifeguards" we know will continue to sing in beautiful harmony for a long time to come.

The "LIFEGUARDS" were born as a result of a challenge issued by the Ladies' Section of the Dowlais Male Choir to provide entertainment for a "Noson Lawen" evening to celebrate St. David's Day in March, 1977.

A group of choristers met in a local pub, The White Horse Inn, Twynyrodyn, after practising with the male choir. The challenge by the ladies was put to the group and discussed at length, and three members decided to accept the challenge.

These three were Wyndham Carey, Bill Edwards and Len Hargreaves. A further eight were recruited to the cause: Carl Llewellyn, Philip Adams, Ivor Jones, John Jenkins, John Mitchell, Gerwyn Williams, Grahame Clark and Don Barry. Within a few days a "Harmony Group" was formed and members discussed and made up a programme ready for the "Noson Lawen". Being all fired-up and ready to perform, they found out at the last minute that they were the sole entertainment for the evening but a successful evening proved to be the first of many.

As a result of the performance, quite a number of requests were received by the group. Because of these requests, the group decided that if they were to perform at any further functions, they would ask for a fee for their services, which would be donated directly to a charity of their choice.

The name "LIFEGUARDS" was decided upon because of the charitable nature of the group. A performing uniform was devised to link charity to the traditional garb of the early lifeguards, namely the bathing costumes hooped in red and white, and hooped in black and white. This "uniform" for stage performances became the official logo of the "Lifeguards", whose motto is "Cynghanedd mewn Bywyd" ("Harmony in Life").

After many years of weekly practice and a few hundred performances, the group was now formally established and, as a result, decided to apply for "Charitable Trust Status". This was granted in 1986. The concerts that the Lifeguards have performed since 1977 number approximately 460 and, hopefully, will be celebrating their 500th performance on stage.

Practice venues for the "Lifeguards" have changed throughout the years for many different reasons. Local hostelries such as The White Horse, Twynyrodyn, and Farmers Arms (The Spite), Narrow Gauge and Imperial Hotel, Merthyr, have been used after the practices of the Dowlais Male Choir. The group presently meets for practice on Wednesday and Sunday nights at the Merthyr Conservative Club.

Usually practices take the form of singing a variety of songs, mainly old favourites "to get it right on the night". However, there are occasions when no singing is done. We have discussions on songs to be sung, new songs to be learnt, the business of organising transport to venues near and far, the dress for the evening and many other aspects in relation to a particular concert.

The "Lifeguards" to date have quite a repertoire, in that they sing songs from many eras, songs from shows, songs from the "Deep South" (not South Wales), songs from the two World Wars and, of course, songs from Wales, including many Welsh hymn tunes. Reference to some of the songs will be made further into this script.

The stage costumes of the "Lifeguards" reflect the songs they sing. They have regular changes of costume, i.e., the distinct red and white, and black and white hooped bathing costumes with straw boater head-gear. The bow tie, white shirt and waistcoat costume and the old Welsh traditional costumes of "Dai Caps", mufflers and black waistcoats which are used for the "Welsh Scene". One other costume is used – that of Dickensian outfits for use in the weeks running up to Christmas, when the lads sing carols in local pubs, clubs and hospitals, using collecting tins for charitable donations.

Little did they think that 20 years on the group would still be together after such humble beginnings. Changes of faces, venues and songs, but they are still together and, hopefully, will be for many years to come.

The Growth of the Lifeguards, or "This Is Your Life!"

1st March, 1977

First "Noson Lawen", held in the Guest Memorial Club, Dowlais. Three concerts were performed this year.

1978

The concerts in 1978 were significant, not because of the venues but because of the artists that they appeared with, namely: Bryn Williams of "Black and White Minstrel" fame, singer Bryn Phillips and Malcolm Nash, ex-Glamorgan Cricketer.

Fourteen concerts were performed in this year.

1979

This was the year the "Lifeguards" were invited by Alan Osborne to appear in his musical *Terraces*, based on Merthyr Tydfil.

The group performed for a fortnight at the "Chapter Arts Theatre", Cardiff, with Sue Jones Davies of *Rock Follies* fame and Bob Blythe, a prominent Welsh actor.

1980

Many concerts were performed locally, but appearing with Philip Madoc in "Baverstocks Hotel" on an International Rotarian night, put the icing on the cake.

1981

In this year, twenty-two concerts were performed but the "Lifeguards" derived their greatest pleasure and enjoyment by organising and performing in their first OLD TYME MUSIC HALL AND VARIETY SHOW at the MINERS' HALL in MERTHYR TYDFIL.

This proved to be so highly entertaining and popular to capacity audiences that they were asked to organise another show for 1982.

1982

The "Lifeguards" were invited to the Mayor's Parlour by Councillor Mona Shankland in recognition of their work for charity.

The OLD TIME MUSIC HALL Concert was repeated and they paid a second visit to HOPE HALL to sing for the DANYGRAIG CHESHIRE HOMES CHARITY.

1983

The 20th of September was a "Red Letter Day" for the lads as they celebrated their 100th concert at HOPE CHAPEL.

They also entered a "CASTLES OF WALES" competition and came third out of over 100 entries. The judges included MAX BOYCE and OWAIN ARWEL HUGHES.

1983 was also the first time they dressed in the Dickensian outfits for the Christmas Collections. They collected £500 for the Welsh Kidney Research Fund and presented the money under a lampost outside the White Horse Inn, Twynrodyn. It was after this event that they decided to give all other monies raised to local charities.

1984

The "Lifeguards" were part of a well-known cast used to open "THE ROSE THEATRE", TEWKESBURY, owned by STAN STENNET.

The collection at Christmas in this year amounted to £1,000, which was given to the charity "THE TALKING NEWSPAPER". Thirty-four concerts were performed this year.

1985

The "Lifeguards" made their first commercial tape, the title of which was *In Harmony*. They were indebted to Chris Kelly (Conductor and Leader of an Army Band), who gave of his expertise conducting the "Lifeguards" prior to and during the recording.

In May there was a highly beneficial yet unsuccessful venture by the group to audition for a B.B.C. Light Entertainment Show. The singing was up to standard but, according to the people who mattered, movement on stage was too static and they failed to gain a "spot" on British Television.

This was the year of an opening of a restaurant called "GLUTTONS" in Porthcawl. An appearance and singing at this event brought traffic to a standstill in the main high street.

Fifty concerts were sung this year. The most memorable was singing in ST. DAVID'S HALL, CARDIFF for the COMMONWEALTH GAMES APPEAL FUND, which was hosted by SIR GERAINT EVANS.

The amount collected at Christmas was given to the "BABY SCANNER UNIT" at PRINCE CHARLES' HOSPITAL. This totalled £1,200.

1986

The group were invited to the GRAND THEATRE, SWANSEA, to take part in a concert for the COMMONWEALTH GAMES APPEAL FUND.

They also appeared for the opening of LEEKES, LLANTRISANT and the CROSSHANDS DEPOT.

In October they took part in the CHRISTIE TYLER INTERNATIONAL FORTNIGHT at the PARK HOTEL, CARDIFF. They appeared during every night of this festival.

A GRAND CHRISTMAS CONCERT was their next performance, held at the CATHOLIC HALL, MERTHYR TYDFIL, in aid of the URDD NATIONAL EISTEDDFOD, which was held in MERTHYR the following year.

1987

So successful was the production of the first tape, a second tape was made and was entitled *Hiraeth and Harmony*. This tape included the songs from the Welsh Scene and brought tears to many listeners' eyes.

In March at the "HOLIDAY INN", CARDIFF, they were requested by the VARIETY CLUB OF GREAT BRITAIN to appear with a host of "stars" and helped to raise £5,000 in one evening.

In May the "Lifeguards" and their wives made their longest journey after being invited by the HOOVER COMPANY, CANTON, OHIO and the CANTON CHORALE to give concerts in the U.S.A.

Five concerts were staged in and around CANTON, URBANA, RADNOR and COLUMBUS, the State Capital. A weekend was enjoyed by all in NASHVILLE, TENNESSEE, even though there were no formal concerts on the itinerary.

Music and friendship continued to be the joint themes of the tour. Americans who had come to NASHVILLE to hear their own country music were soon tapping their toes to the strains of "MOLIANWN". While cruising on the river boat *The General Jackson*, the "Lifeguards" were congratulated time and time again on their singing.

When everyone had said their good-byes at the end of the successful tour, little did they think that they would hear these voices again so soon.

Because of the delay in their flight from NEWARK, NEW JERSEY AIRPORT, the lads dug deep into the reserves of their voices to treat their fellow-travellers to an unscheduled concert at the airport concourse.

They made many friends and fans across the Atlantic. The letters to the *Merthyr Express* and other South Wales newspapers were testimony to their high esteem in the U.S.A. The monies they earned on this tour were donated to MENCAP and amounted to £1,500.

1988

The highlights of this year started when they were invited to participate in an "OLD TIME MUSICAL" to commemorate the 75th Anniversary of the "PARC AND DARE HALL" in TREORCHY. Those taking part included GLYN HOUSTON (film actor), BEVERLEY HUMPHRIES (television singer), BRYN WILLIAMS (Black and White Minstrel *fame) and* PAUL SHANE (*Hi-Di-Hi*, Actor/Comedian).

A further invitation came from NORMANDY, FRANCE, which the "Lifeguards" accepted. A week-end was enjoyed singing for 500 French children and their parents.

Toward the end of the year the "Lifeguards" donated £1,000 to the McMILLAN NURSES' APPEAL FUND during an all-night BOWLING COMPETITION organised for the MAYOR'S APPEAL at RHYDYCAR INDOOR BOWLING STADIUM.

1989

The "Lifeguards" were on the move again after an invitation to sing during ST. DAVID'S DAY CELEBRATIONS at BAHRAIN in the MIDDLE EAST.

Instigators of the invitation were members of the BAHRAIN WELSH SOCIETY, led by BOB GILCHRIST, a Merthyr man working for a prominent British Company, Watson Hawksley. Again the "Lifeguards" were indebted to those of the Welsh Society for their friendship and hospitality.

While in BAHRAIN, the "Lifeguards" were asked to perform on a Saturday night at the "BRITISH CLUB". When the group arrived they found they were sharing the stage with the world-famous American group, "THE DRIFTERS".

The "Lifeguards" sang at twelve venues during this tour. Apart from the "BRITISH CLUB" the "Lifeguards" will remember their renditions on the British War Ship, *H.M.S. Hermione*, berthed in BAHRAIN and whose Captain was Welshman OWEN JARRETT.

The Rugby Football Club at SAAR and in the office of SHEIKH RASHID BIN KHALIFA, MINISTER OF TOURISM AND INFORMATION.

The charitable donations on this tour helped to raise funds for a local children's home in BAHRAIN.

In October the group sang at the CREST HOTEL, CARDIFF, in support of the COMMONWEALTH GAMES APPEAL FUND.

By the end of this year, the "Lifeguards" had performed in 324 concerts/ engagements in a variety of venues, including Old People's Homes, where they were humbled to see the way some people get on with their lives despite terrible handicaps.

Concerts in Church, Chapel and Village Halls were received enthusiastically by all who attended.

1990

January and February were frantic months of rehearsal for the return visit to BAHRAIN. The final rehearsal was held at HOREB CHAPEL, PENYDARREN, to a very appreciative congregation on a Sunday evening.

Late February saw the start of a long journey to BAHRAIN, arriving in the early hours of the morning. The Welsh Society ST. DAVID'S DAY FESTIVITIES had begun. The hosts on this occasion were friends made on the previous visit.

Concerts were held in the BRITISH CLUB, THE DILMUN CLUB and culminated in a large dinner-dance and concert at the HOLIDAY INN HOTEL, BAHRAIN. Welsh men and women had travelled from many Gulf States, especially SAUDI ARABIA, for this event. Also present were the BRITISH AMBASSADOR in BAHRAIN and the COMMODORE AND OFFICERS OF U.S. GULF FLEET anchored in BAHRAIN.

The Commodore and officers were from the Command Vessel, *U.S.S. La Salle*, which was the first ship into KUWAIT HARBOUR after liberation at the end of the GULF WAR.

The "Lifeguards" made many visits during their stay in THE GULF. Mr. David Mantle made a presentation of a Welsh Miner's Lamp to the Minister of Tourism and Information. The group also visited the recently-built BAHRAIN NATIONAL MUSEUM; the very impressive "GRAND MOSQUE", built and funded by a BAHRAINI MILLIONAIRE, the renovated "ARAD FORT" of PORTUGUESE origin, the GOLD SOUK in MANAMA; a Soap Box at JEBEL DUKHAN in the desert and an evening spent in the desert under the stars, culminating with a camel ride and typical Arab Desert Feast.

A Pearl Merchant's house was also visited and an afternoon was spent cruising the Bahraini Coastline and "HARBOUR" on a private launch.

On their return to the U.K., the "Lifeguards" were in business once again, doing many local concerts in the months ahead.

1991

Early in 1991 the "Lifeguards" donated £600 to the PRINCE CHARLES HOSPITAL "EYES RIGHT LASER APPEAL". Two crossings of the "border" were made early in this year. One was to sing at the EVESHAM TOWN HALL at the invitation of MAYOR, MR. PHILIP WALKER, a Penydarren-born gentleman.

The second crossing was made on a very windy, rain-lashed Severn Bridge to celebrate the 25th ANNIVERSARY OF THE THORNBURY WELSH SOCIETY.

In October, the "Lifeguards" joined forces with Gareth Gwenlan, B.B.C. T.V. Producer of *Only Fools and Horses* (a Cefn Coed Boy), who compered an evening's entertainment at the Community Centre in aid of the Carmel Chapel Restoration Appeal.

1992

Highlights of this year were concerts sung and new friends made north of the border in NEWCASTLE AND JEDBURGH, SCOTLAND. A harmonising rendition of *Scotland the Brave* was enthusiastically received in many venues visited on this tour.

1993

Apart from again singing locally, there were three highlights in this year which came close together in the autumn months.

In September the "Lifeguards" sang in the MUNI ARTS CENTRE, PONTYPRIDD. Sharing the stage that evening was JOHN EDWARDS of "WENGLISH" fame.

A trip to IRELAND followed in October. The "Lifeguards" found new friends in KILNENNY and THURLES. Mr. Sean O'Neil, secretary of the KILKENNY GOLF CLUB, was instrumental in arranging performances at Kilkenny Golf Club, Thurles Golf Club, "John Cleere" Pub/Theatre, New Park Hotel, "LANGTONS" (Irish Pub of the year in 86, 87, 88, 90, and Super Pub of the Year in 1992). The famous SMITHWICKS IRISH BREWERY, THE MODEL SCHOOL, KILKENNY and ST. MARY'S CATHEDRAL, where the "Lifeguards" were applauded in a Sunday morning service. Thanks go to the publicans of the PANT CAD-IVOR INN, Pantysgallog, for their sponsorship of the successful Irish Tour.

In November the "Lifeguards" supported GEORGE MELLY and band at the RHYDYCAR LEISURE CENTRE, and then continued to practice their Christmas Carol repertoire for their visits to Pubs, Clubs and Old People's Homes.

1994

A performance was made on the stage of the COLISEUM, ABERDARE, supporting JOAN REGAN in the "D-Day" Celebrations and in August a visit for a first taste of the VICTORIAN FESTIVAL at LLANDRINDOD WELLS.

1995

Local performances predominated in the early part of the year and the "Lifeguards" were invited to the opening of CARMEL CHAPEL, CEFN-COED-Y-CYMMER, where VISCOUNT TONYPANDY (GEORGE THOMAS, EX-SPEAKER OF THE HOUSE OF COMMONS) gave a sermon and unveiled a commemorative plaque. The "Lifeguards" had contributed their services on numerous occasions prior to the inauguration and dedication of the Chapel.

A second visit was made to the LLANDRINDOD WELLS VICTORIAN FESTIVAL in August, after being received with enthusiasm a year previously.

The last major performance was at the invitation of the famous SWANSEA ACCORDION BAND to their ANNUAL CONCERT, held at the PENTWYN LEISURE CENTRE, GORSEINON, SWANSEA, where the "Lifeguards" supported the band and T.V. personality-comedian, JOHNNY TUDOR. A memorable night was had by all.

The "Lifeguards" have made many friends at home and abroad, continuing to make contact with many admirers throughout the world. The group are encouraged when glowing letters of thanks and support arrive after most performances. Some of these letters were published in the *Merthyr Express*, especially after the tour in the U.S.A.; examples are given in this essay.

They are not only recognised as a "very professional" group for their singing but also for their humour, which seems to radiate in their presence. The "Lifeguards'" ' repertoire is extended by the humour of Len Hargreaves who, in between songs, is not without a joke or two. This humour is greatly enhanced by the unexpected happenings of false moustaches dropping off, or members of the group who ad-lib in the middle of Len's "serious humour"! A humour which, although appreciated by the audience, may not be shared by the "serious joke-maker"!

Naturally this humour, together with the singing, keeps the group going. Every "Lifeguard" past and present has some story to tell.

Over the last eighteen years there have been many "Lifeguards" who no doubt have their own special tales to tell. The following stories are just a taste of the unexpected humour that has been experienced by all in the group at one time or other.

One of the first incidents that comes to mind is being locked outside the

TREHARRIS SALVATION ARMY HALL on a freezing winter night in swimsuits, because our normal clothes were in the hall and the caretaker had locked up for the night and gone home. After half an hour of standing in the cold and looking exceedingly strange to all who passed by, the caretaker was located and returned to let us in. We didn't recover for a whole week.

At a BEDLINOG Concert, in the middle of a song a rather large spider came down from the ceiling into the middle of the floor. Singing stopped and general confusion prevailed as ladies screamed and jumped on tables and chairs.

At LONDON HEATHROW AIRPORT, the "Lifeguards" were stopped by Customs Officers, who went through all the cases and hand-luggage. We were taken into a room to be "interrogated" by the officers, who thought we had concealed "SEMTEX" in our luggage. There was much hilarity when we finally told them that three of us were carrying LAVA BREAD in plastic bags, presents for the Welsh expatriates in BAHRAIN.

It seems all too easy and uneventful these days when travelling abroad, but not for some. Steve Williams's passport could not be found at one airport en-route; panic-stricken "Lifeguards" searched high and low until eventually the passport was found in the inside pocket of another member's blazer. After all, every blazer looked the same. As you can imagine, Steve took plenty of "flak" after that episode.

A pleasant day's cruising in the GULF turned into the incident of the tour. While manoeuvering in the GULF off BAHRAIN in a private vessel for the day, the "Lifeguards" were arrested by a BAHRAIN COASTGUARD PATROL/PILOT BOAT and asked to follow them to port. It transpired that our vessel had gone too close to the AMERICAN FLEET anchored and protected by huge barges in BAHRAIN HARBOUR. A charge-sheet was written out but the FIRST OFFICER aboard the *U.S.S. la Salle* had seen what was happening and drove his "Willey Jeep" like Steve McQueen down the jetty. He explained that the "Lifeguards" were not terrorists but friends of "THE FLEET". He had come to the rescue before the patrol had time to take us off the Motor Cruiser. There was much laughter after this event and gifts of Welsh Flags for the U.S. Navy hats were exchanged on the jetty. The charge-sheet, written in Arabic, is still in the possession of one of the "Lifeguards".

On an evening visit to the desert on the same tour, the "Lifeguards" had been told to expect typical Bahraini hospitality. A camel ride had been arranged before an Arabian desert chicken dinner/buffet in a large tent. One of the "Lifeguards" who happened to be last in the queue and who shall remain nameless, commented on the fact that having seen the remains of a carcass on a massive oval plate, it must have been the biggest "chicken" in the desert. He was told later, after the meal, that it was no "chicken" but a whole sheep's carcass. The beverage for the evening – cans of Fosters Lager – must have had their effect! Now every Christmas the rest of the "Lifeguards" test his knowledge of poultry at every opportunity.

On the return journey from the Irish Tour in the early hours of the morning, the hired mini-bus in which the "Lifeguards" were travelling, ran out of diesel. There was just enough left in the tank to negotiate a hill east of Carmarthen. Once over the ridge, the bus had to free-wheel for miles. Not knowing where the next filling station was at that time of the morning, there were plenty of suggestions from those on board as we glided silently downhill.

Eventually the bright lights of a filling station could be seen quite a distance ahead. The filling station seemed to be on the other side of the roundabout. By this time, the road had already flattened out, so there was the need for more speed to negotiate the roundabout. It was the first time any of the "Lifeguards" had travelled in a mini-bus using only "two wheels".

There were the usual shouts of dismay but the bus eventually made the diesel pump without the aid of a push – relief from all on board that we were able to continue homeward bound.

There is one other bit of humour connected to a "FISHERMAN'S FRIEND" (the lozenge for coughs and colds) but you will have to ask one of the "Lifeguards" about this little episode; whether you get a reply or not will depend on which member you approach!

Past and present "Lifeguards" will have their own stories to tell and will, no doubt, be very reminiscent about these and the songs sung during their time spent with the group.

The present "Lifeguards" still enjoy rehearsing the old favourites, such as "The Old Songs" – *Grandfather's Clock*, *Annie's Song*, *Love Me With All Of Your Heart*, *This Little Light Of Mine*, *Lullaby of Broadway*, *Dream*, *Moonlight Bay*, etc., not to mention the Welsh Favourites: *Myfanwy*, *Molianwn*, *Mi glywaf dyner lais*, *Cartref* and many Welsh hymn tunes.

New songs are tried our regularly, especially one with natural harmony, and if the group agrees they endeavour to practice until the songs are ready to include in a performance.

Present Members of the "Lifeguards"

Len Hargreaves	Bill Edwards	Ken Morris
Colin Griffiths	David Mantle	David Lewis Jones
Lionel Davies	Mike Kerrigan	Steve Williams

Past Members

Don Barry	Philip Adams	Wyndham Carey
Warwick Rowlands	Carl Llewellyn	Brian Stonehewer
Grahame Clark	Nigel Santos	Ivor Jones
Gerwyn Williams	Mike Richards	Dominic Baker
Richard Williams	Barry Gardner	John Jenkins
Peter Evans	Mostyn Reynolds	John Mitchell
Brian Cole	Ken O'Neill	

The commercial tapes of "The Lifeguards" mentioned previously are still available (1: *Harmony*, 2: *Hiraeth and Harmony*) from the Secretary, Ken Morris, Tel: 01685-370036 or from any Lifeguard member.

Recently, with the aid of local hotels, hostelries and a local video company, the Lifeguards have made their first video, which promotes Wales and its songs.

The video, *Hiraeth am Gymru* is also available from the same source as the tapes.

Thank You

There's a group of men in Merthyr,
The Lifeguards is their name.
Just ordinary fellows –
They have no claim to fame.
They have many things in common,
One is their love of song,
When the working day is over
They sing all evening long.
The music that they make
Is a joy to any ear,
Their harmony so beautiful
It often brings a tear.

Another common factor
Is their spirit of compassion.
(Such a quality, these days
Is rather out of fashion.)
They love to help the needy,
Underprivileged and poor,
To cheer them with their singing
And also – what is more,
They pass around the hat
To anyone who's willing
To help all those less fortunate
Who are grateful for a shilling.

This group of men in Merthyr
Got together last December
And did something so wonderful,
We always will remember
How they dressed in Wakes' attire
And with lantern in the hand,
They travelled many miles,
This jolly looking band.
They sang the Christmas songs
Everybody loves to hear.
The listeners' hearts were filled
With old-fashioned Christmas cheer.
People flocked to hear them
Collecting boxes passed around.
Some gave a few pennies,
Many gave a pound.
When the season ended
And the lanterns put away,
The money was all counted.
"How much was it?" did you say?
"One thousand pounds," I answer
And those Lifeguards, of one mind
Gave it to the Talking Newspaper
Association for the Blind.
To that super group of Lifeguards
We offer grateful thanks
For their voices like the angels
And their hearts like Sherman tanks.

Maureen M. Pulman

Old time musical, Miners' Hall, Merthyr, 1981. (Photo courtesy John Yates.)

Lifeguards in Dickensian outfits, Christmas, 1983.

Aboard private launch, Bahrain Harbour, 1990.

Coastguards' vessel that arrested Lifeguards' launch, 2nd March, 1990.

The Welsh Scene, Bahrain, 1990.

Happy Birthday, Lifeguards, Bahrain, 1990.

Smart lads! Holiday Inn, Bahrain, 1990.

Dave Mantle presenting a miner's lamp to the Minister of Tourism, Bahrain, 1990.

At the gold souk, Manama, Bahrain, 1990.

Lifeguards, gold souk, Bahrain, 1990.

With Irish friends, Jebel Dukhan, Bahrain, 1990.

Soap Box Derby, Rotary Club, Jebel Dukhan, March, 1990.

Lifeguards watching Soap Box Derby, Bahrain, 1990.

Lifeguards at the National Museum, Bahrain. Bob Gilchrist, far left. Curator, fifth from right.

The British Club, Bahrain, March, 1990.

Sheik Omar Sharif Jones receives Welsh, Irish and Scottish visitors, Bahrain, 1990.

"The Lads" outside John Cleere's Pub/Theatre, Kilkenny, October, 1993.

Sustenance in a Thurles Pub before concert at Thurles Golf Club, October, 1993.

With our hostess Margaret at Kilkenny, October, 1993.

Shopping in Kilkenny, Eire, October, 1993.

Kilkenny Golf Club, with Club Secretary Sean O'Neill, October, 1993.

Enjoying Irish cwrw, Kilkenny, October, 1993.

Author of this essay, "THE LIFEGUARDS", David Lewis Jones of Pant, relaxing in a typical Irish Pub at Kilkenny, 1993.

Lifeguards' annual Christmas Dinner at The Tredegar Arms, Dowlais.

Stopped off at Gretna Green, Scotland Tour, 1992.

The Lifeguards on the steps of Cyfarthfa Castle, Merthyr Tydfil, 1991. (Photo courtesy of Shell Photographic Service.)

Commonwealth Games

CAEREDIN 1986 EDINBURGH

Tonight's show owes its origin to Sir Geraint Evans, C.B.E., who is Chairman of the Welsh Commonwealth Games Committee.

Appointed as director of operations was Mr Bryn Thomas, B.E.M.

Anything is possible with Bryn in the driving seat, but tonight's show will linger in the memory longer than most with a mixture of Billy Smart's Circus, The Cardiff Military Tattoo, Come Dancing, Saturday Night at the London Palladium and Dr Who.

Bryn is a wizard in his own right when it comes to producing glittering entertainment, and with his experience and expertise he makes a gigantic task appear as easy as winning a Gold Medal.

We hope you will enjoy tonight's performance and we thank you for your support.

Our special thanks go to Sir Geraint Evans for his enthusiastic leadership, Mr Bryn Williams and Mrs Maralyn Caramella.

PROGRAMME

Band of the Royal Welch Fusiliers
Director of Music W.O. E. G. Mooney

Ladies Keep Fit Association of Wales
Leader – Jenny Jones

Côr Meibion Aberafan
Musical Director – Clive Phillips

The June Bois Dancers
and
Dawnswyr-Gwerin – Pen-y-Fai
Welsh Folk Dancers

Mike Doyle Entertains

Our Salute to the Commonwealth Games

INTERVAL

The Band of the Royal Welch Fusiliers appear by permission of the Commanding Officer, Lt.Col. T.L.M. Porter, M.B.E.

Lewis Merthyr Band
Director of Music Mr C. Brian Buckley

Côr Meibion Aberafan

Triban

Owen Money – The Laughter Maker

The Life Guards – Barber Shop Singers

Fire Brigade – Wales top show band

Grand Finale

National Anthem

Hospitality Chairman
Michael E. McCrane

Announcers:
Mr Alun Williams, M.B.E.
Mr David Parry Jones

Festival of
Industry and
Culture

RHONDDA
BOROUGH
COUNCIL

Present

OLDE TYME MUSIC HALL

at the

Parc & Dare Theatre, Treorchy

on

Saturday 29th October 1988
at
8-00p.m.

With your Chairman for the Evening

Mr. Glyn Houston

Presenting
A Night of
Splendid Entertainment

Programme for the Evening

- Overture -

✤ - Chairman for the Evening - ✤

Glyn Houston

✤ - The Dot Watts Dancers - ✤

- The Lifeguards -

✤ - Bryn Williams - ✤

- The Cingalees -

Interval

✤ - The Dot Watts Dancers - ✤

- Beverley Humphries -

✤ - Parc & Dare Band - ✤

- The Dot Watts Dancers -

✤ - Paul Shane - ✤

- Finale -

Office of the Mayor

Urbana, Ohio

Proclamation

WHEREAS, The LIFEGUARDS present "Hiraeth and Harmony", Friday, May 22, 1987, at the Champaign County Library Auditorium, sponsored by the Champaign County Arts Council; and

WHEREAS, on May 22, 1987 Urbana will be treated to a delightful and light-hearted musical evening which will combine the folk music of Wales with popular favorites from both Britain and America. Although they share similarities of repertoire and presentation with American barbershop music, their harmony is unique to the valleys of Wales; and

WHEREAS, the westernmost principality of the island of Great Britain, Wales enjoys one of the richest musical traditions in Europe. Musical groups of all kinds and especially vocal ensembles are sources of municipal pride. Formed in 1977, The Lifeguards numbers twelve men from the borough of Merthyr Tydfil in the Taf valley of South Wales. They are a registered charity and use their talents to raise funds for needy causes. The Lifeguards have completed more than 250 engagements in venues ranging from village halls and nursing homes to the premier concert halls of Wales and England. This is their first international tour; and

WHEREAS, their program in America, "Hiraeth and Harmony", takes its theme from the title of their most recent recording. "Hiraeth" theme is a Welsh word which defines a special kind of longing or homesickness for all things Welsh. The Welsh portion of the evening is sure to give American audiences "just alittle touch of hiraeth." The remainder of the concert will find audiences marking time to the upbeat rhythms of some of their all-time favorite melodies; and

WHEREAS, admission to the concert is free. The Lifeguards and their wives, dressed in Welsh costumes, will accept donations for souvenir programmes and will have tape recordings for sale. All proceeds of their American tour will go the aid the mentally handicapped and underprivileged children of the borough of Merthyr Tydfil.

Lewis B. Moore

Lewis B. Moore
Mayor.

Letter from America, 1987.

Mrs. E. M. Pence
614 South Main Street
Urbana, Ohio 43078 U.S.A.
June 2, 1987

Editor
Merthyr Express
Celtic Newspapers, Ltd.
Merthyr Industrial Estate
Pant
Merthyr Tydfil
Mid-Glamorgan
South Wales
United Kingdom

To The Editor:

During the American Revolutionary War there often rang out the cry, "The Redcoats are coming!" . . . a warning that British troops were approaching.

For several weeks prior to May 22, posters scattered around this small central Ohio town carried another announcement, "The Lifeguards are coming."

The Lifeguards have been and gone, leaving behind memories, not only of their music which was received with standing ovations wherever they performed, but also of their warmth, friendliness and good humor, even when delays, failure of air conditioning systems, and temperatures hovering around 90 F with unbearably high humidity, all combined to make exceedingly uncomfortable conditions.

Each host family has its own memories of these Welsh men and women who came from places with strange sounding names like Pontsticill, Twynrodyn, and Pantyscallog. Already these memories are being shared around this community of 12,000 where I taught for 25 years before I retired.

I am a native of Merthyr Tydfil. I was born in Caeracca, Pant in 1921 and received a sound education in Pant School and Cyfarthfa. I left Wales to go to college in 1940, but I have made frequent trips back to Merthyr during the 47 years I've been one of the "Cymry ar Wasgar."

Since the Lifeguards' Concert I am reminded of John F. Kennedy's speech to the people of Berlin. He expressed his admiration for the people of that city in his opening words, "*Ich bin ein Berliner*" . . . I am a Berliner. I am repeatedly being greeted by friends and acquaintances who tell me of their Welsh roots . . . mixed as they are among the roots of England, Ireland, Scotland, Germany, etc. I am learning it is now very right to say in Urbana, "I am Welsh."

I have always been proud to claim my Welsh heritage. I am proud of the fact that my daughter, a frequent visitor to Merthyr, is President-Elect of the Welsh Society of Central Ohio; I have never been more proud of the land of my birth and of Merthyr Tydfil than when my daughter presented to an Urbana audience, "The Lifeguards from Merthyr Tydfil, South Wales."

May the Lifeguards enjoy ever increasing success in their efforts to spread good will and happiness as they give their support to worthy causes.

Urbana thanks Merthyr Tydfil for sending its native sons and daughters. They were the best of ambassadors.

Thank you, Lifeguards, for reinforcing the message I have been spreading during the forty-one years I have lived in America, "The Welsh are a great people!"

Sincerely,

Evelyn M. Walters Pence

Another letter from America, 1987.

Anne E. Mayer
Arosfa
212 West Reynolds Street
Urbana, Ohio 43078
U. S. A.
June 4, 1987

Editor
Merthyr Express
Celtic Newspapers, Ltd.
Merthyr Industrial Estate
Pant
Merthyr Tydfil
Mid-Glamorgan
South Wales
United Kingdom

To the Editor:

Several years ago following this group's successful effort in 1983 to raise money for kidney research, the Merthyr Express printed an article about the Merthyr based close harmony group, The Lifeguards, with the headline, "Singing Sensations." That headline was certainly prophetic of the kind of reception the group received during their recent American tour. The twelve singers and their families returned to Merthyr on June 1 after a rigorous 10-day concert tour that included five scheduled concerts and additional impromptu appearances.

My husband, Albert, and I count it a real privilege to have been associated with this group over the past five years. It has been a wonderfully rewarding experience for us to have played a small part in introducing our friends, The Lifeguards, to American audiences. This is especially so as Merthyr Tydfil is my mother's native town and much of the tour was based in my father's home territory of central Ohio.

Hundreds of Americans have learned a new word, "hiraeth," and have been introduced to the best of a very special part of Britain as a result of The Lifeguards' American visit. Their American program was entitled "Hiraeth and Harmony" and contained a delightful blend of popular favorites from both sides of the Atlantic and Welsh music. The middle segment of the concert was a beautifully narrated interpretation of the musical heritage of Wales. It was fascinating to watch both general American and Welsh-American audiences become immeresed in the power, emotion, and beauty of this section. Be it "hiraeth" for the land of their ancestors or appreciation for beautiful music, expertly interpreted, as tune followed tune the atmosphere became electric and often times tears of longing began to flow.

The tour included concerts before a wide variety of audiences. It opened in my home town, Urbana, Ohio, a county seat of about 12,000 people under the sponsorship of the Champaign County Arts Council. It included concerts in major metropolitan areas like the state capital, Columbus, where arrangements were made by the Welsh Society of Central Ohio and Canton where the joint hosts were the Hoover Company and the Canton Chorale.

Not the largest audience but certainly the warmest welcome came on May 25th when The Lifeguards were part of the Memorial Day and Heritage Days activities in the tiny village of Radnor, Ohio. Radnor and its surrounding farms were founded by people from Radnor in mid-Wales. Virtually every resident of the district was in attendance at the concert. The Lifeguards had contacted government officials in Radnor who had sent an impressive historical map of the Radnor area as a gift to the people of Radnor, Ohio. The residents of the Ohio Radnor reciprocated with the gift of an Ohio flag and a history of their village. In many ways Radnor, Ohio had grown away from its Welsh roots but by the end of The Lifeguards' visit plans were developing for St. David's Day celebrations and student exchanges.

Memorial Day in the United States is a time for remembering the sacrifices of those who have fought for their country. At the ceremonies in the village cemetary at the war memorial British troops were remembered along with American veterans as the haunting strains of Taps echoed and re-echoed across the corn fields. For someone like me whose parents met as a result of World War II, these joint prayers were symbolic of a welding of the two places in the world I hold most dear, and for other Welsh-Americans they reaffirmed the need to once again make contact with the land of their ancestors.

Measured by any standard of musical excellence and audience appreciation, The Lifeguards' American tour was a resounding success. But another real triumph of these ten days came outside the concert halls as friendships blossomed between The Lifeguards and their families and their American hosts. There were small reunions since several of the singers had participated in the Dowlais Male Voice Choir tour in 1982 and in exchanges with the Canton Chorale. Many, many new friendships were formed which will no doubt grow in the years ahead.

This tour was a special one too because the group was small enough that they could bring their wives and other family members along. The ladies were attired in Welsh costume for all the concerts and added a very colorful note to the Memorial Day parade in Radnor. Their presence also reinforced the fact that lasting friendships were being formed by family groups who share many commonalities of daily life even though an ocean separates their homes.

With emotional ties still so fresh at this point, that ocean seems like an endless, alien barrier. But there are countless memories in the hearts of the hosts of conversations on porch swings and patios, of tours of local landmarks, and yes, most dramatically of beautiful music combined with laughter and friendship. Thanks to their most recent recording also called, "Hiraeth and Harmony," American fans can refresh those memories whenever they feel again the pangs of hiraeth.

Following the five Ohio concerts the group enjoyed a weekend in Nashville, Tennessee. Eventhough there were no formal concerts music and friendship continued to be the joint themes of the tour. After a visit to the Grand Ole Opry members of the group were invited to sing at the Pickin' Palace at the Opryland Hotel when the local performer discovered he had a group of fellow musicians in the audience. Americans who had come to Nashville to hear country music were soon tapping their toes to the strains of "Molianwn." The applause was enthusiastic and memories were formed only to be reinforced the following night when members of that audience recognized the singing Welsh visitors during a cruise on the paddle wheel river boat, The General Jackson, and made a special effort to congratulate them on their singing.

We left The Lifeguards in the Nashville airport with the final cords of "We'll Keep A Welcome in the Hillsides" still ringing through the terminal. We thought that the singing was over and only the long trip home remained. However, when their transatlantic flight was delayed several hours, these weary singing ambassadors found a reserve supply of energy and treated their fellow travellers to an unscheduled sixth concert at the Newark, New Jersey airport. That act once again symbolizes the joint theme of friendship and love of music that characterized The Lifeguards' American tour.

We their American friends and fans, wish The Lifeguards continued success in their ongoing mission to spread friendship and happiness through their musical talents, as they raise funds for charitable causes. This letter comes from all of those who participated in the tour, with the fervent wish that this trip on the occasion of their tenth anniversary was The Lifeguards' first American tour and will be followed in the years to come with additional joyous reunions and more beautiful music!

Sincerely,

Anne E. Mayer

(Mrs.) Anne E. Mayer

In Search of Thomas Marchant Williams (1845-1914)

by Huw Williams

Introduction

"Death has been unusually busy among the public men of Wales," observed R. A. Griffiths, Deputy Stipendiary Magistrate for the Merthyr Tydfil and District Courts (*Merthyr Express*, 7th November, 1914). As he was speaking at the end of October, 1914, he may have possessed a perception of events to come well beyond contemporary opinion and knowledge, since the pages of the South Wales press which had reported his remarks were taken up with the first onslaught of war in Flanders and along the increasing length of the Western Front: The Great War of 1914-1918 had started. Actually, Griffiths was being very precise in his references that day at Merthyr Tydfil's Police Court. He alluded to Sir Edward Anwyl, the noted Welsh scholar who had recently died at the beginning of August, 1914. He could have added in the same breath Sir W. T. Lewis, the first Lord Merthyr, who had passed away at the end of the same month. Griffiths, however, was specifically paying tribute as duty bound to the late Stipendiary Magistrate for the district, Sir Thomas Marchant Williams, who had died at Builth Wells on 27th October, 1914. The pages of the contemporary press were fulsome in their obituary and reflection towards this well-known public servant and Welsh man of letters. Generous tribute to Williams lavishly occupied local news columns and war was relegated briefly to another day in at least one editorial of the *Western Mail* (28th October, 1914).

History is a funny old business! Such a phrase comes to mind here. It

Caricature, Sir Thomas Marchant Williams.

presumes to ascribe to the past certain motives, actions and reactions which may bear little or no resemblance to the realities of the time, then or now! History "compartmentalises" for the benefit of the reader: it seeks to make sense of the past in manageable portions and ultimately there is nothing wrong with that approach. Here is Thomas Marchant Williams as a case in point. A life and career in the main spanning some seventy years or so from 1845 to the start of War in 1914 can be perhaps best understood and analysed in terms of crucial dates and phases which allow this review to fall within four main sections or sub-divisions thus:

I. The years 1845 to 1885, covering Williams's early period as an educationalist, his appointment to London and his active involvement in London Welsh society.
II. The years 1885 to 1900, analysing Williams's abandonment of political ambition, his return to South Wales in a new, legal career and his abiding concern with Welsh political and cultural matters, notably through several influential publications.
III. The years 1900 to 1914, in the first instance portraying Williams as a highly active force in educational, cultural and literary life in Wales, again undertaken through the medium of several influential publications, not least of which was his own magazine, *The Nationalist*.
IV. The years 1900 to 1914 again, but this time examining Williams specifically in his role as Stipendiary Magistrate for Merthyr Tydfil and Aberdare Courts and as a major contributor to town and valleys' life and morales until his death in 1914.

This essay intends to look at each of these sections in turn and seeks to place Williams, in conclusion, in a proper historical context of time and place.

I. 1845-1885

Contemporary opinion was unanimous in praise to a great Welshman on news of Williams's death at the end of October, 1914: "one of the most prominent figures in Welsh nationalism," stated *The Aberdare Leader* (31st October, 1914). Born the son of a Gadlys coalminer in the Cynon Valley on 31st July, 1845, Williams received a sound education at Aberdare's Park Schools, Trecynon, the first British School opened in the town and better known throughout the area as "Ysgol Y Comin" and where Dan Isaac Davies, as head teacher, exercised an enduring influence on a succession of young up-and-coming Welsh men. Williams was one of the second batch of pupil-teachers to emerge from this patriotic Welsh forcing house of ideas and language in the formative years of mid-19th century South Wales. He then proceeded to Bangor Normal College to train as a teacher and where, under the influence of its Principal, John Phillips, the young Williams was imbued with "that enthusiasm for Welsh nationalism which so largely influenced his career" (*Western Mail*, 28th October, 1914). He was subsequently appointed a master of method at that College and at the same time held a post of head teacher at the Garth School in Bangor. Another headship followed, this time at Amlwch School on Anglesey and thereafter Williams moved to a further teaching post in Yorkshire. He had enroled as one of the first undergraduate students at the newly-founded University College of Wales at Aberystwyth but it was from the University of London as an external candidate while at Bangor that he obtained a Bachelor of Arts degree with Honours. Years of study, teaching and administration in education had left their mark and, in 1874, he was appointed as an Inspector of Schools for the Metropolitan Area under the old London School Board, a post he held at London until 1884.

A career in the Metropolis gave Williams the ideal opportunity to indulge passionately and enthusiastically in London Welsh life, something which remained a constant influence for the rest of his days, even when he had moved back to South Wales after 1885. Here in a vibrant capital city, Williams became a founder member of the reconstituted Honourable Society of Cymmrodorion in November, 1873, although according to the official historians of that Society, his name does not appear in the inaugural minutes. Williams, in subsequent recollections, was always adamant that he was indeed present and in attendance at that meeting! He soon made his mark in London's Anglo-Welsh educational and literary circles. A consultative paper offered by him to the Honourable Society in February, 1877, and subsequently published under the same title that year as *The Educational Wants of Wales* contained an outline provision for education in the Principality of Wales and several suggestions for further reform to the curriculum with the ultimate view, in Williams's opinion, of gaining a parity for the Welsh language in the classroom. Despite his self-enforced exile in the Metropolis during the later 1870s and early 1880s, Williams was heavily involved in Welsh educational matters, using his vantage point in the capital to pronounce on a wide range of issues; and he remained as a sort of freelance consultant on all matters to do with the state of education in Wales for the rest of his life. In 1883 he married one Elizabeth Wilding of Rhydyfelin, near Builth Wells:

there were no children from this union. This mid-Wales connection through marriage would assume an increasing importance to Williams in his later years. Indeed, neither Merthyr Tydfil nor Aberdare were domestic abodes on his return to these valleys after 1885, he preferring the convenience of Cardiff as a centre for his literary and cultural pursuits and his home at Rhydyfelin on the banks of the River Wye as an escape from work, surrounded there by his books and collections of fine porcelain and pictures.

In 1885 he was called to the Bar at London's Inner Temple and thereafter returned to his native South Wales. The first formative phase of Marchant Williams's career could thus be considered ended with his marriage and his forsaking a continuing career in education which seemed to hold out so much promise. London life had served him royally: he had risen to rapid prominence within the influential orbit of London Welsh society. He would serve in later years as Honorary Secretary of the London Welsh Charitable Aid Society; he was and remained a prominent member of the Council of the Honourable Society of Cymmrodorion. This latter role he especially treasured for the whole of his life and it proved of no mean importance to him in his career and involvement in contemporary Welsh affairs.

II. 1885-1900

The years 1885-86 were a personal watershed for Williams in another crucial sense. In his earlier days in London he had caught the eye of the political Establishment as an ardent Liberal and at one time took his ambitions as far as actually standing for one of the London Parliamentary Divisions as a Liberal candidate. The schism within the national Liberal Party over the vexed question of Home Rule for Ireland, which brought down Gladstone's third premiership in 1886, found Williams, along with a handful of like-minded Welsh Liberals, leaving the main-stream party line and taking up with the Liberal Unionist cause. Despite his shift in allegiance, Williams remained in favour with broad Welsh Liberalism and served as Secretary of the Liberal Unionist Association for Wales, although Lloyd George, one of Williams's political contemporaries, had soon brought Welsh Liberalism back to the fold of Gladstonian-style politics by the early 1890s. The revolt in Wales did not last long; Liberal Unionism had after the General Election of 1892 effectively disappeared from Welsh history (Morgan). Through the typically independent action that he had taken, Williams found himself rather out on a limb and somewhat removed from the majority-held tenets of late 19th century Welsh Liberalism. This self-realisation may well have governed the next stages in his career. With his transition to the legal profession, Williams had effectively relinquished all practical ambitions in politics and thereafter confined his involvement to a series of personal, lifelong friendships with the likes of the Duke of Devonshire, Joseph Chamberlain, who had instigated the Liberal Party split in 1886, Lord Pontypridd (Sir Alfred Thomas) and with Lloyd George himself.

His move to law also left Williams free to employ his pen to an acerbic effect as a most perceptive and caustic observer on the Welsh political scene in the remaining decade and a half of Queen Victoria's reign and for an equivalent period of her successor's reign in this century. It was during this phase of his career and through his several writings that he acquired that unique style of enquiry and satire which would draw to him the dubious accolade of the nickname, "The Acid Drop", in later life. Williams had departed from London in 1885 and joined the South Wales circuit as a Deputy Clerk to the Assize Courts. He brought with him from London a finely-tuned personal belief in a contemporary Welsh nationalism. Had he remained in active politics, he would surely have embraced the ethos and dynamism of Cymru Fydd ("Young Wales"), however short-lived it proved to be as a political movement in the 1890s, and would surely have been one to contemplate alongside the likes of his more famous contemporary, Lloyd George. Such, indeed, had been the impact of the young, politically aspiring Williams that at one time he had been allegedly countenanced as a rival candidate to Lloyd George for the Carnarvon Boroughs! (*The Aberdare Leader*, 31st October, 1914). Yet, true to form, he took an independently-minded stance with regard to political matters. "Although a most fervid patriot," noted *The Aberdare Leader* of 31st October, 1914, "he was the Ishmael of the orthodox Welsh Nationalists". He confined his participation to his trusty pen, his irascible wit and a dry humour. He was a shrewd raconteur, "the personification of Welsh nationalism," observed one newspaper tribute, and the focus around which revolved the national ideals of his fellow countrymen (*Western Mail*, 28th October, 1914).

After 1885, once he had eschewed political ambition, it allowed Williams the necessary latitude for a large measure of scurrilous commentary on the political and related contemporary issues of the day, but never at the expense of his lifelong-held beliefs in an overriding patriotic fervour for the land of his birth. "The New Wales owes a great deal to the late Sir Marchant Williams," commented the *Western Mail* in its obituary notice of 28th October, 1914. "His nationalistic ardour and the variety of his interests made it inevitable that he should be associated with many of those movements which gave colour and direction to public affairs. Unlike many Welsh people he thought little of political activities as a nationalist instrument. He saw that external consciousness and regional culture did not depend upon political activities."

This last extract seems to sum up Williams's very life force and a self-dynamism which dictated his rich involvement in Welsh matters for nearly half a century. "Many of those movements which gave colour and direction to public affairs" included his role as Chairman of the Executive Committee of the National Temperance League. He had always been an ardent teetotaller, brought up in the "straitest sect" of his parents' Aberdare-based, Calvinist Welsh Methodism. Many a court ruling from Stipendiary Magistrate Williams in later years would be governed by this tenet. In South Wales it was perhaps as an active eisteddfodwr that he ranked most prominently in his day. "It was in the Gorsedd circle that he was in his element and bards and men of letters were his favourite associates" (*The Aberdare Leader*, 31st October, 1914). He served as Honorary Secretary of the National Eisteddfod Association, of which he was a founding member at the Caernarvon Eisteddfod of 1880. He claimed in his latter days to be the oldest surviving person connected with the eisteddfod movement in its 19th century guise, having attended virtually all of the meetings since 1861; at his death he was Chairman of the Association (*Western Mail*, 28th October, 1914).

He was a close acquaintance of some of the best-known bards of the day: "Mynyddog" (Richard Davies, 1833-77) and "Ceiriog" (John Hughes, 1832-87), to name but two, were especially dear to him. Under his own bardic title of "Marsiant", Williams flourished as a lyricist and a poet of some note and he was a frequent contributor to the popular press in both English and Welsh, where he pronounced on a wide compass of literary and antiquarian topics. "He loved the eisteddfod intensely and loved all the ardent devotees of awen a chan", noted *The Aberdare Leader* for 31st October, 1914. In August, 1885, at the Aberdare National Eisteddfod, Williams found himself alongside his old mentor and inspirational tutor, Dan Isaac Davies, at the inauguration of The Society for the Utilization of the Welsh Language, better known in Wales as "The Welsh Language Society". As an educational reformer, as an undoubted nationalist and Welsh patriot, Williams had become engaged on a crusade to seek equality for Wales and for its language within the schools' curriculum, within educational circles in general and indeed throughout all facets of national life.

In 1889 Williams published a satirical novel, *The Land Of My Fathers*, in which he gently but not threateningly poked fun at some of the shortcomings of the educational system then existing in Wales. An improbably but deliberately named group of characters are thrown up as the epitome of educational backwardness who, in the end, gain their just deserts. Thus Williams sets before the reader Mr. and Mrs. Gubbins, appointed to the local School Board, who wreak havoc on the school in their charge in collusion with and supported by Her Majesty's Inspector, the Rev. Mr. Drizzle, aided by his Assistant, Mr. Blight. They are set in contrast against the almost saintly Miss Enid Vaughan, head teacher of the local girls' school and who typifies the new ideals of educational practice hardly recognised by the other four. The book, however, tries to convey a wider picture of Wales which the author sets out in the Preface, where he endeavours "to throw a little light on some of the aspects of the present social, religious, and political condition of the Land of my Fathers, and, especially also, to deal a blow at the narrow sectarian spirit which pervades all departments of public life there, to the detriment of every good cause and the hindrance of the progress of my countrymen in well-doing and well-being." What comes across ultimately is an almost stereotypical Wales which reflects the age and way of thinking in keeping with the unquestioned comforts of late Victorian prosperity. Social cohesion is underpinned in a series of cameo portraits: the tenant farmer, Mr. Caradoc Pugh and "his bright little wife" (who is never named), living at Birch Grove, an ivy-covered farmhouse standing above "one of the loveliest valleys of Wales" and who are on homely terms with their landlord, Squire Broadmead. There is the newly-arrived Captain Capper as tenant of The Grange to add substance to this socially acceptable equation; several clergy are introduced, ministering to the non-conformist chapels of the town of Ystrad. The Rev. Urien Rheged is a touring preacher on the non-conformist circuit, for example; the Anglican Church is served by the Rev. Septimus Moggs. The broad Liberal issues of disestablishment of the Anglican Church, temperance ("Drink is a creeping thing"), local eisteddfod, education and self-betterment are aired through dialogue in the form of a series of inter-relationships between the sons and daughters of the leading characters; here, friendships cross social and class divisions but never question them or even seem conscious of their being. It is a safe Wales, of continuity, community, religion and respectability and linking these forces together are the two powerful concepts of language and nationality. A popular "Welshness" is meted out by Williams, who is just one in a company of contemporary Anglo-Welsh authors producing persuasive, popular tracts for the period 1880 to 1920. It is one example in many of what Dai Smith stridently calls "a determined production of Gwaliakitsch of an iron-souled feyness that was out to lobotomise all the Welsh on behalf of some of them". Moggs, Capper and Vaughan are disposable in the fashion of a Victorian melodrama. Righteousness wins through in the end in terms of a Pugh-Broadmead alliance, of Olwin Pugh, daughter of that family, and Hubert, son of the Squire. An existing social order is thus sealed and educational purity, despite (or because of) the sacrifice of Enid Vaughan is secured for future generations. There is not a hint of iron or coal in this picture of rural Welsh quietude which might reflect some of the realities of a Merthyr Tydfil or Aberdare in the late 19th century. It was in essence a Wales depicted by Williams that was beginning to lose touch with the increasingly stark existence of a new creed of Syndicalism on the South Wales coalfield: strikes and lock-outs were to be the punctuation marks of this new, challenging social order in the last few years of the 19th century and certainly into the next century. It was an agenda for a Wales which Williams's literary eye, yearning for an ordered, earlier, rural and quaint Wales of Gorsedd, Eisteddfod and literary purity could not address and failed to understand.

A personal decision to enter the legal profession effectively barred Williams from any overt political ambitions he may have harboured after 1885. He was never, in the words of the *Western Mail*, "a politico-maniac". After 1886 he enhanced and refined his perceptible grip on the pulse of Welsh political and cultural life mainly through his contributions in journals and the popular press on numerous wide-ranging issues of the day. "His detachment from party ties, his studious habits and his judicial insights would have made him as keen a critic of party conventions as he was of other interests which occupy a space in public affairs in Wales", observed the *Western Mail* (28th October, 1914). His personal friendships with the men that mattered in Welsh political and public life served him with the finest raw materials for a widely read, satirical and highly-jaundiced series of pen portraits entitled *The Welsh Members of Parliament* (1894). Compiled by Williams and with illustrated caricatures supplied by Will Thomas, the book seems from today's vantage point a rather anodyne, timid affair, only slightly scurrilous in its invective towards a collection of Welsh political figures, some, who it could be said, had already arrived and those who were still on the make! Here is Williams, for example, on Lloyd George, where it did not take an abundance of political acumen to foresee the potential in such a charismatic public figure. "Take him for all in all, he seems by far the best-fitted of the Welsh members for the leadership of the National party in the House of Commons... He is quick-witted; he is eloquent; he is daring; in a word, he is perhaps the truest Celt that Wales has ever sent into the House of Commons". In the opinion of the *Western Mail* this book revealed Williams at his best, as a political satirist and a shrewd, lively and entertaining commentator on the political scene as viewed from Wales. Another book, a satirical novel again, found Williams continuing in a similar vein. *The Missing Member* was "a rollicking political tale with a vivid drawing of a well known London club" (Evans). It was somewhat of a marriage of styles, of Williams as a rather sentimental novelist and his almost self-appointed role as a Celtic lobby correspondent pronouncing on Westminster affairs on behalf of the Welsh nation. Its focal point, not surprising given Williams's political colours, centred around the National Liberal Club in London.

III. 1900-1914

In 1900 Williams's career took another significant turn with his appointment as Stipendiary Magistrate to Merthyr Tydfil and District Courts. His writings continued apace, indeed increased in output and in their invective towards the subject matter being addressed. In the first decade of the 20th century he continued as a prolific contributor to the national South Wales press; he was an essayist, an eisteddfodwr, adjudicator, poet, critic and writer on a wide range of matters concerning Welsh and "Welshness". In 1907 a collection of his lyrical poems, *Odlau Serch A Bywyd* (Lyrics of Love and Life) was published by the Educational Publishing Company of Merthyr Tydfil and Cardiff. It was a reflection of Williams's own partiality towards that literary form of expression. Such was the keenness of his poet's eye that he could, seemingly effortlessly, make a literary contribution almost at an instant, guided by the sharpness of his brain and aided by an equally sharp pen and his own total self-immersion in the Welsh traditions of metre and line. He is accredited, for example, with translating into Welsh Omar Khayham's long poem on the subject of "Wine". Williams's Welsh version reads as "Efengyl Y Pagan" ("The Pagan's Gospel") and the whole task of translation was undertaken on a train journey from Cardiff to Builth Wells! (*Merthyr Express*, 11th April, 1908).

In 1904 Williams became "Sir Marchant Williams", knighted in recognition of his services towards Welsh life and in particular to the National Eisteddfod and to the University of Wales. Given his North Wales connections from his earlier days as a trainee teacher and head master there, it was not surprising that he should be closely involved in the establishment of a University College of Wales at Bangor in the early 1880s. He was equally active in the foundation and well-being of the new South Wales University College at Cardiff in the same decade. He served as a representative of the Treasury on the Court of the University of Wales, was a member of the Council of the National Museum of Wales and of the Welsh National Library. In close co-operation with his contemporary, Sir W. T. Lewis, he was an instrumental force behind the scenes in securing the opening of a School of Mines at Treforest just before the outbreak of war in 1914.

In his dealings with the University of Wales, Williams, true to form, did not suffer fools gladly and was an irascible presence throughout these formative years of this institution once it had been granted its Royal Charter in November, 1893. He was "one of the most colourful, cantankerous and fearless figures in the University Court" (Jenkins) and never enjoyed easy working relations with several of his fellow members. Gilbert Norwood, Professor of Greek at Cardiff, once observed that he "could not bear to be agreed with by the wrong people" and his mischievous behaviour, sometimes deliberately disruptive "tea-cup storms" in the Court, attracted much attention in the press. Williams was not alone, however, in thinking that the University Senate, established in September, 1894, was a wasteful and unwieldy device, although it survived until 1920. (Principal E. H. Griffiths facetiously commented that guiding the Ten Commandments through the Senate would take at least nineteen months!

In his magazine, *The Nationalist*, Williams expressed his outrage at the refusal of the Court of the University of Wales to hold its Annual May Meeting at Merthyr Tydfil in 1907 on the grounds of its inaccessibility to the Professors and Principal of the North Wales University College of Bangor. The same thing and for the same reasons happened in 1908, this time the venue being Pontypridd; instead the town of Llandrindod Wells was favoured. "A University that cannot conveniently hold its Annual meetings except in little places in North and Mid Wales that are far away from the vast population of Glamorganshire and Monmouthshire, must sooner or later cease to be known as the University of Wales, and must be described as the University of North and Mid Wales" (*The Nationalist*, January, 1908). Neither did he tolerate much in the way of any youthful exuberance as displayed by the University's students on graduation or "capping" day which did the rounds of the then three constituent colleges before 1914. A ceremony at Cardiff in 1909 dissolved into uproar as students blew trumpets, tossed flour bags and sang *Sosban Fach* and *The Wallaby War Song*. Stipendiary Williams, mindful of his role in that office and therefore no stranger to scenes of disorder, suggested that unless the University authorities could maintain order, the ceremony of conferring degrees might find a more suitable home at Merthyr Tydfil's Police Court! (Jenkins.)

The main vehicle by which Williams could utilise his particular satirical observations and musings on matters of the day was one of his own creation, as editor and chief contributor to *The Nationalist*. Sub-titled as "a non-political magazine for Wales", it ran from March, 1907, until October, 1912, firstly as a monthly, threepenny issue until May, 1909, and thereafter as a quarterly, costing a shilling in its final years. In its first issue, March, 1907, and on the very first page in its address "To the Reader" Williams set out the aims of this publication:

> "Nationalism is wider that sect and deeper than party. This magazine directly and specially aims at fostering among the Welsh people of all sects and of all parties a true national spirit. It will encourage the study of the language and literature of the Welsh people, and will promote the development and extension of the educational system of Wales on national lines, and the advancement of every cause and every movement that tend to make the sons and daughters of Wales proud of the Land of their Fathers."

Thereafter in each issue Williams indulged his pen and brain in equal sharpness in a series of erudite and well-crafted essays on a wide range of Welsh cultural and historical topics, preferably when there was some tangible connection with the Gorsedd or an eisteddfod. A group of well-appointed authors and critics of the day acted as contributors, although Williams took the lion's share of articles; notes and correspondence featured in these pages; books were received and reviewed, gossip was dissected and analysed per month. Here was Williams at his most acidic and sarcastic and opinions offered were not always in keeping with an overt generosity of academic manners. A four and a half pages critical review of Professor John Morris-Jones's collection of poetry, *Caniadau*, is probably the best-known example of Williams's caustic wit. The author was the much-respected Professor of Welsh at Bangor and one of the foremost scholars of his day on Welsh poetry. The collection was considered at the outset of this review to be "a book of hand-made paper and 'machine-made' poetry". The review continued: "The paper will live, for it is excellent; but the poetry, we confidently yet regretfully predict, will be consigned in due course to that great heap of uninspired and neglected verse that cumbers the field of Welsh literature." (December, 1907). Such stinging words were just the first paragraph of review! Further skirmishes along the same lines and between these two same protagonists – a clash of poets' temperament, perhaps – had prompted the *Western Mail* to fashion an intriguing piece on "Sir Marchant's Humour" (16th June, 1909).

It was from such outbursts as this in the pages of *The Nationalist* that Williams garnered the nickname "The Acid Drop" and by which he became popularly known in Welsh literary circles and perhaps, to some extent, in his legal judgements at court as well. A regular item in the magazine from July, 1907, surely penned by editor Williams and intriguingly entitled "The Musings of a London Welshman", took the reader gently through issues of interest appertaining to Wales and Welsh life. Under this literary device in the issue for January, 1910, a series of amusing and satirical pen-portraits were offered as examplars to be followed in anticipation of a Dictionary of National Biography being published, dealing exclusively with living Welsh men. E. H. Griffiths, Principal of the University of South Wales and Monmouth, was employed as a contributing "author" to pronounce on Sir Marchant Williams himself as one of these sample biographies. The short piece concluded this: "He doesn't drink; doesn't smoke; doesn't play golf and doesn't run a motor. His only recreation is to sit as Stipendiary Magistrate at Merthyr Tydfil."

IV. 1900-1914

In March, 1900, following the death of W. M. North, Williams took up the vacant position of Stipendiary Magistrate for Merthyr Tydfil and District and where he remained until his death in October, 1914. The post by now had included not just Merthyr Tydfil and Aberdare Courts but extended as far as Mountain Ash as well. Williams followed a long and distinguished line of eminent magistrates who had pronounced on the daily affairs of the district. It had become a paid post from the early 1840s and had devolved into the hands of a legally-trained appointee. It was clearly seen by some incumbents as a stepping-stone towards higher office: thus H. A. Bruce, the future Lord Aberdare, held the Office from 1846 to 1853 before succeeding Guest as the Member of Parliament for the town. Of business and industrial stock themselves, these early magistrates were not, however, loathe to take on the ironmasters' interests where appropriate as the ever-expanding communities of Merthyr Tydfil and Aberdare threw up more and more circumstances calling for legal intervention and judgements. William Meyrick, lawyer and magistrate's clerk, gained a lucrative earning from such differences with the ironmaster fraternity in matters of law; in 1851 ironmaster Fothergill was summonsed by the then magistrate, Bruce, for keeping an illegal truck shop at his Aberdare Works. The fraught times of the 1840s in Merthyr Tydfil taxed the first legally-trained stipendiary, T. W. Hill, to the utmost. "For many years," cited the town's historian, Charles Wilkins, "he checked the brutal tendencies of the lower classes and taught lessons of worth to agents and ironmaster, always insisting on open court and favour to no one party more than another."

To judge from contemporary press coverage, week in and week out, of the local police courts at Merthyr Tydfil, Thomas Marchant Williams, as Stipendiary Magistrate presiding, was carrying out much the same order for the first decade and a half of the present century as his predecessor Hill had done for an earlier period, suppressing, according to his deputy, R. A. Griffiths, drunkenness, brutality and all forms of vice and dishonesty (*Merthyr Express*, 7th November, 1914). Williams left it in no doubt that he was a committed temperance reformer and a total abstainer (though not a prohibitionist). Cases of drunkenness before him found few lenient remarks and little favour: "To him there was no excuse for intemperance, as the 'drunk and disorderlies' hauled before him found to their cost." (*Merthyr Express*, 31st October, 1914). That he was his own man, believing in and acting upon his own counsel there was no doubt, as this review of his career has already suggested. The accusation soon followed his death that, as a man of strong personality and will, he was fond of getting his own way in the court; that he rarely consulted the local magistracy (especially those at the Merthyr Tydfil courts, noted *The Aberdare Leader* quite pointedly!) in deciding the cases that came before him. A glance at his career from 1900 lends some credence towards this view. Williams was almost immediately in conflict with the town's local justices less than a year after his initial appointment over the issue of "irregularities and bench packing", to quote the *Merthyr Express*. A detailed correspondence ensued in the early part of 1901 as to whether or not the proper consultative processes had been followed. It was a Dowlais Works-based caucus of Dr. Cresswell, William Evans, E. P. Martin and others who railed against Williams's highhandedness and the matter was sent to the Home Department at Whitehall for advice and a higher ruling. Nothing more seems to have emerged from these wranglings and an uneasy peace became the order of the day between these parties.

The charge that Williams often acted in a cavalier manner rumbled on, to judge from contemporary anecdotage gleaned from the local press. It was suggested that he took the most direct, commonsense view "and was not governed by legal technicalities and red tapeism." (*The Aberdare Leader*, 31st October, 1914). He was never long in deciding a case; some of those who did business with him in court complained that he had decided cases before hearing both sides; that even when he did consult, his remarks and questions during evidence showed his leanings. Woe betide the magistrate who dared to cross his purpose and declare against him, noted *The Aberdare Leader*! The same newspaper source might, however, be fairly accused of slightly irreverent mischief-making on behalf of one of its fondest sons in taking his part against "the Great Unpaid" – the local magistracy of the Merthyr Tydfil courts – who sent their pleas on more than one occasion to the senior Member for the Borough, D. A. Thomas, for redress against their full-time magistrate.

As Stipendiary Magistrate, Williams was also a well placed legal and literary-minded public figure and was therefore often involved in the capacity of a mediator and an adjudicator on several coal-based disputes which were beginning to bedevil the South Wales valleys in the 1900s. In August, 1908, he was persuasive enough in getting the combined force of some 5,000 to 6,000 Powell Duffryn colliers of the Aberdare Valley to return to work by bringing together the miner's agent, C. B. Stanton, and P. D.'s general manager, E. M. Hann, towards an amicable settlement. A sign of the times, however, was in the nature of this temporary truce: that the sixty-seven collier defendants would not be charged with breach of contract for the present and the Company's claim for damages was left to lie adjourned for a month. The matter was to be put before the coal industry's Conciliation Board at a later date (*Merthyr Express*, 29th August, 1908). It was merely, on reflection, postponing an inevitable, more bloody show-down between masters and men for another day which, in the circumstances, if he had indeed realised their full implications, was all that Williams could reasonably do. In late November, 1910, he was involved in the capacity of an honest-broker again, this time between the increasingly warring factions engaged in the Cambrian Combine dispute gripping the Rhondda Valleys and which included, of course, the Tonypandy Riots earlier that same month. Together with D. Lleufer Thomas, his stipendiary equivalent for Pontypridd and the Rhondda, Williams engaged in talks with General Macready, the Government's military commander, and the local Members of Parliament, towards seeking some kind of settlement. What Williams's precise role was within these protracted engagements and his actual contribution towards any outcome, are issues less clear to allow for measured comment here. Before ill-health prevented him from taking an active part at the courts from late spring, 1914, one of Williams's last cases found him in the role of an accomplished mediator once more, in seeking some form of reconciliation between several Dowlais Roman Catholic parents who had been summonsed in relation to a local school boycott which had been implemented by them from the beginning of the year. Williams's indisposition through failing health did not allow him to arrive at any definitive ruling on this vexed question before his death.

A fragile health by 1913 halted Williams's participation in public affairs and a trip to Canada and the U.S.A. that year did him no good whatsoever in aiding his recuperation. A recommended restorative voyage to warmer climes, to Madeira at the end of 1913, was also ill-judged and twice he had to endure live-saving surgery on board ship. True to form, while laid up in a Spanish hospital, Williams took time to write a poem alluding to his own duel with the Angel of Death and how he narrowly escaped with his life. This time, anyway! Failing health dogged him into the following year and, despite rallying several times, he died at Rhydyfelin, his home near Builth Wells, on 27th October, 1914. The funeral service at St. John's Church, Builth Wells, was conducted by the then Archdruid of Wales, the Rev. E. Ben Rees (Dyfed); Williams lies buried in that same churchyard. One of the last visits he had made to his native Aberdare in 1914, apart from attendances at the Police Court, was to attend the unveiling of a statue in the public park to the late Lord Merthyr, his contemporary for so many years in local public life. Thus two revered and respected representatives of an earlier, Victorian Wales, had departed within two months of each other on the threshold of World War in 1914. It was the parting of an old order in so many ways.

Conclusion

Thomas Marchant Williams was a man of his time and therefore deserves to be judged by the precepts of that time and place. His life and career encompasses the middle and late 19th century of a dominant Welsh Liberalism and the first decade and a half of the present century to the eve of The Great War. In political terms, the years 1880 to 1914 were very much the age of Lloyd George (Morgan). Williams, although confined to the margins for much of that era by his own choice was, nevertheless, a key player during that period. He embraced the core of a Welsh Liberalism despite his shift from the centre over Irish Home Rule in 1886: disestablishment of the Anglican Church, land reform, temperance reform, educational parity, a measure of Welsh nationalism and national equality, but within a Great Britain rather than separate from it, were the hallmarks of this radical, non-conformist, Liberal, democratic politics and Welshness down to 1920. Williams harboured no doubts about any of this political philosophy and way of seeing Wales in relation to the rest of Great Britain. His literary outpourings testify to that! In terms of local literature, he ranks alongside a rich company of writers in the district of Aberdare, Mountain Ash and Merthyr Tydfil; journalists, educational reformers and eisteddfodwr can count him as one of them in rekindling the fullest expression of an older Wales, based on the observance of the Gorsedd, the National Eisteddfod, muse, poetry, music and the Welsh language. They ensured that this rich diet of culture was being brought to a far wider audience through the mass circulation of books, newspapers and learned journals. Williams certainly made his unique contribution on this score! The likes of Jonathan Reynolds (Nathan Dyfed, 1814-91) and David Williams (Alaw Goch, 1809-63), both Aberdare-born bards, appear as parallel figures of a generation earlier than Williams in South Wales cultural life and instrumental in that local renaissance of eisteddfodau and Gorseddd activities in Merthyr Tydfil and Aberdare which Williams would continue into the present century. Thomas Stephens (1821-75), essayist and *literateur*, Joseph Parry (1841-1903), musician and composer, Charles Wilkins (1831-1913), writer and historian and D. M. Richards (1853-1913), Aberdare-based journalist and eisteddfodwr, are just four literary spirits in whose company Williams can truly belong as purveyors to a new urban audience of ideas and views about Wales which, ultimately, derived from an earlier time and, without which, they would all argue to a man, their own period of the late 19th century and the early 20th century would make that much less sense.

Certainly Williams was a mixture of contradictions, in a life and career that seemed on the face of it to be clear-cut in its intentions, destinations and outcomes. Independently-minded in all he touched, his career and his strongly-held beliefs that shaped that career, very often pulled him in opposite directions that more often than not began to flow against the dynamic tide of forces shaping an emerging 20th-century Wales. An ardent educationalist from the outset, he left a highly-promising career for law in 1885; an aspiring

Liberal candidate in the making, he deserted to the Liberal Unionist cause after 1886 and never re-entered the political arena. A fierce teetotaller, he was against outright prohibition of alcohol; raised as a strict Calvinistic Methodist, this was the very creed of which he was most critical in later years. A leading light in the higher education movement in Wales and in particular in the well-being of the new University of Wales, he was highly critical of many of that institution's administrative and policy decisions. He was a literary Welsh nationalist, fired by a Wales of yesteryear yet, by the 1900s, found himself increasingly out of step with that new decade; a temperate (literally) magistrate at court, his outlook took little cognizance of the changing South Wales (and Merthyr Tydfil) after 1900, with deeply-set strife embryonic in the Valleys' culture and daily life outside his court. On reflection, his seemed to be ironically almost a timely death in 1914, along with so many of his contemporaries who had journeyed from the mid-19th century, moulded by those mores of a high, Victorian way of life. Wales would never be the same after The Great War. Williams and his contemporaries of the old school of Wales would have been hard-pressed to cope with the "New Wales" of the 1920s and 1930s. Even the most mercurial of his contemporaries of that era, Lloyd George, found post-war life unfulfilling and perplexing.

Whether in the enclaves of the Eisteddfod Association, in the Councils of the Welsh University or on the Magisterial Bench, observed *The Aberdare Leader*, "he was essentially a man of action and a man of method" (31st October, 1914). The same obituary source actually likened Williams in many ways to the famous writer and fellow-satirist, Jonathan Swift, although Williams, it should be stated, bore no malice towards anyone. If he had not practised the use of his tongue and pen, the account continued, doubtless he would have been obliged to find an outlet for his pugnacious nature with his fists! "It is doubtful if any Welshman was as well known personally to the people of Wales as Sir Marchant Williams," boasted the *Western Mail* (27th October, 1914). This essay has tried to redress some of the balance that time invariably distorts and has sought to rescue Williams from the condemnation of obscurity at the end of this century, some eighty years after his death. At the time of writing, as the present author prepares for one of life's rituals – jury duty at Merthyr Tydfil Law Courts – what may be the chances of stumbling on the ghost of Thomas Marchant Williams in those corridors and court rooms in the next few weeks? Indeed, History is a funny, old business!

References

There is no known collection of Williams's papers or memorabilia from which to draw information. He appears with regularity in the pages of the contemporary South Wales newspapers and in this respect primary details of his life and career are best found from the dubious vantage point of obituary notices in the local press for late October and early November, 1914, notably those contained in the pages of *The Aberdare Leader*, *Western Mail* and *Merthyr Express*. Full references are cited in this essay. Vincent Evans's obituary account in *The Transactions of the Honourable Society of Cymmrodorion* (1913-14) is worth consulting as a contemporary source. From the Welsh language press, see the obituary details in *Y Geninen* (Dydd Gwyl/March, 1915).

A biographical note, several years removed from Williams's death, is found in Thomas Hughes's *Great Welshmen Of Modern Days* (1931). A succinct pen portrait in Welsh can be located in Daniel Williams's *Pedwar Eisteddfodwr* (1949). Incidental biographical details are cited in the standard texts: *The Dictionary of Welsh Biography* (1959) provides notes on Williams and his contemporaries and *The Oxford Companion to the Literature of Wales* (1986) contains useful literary references on Williams and his circle.

Any account of Merthyr Tydfil's history has need of reference to the town's historian and a contemporary of Williams; *viz* Charles Wilkins's *The History of Merthyr Tydfil* (Second edition, 1908); however erratic a source, which contains useful details on the local magistracy (pp. 363-375). More recently, this Society's Secretary, Hugh Watkins, has provided an account of this magistracy in "The Magistrates and Courts of Merthyr Tydfil 1680-1977" in *Merthyr Historian* Volume 4 (1989). On cultural and literary forces influencing the town during Williams's formative early years, see my essay, "Jonathan Reynolds (Nathan Dyfed) 1814-1891: Local Eisteddfodwr" in *Merthyr Historian* Volume 6 (1992).

The historical background in which Williams was a key player can be traced in several authoritative and indispensable works by Kenneth O. Morgan, notably his *Wales in British Politics 1868-1922* (Third edition, 1980) and *Rebirth of a Nation: Wales 1880-1980* (1981). See also the same author's contributory essay, "David Lloyd George and Wales", to *Wales 1880-1914*, eds. T. Herbert and G. E. Jones (1988) which, incidentally, contains an extract from Williams's satirical sketch on Lloyd George referred to in this essay. See also David Smith's editorial introduction to *A People and A Proletariat: Essays in the History of Wales 1780-1980*, ed. D. Smith

(1980) and his concluding essay therein, "Wales Through the Looking Glass", for a typically perceptive overview on turn-of-the-century Wales.

On Williams's role in the University of Wales movement, see Geraint H. Jenkins's admirable account, *The University of Wales: An Illustrated History* (1993).

Best of all, the reader is directed to Marchant Williams's own writings. The larger public reference libraries and university collections in the area hold back numbers of *The Nationalist* and possibly the occasional copy of *The Land of My Fathers* (1889) and *The Welsh Members of Parliament* (1894).

Acknowledgements

Many thanks are owed on behalf of ALL local historians to that largely undervalued species, the local reference librarian, in this instance those most helpful and patient of souls serving Merthyr Tydfil, Aberdare and Cardiff libraries, for the numerous reference items secured in the research and writing of this article.

Finally and once again, my colleagues of many years' standing, Fred and Vida Holley, have generously put at my disposal a wealth of materials appertaining to the subject of this essay; and not least have been copious references from the contemporary South Wales press and back numbers of *The Nationalist* magazines. Dr. and Mrs. Holley truly have saved the wearied feet, eyes and brain of this particularly beleaguered historian striving to fashion an essay which continuously over-runs the required deadlines set! I am in their debt. I trust they approve of and recognise the Thomas Marchant Williams who has emerged onto these pages at the end of this travail.

October, 1995.

Ladies of Letters

by Ray Jones

Some Aspects of the Social History of Merthyr and Treharris – as revealed in the 19th century correspondence of a mother to her emigrant son, and of a new bride, on honeymoon, to her sister.

*****

Part of the excitement and pleasure of historical research stems from the unexpected primary sources that "pop-up" from time to time, which give original insights into the daily lives of ordinary people in days gone by.

Purely chance remarks made by a family friend in Exmouth and also by a shop-keeper in Quakers' Yard led to the discovery of letters written in the Nineteenth Century, some of which, again by the most incredible good fortune, were returned to these shores having travelled half-way around the world. Perhaps I should explain that, although born and brought up in Aberfan, my professional life has been spent away from Wales. Since my wife is a native of Treharris it is not surprising that we and our two sons have made frequent visits to Merthyr over the years. Our Welsh affiliations are, of course, well-known to friends and colleagues in Devon. We have lived in Exmouth for over 30 years and it was during one of many nostalgic conversations with some of our West Country friends that it became clear that one of the listeners had a very informed view of "old Merthyr". It transpired that our friend – Mrs. June Bateson of Exmouth – had learned about "historical Merthyr" from letters written by her great-grandmother in 1854, which were a treasured possession of the family. A copy of one of these letters has kindly been loaned to me by Mrs. Bateson, to whom thanks are recorded for also giving permission to include extracts in this article.

Anna Treliving

John Treliving

June's great-grandmother was called Anna Lean and she married John James Treliving in 1854. Her husband was in business. We know that he later became a cloth manufacturer's representative and it seems that, although on honeymoon, John was out and about, perhaps combining business with pleasure, calling on customers throughout South Wales, leaving his new wife to explore the locality alone and also to write letters to her sister, Georgina. In the letter written on 25th October, 1854, Anna starts apologetically by commenting that "getting about so very much" leaves little time to write. It seems that this was a touring honeymoon, since Anna later describes travelling on the "South Wales line of rails" and to Newport, Neath, Swansea and Cardiff. In any event, Anna obviously relished her rail trips... "I have enjoyed getting about very much indeed... on the Taff Vale and... the Vale of Neath line." It is interesting to reflect on the growth of the Railways in South Wales, which were fairly new when Anna and her husband undertook their journeys.

Despite the opposition of the Glamorgan Canal Company, rail transport was forging ahead in the early part of the 19th century. The nine-mile stretch of the historic Pen-y-darran Tramroad was opened in 1799 and this was followed on 21st February, 1804, by the successful trial run of Richard Trevithick's steam locomotive. After a difficult passage the Taff Vale Railway Company's Act received the Royal Assent on 21st June, 1836, thus incorporating the first public railway of any commercial importance in the Principality. The preamble to the Act stated:

> "... the making of a Railway from Merthyr Tydfil to Cardiff... would be of great public convenience by opening an additional, certain and expeditious Means of Conveyance to the Sea for... Mineral and other Produce... and for the Conveyance of Passengers and Goods..."

The main line was opened from Cardiff to Merthyr on 12th April, 1841, whilst the Vale of Neath line was completed on 2nd November, 1853 – barely a year before the young honeymooners Anna and John travelled on it with such pleasure. At the time of writing her letter (from Aberdare) on "Tuesday morn", 25th October, John had "gone over to Aberammon", but on the previous Sunday they had obviously visited Merthyr together – an experience which Anna didn't enjoy.

"I do not like the town," she wrote, "It is so dirty but a large place, and

> in the streets you hear nothing but Welsh spoken and the inhabitants look dirty plain people with their high hats... It will be quite a treat to see a neat lace cap on women's heads. They all wear thick muslin with two wide borders and the girls' heads are terribly untidy – all the hair is combed back in one great rough twist at the back of the head."

Interestingly, "high hats" were being worn in Merthyr at this time, though the general appearance of the population – particularly that of the women – seemed very dowdy to Anna. This was probably a reflection of the general environmental conditions caused by the industrial activity of the town. To live in Merthyr in the 1850s was to live cheek by jowl with blast furnaces and rolling mills as dark and satanic as any in the world. It is little wonder that the locals didn't seem over-concerned about their appearance amidst so much pollution and squalor.

Anna described Merthyr in 1854 as "a large place"; indeed, it was. In the 50 years preceding her visit the population of Merthyr grew from 7,705 to 45,000. The industrialization of the town – in particular the expansion of the iron industry – drew immigrants from a wide area of England as well as Wales. What is interesting in Anna's letter is the reflection that, despite the incursion of so many migrant workers, Welsh seemed to her to be still and overwhelmingly the language in common use in the streets of the town.* She returned to this theme in describing her attempts to find an English place of worship during her Sabbath visit to Merthyr:

> "Sunday we attended the English Baptist Chapel. We had some trouble to find it out. It was some distance from the Royal Hotel and we found it was very little use asking in English [underlined] of the passers by to direct us, the common people very rarely speak anything but Welsh [also underlined!]... in Merthyr on Sunday the people were as busy with their horses and carts as on any other day at the works."

Whilst Nonconformity was firmly established in Merthyr by the start of the 19th century, and whilst the Welsh Baptists had ten places of worship in Merthyr by 1854, it seems that Anna was fortunate to find an English Baptist Chapel there during her stay. It is likely that the first English Baptist chapel was opened in High Street, Merthyr, in 1840, and this may well have been the chapel in which she worshipped on that October Sunday in 1854. No doubt whilst there she reflected on the neglect of Sabbatarian values in the populace at large, as they treated Sunday like any other working day... "busy with their horses and carts", etc.

Anna encountered two more aspects of life in Merthyr during her stay which reinforced her dislike for the town and which prompted her to write: "I wold not live in Wales for anything".

The first was summed up thus: "I saw less of Merthyr Tidvill than any other place on account of the dreadful disease there... The cholera still rages there [and is] not as they hoped on the decrease."

The timing of Anna's honeymoon in October, 1854, coincided with the third of four cholera epidemics which had such a devastating effect on the population of Merthyr in the middle of the 19th century. The first epidemic of 1832 claimed 160 lives, the second in 1849 killed 1,432 people and led to the opening of Pant Cemetery since existing burial grounds were insufficient.

The third epidemic reached Merthyr in September, 1854, and led to 424 deaths. Little wonder that Anna wrote a month later "The cholera still rages..." The fourth epidemic occurred in 1866 when 119 people lost their lives.

Cholera was only one of the infectious diseases which afflicted the population of Merthyr at the time of Anna's and John's visit. They must have been aware of the presence of typhus, small-pox, measles and scarlet fever in the area and, no doubt, were also keenly aware of the insanitary conditions which prevailed in the town. Some years later that most respected and prominent citizen of Merthyr, Dr. Thomas Jones Dyke, wrote "In the eleven years 1845-55, before any works of Sanitary Improvements were begun, the death rate was 33.2 per 1,000." So one has to concede that on this evidence, too, Anna had good reason not to like the town!

The other aspect of life in Merthyr which both impressed and depressed Anna and John was not unrelated to the dire health issues already discussed. It was to do with those prodigious enterprises, the Iron Works. Anna puts it in these words:

> "We had travelled a good deal (all by rail of course) after dark and oh how I have wished for you many a time to see the fires from the iron works. They are just like immense furnaces close together reaching for sometimes half a mile from that to a mile and a half in length and there they blaze away. John says he fancies nothing can nearer approach the idea one forms in their own mind of the bottomless pit. At night tis really awful."

The writer Thomas Carlyle, after a horrified visit, put it more succinctly: "Ah me! It is like a vision of hell, and will never leave me," he wrote, continuing "... those poor creatures toiling all in sweat and dirt, amidst their furnaces, pits and rolling mills."

For over half a century the Merthyr furnaces cast their eerie glow over the surrounding countryside, and almost every visitor made reference to this phenomenon. The great traveller and writer George Borrow also visited the town in 1854. He, too, was impressed by the "blazes" and "a glowing mountain", indeed "so great was the light cast by the blazes and that wonderful glowing object" that Borrow "could distinctly see the little stones upon the road". When he asked "What is all that burning stuff above?" he received the reply, "Dross from the iron forges, sir!" Borrow plucked up courage, later, to visit one of the Iron works. "Cyfartha Fawr... generally considered to be the great wonder of the place." And there he recounts, again in his book *Wild Wales*:

> "I saw enormous furnaces, I saw streams of molten metal. I saw a long ductile piece of red-hot iron being operated upon. I saw millions of sparks flying about. I saw an immense wheel impelled round with frightful velocity by a steam-engine of two hundred and forty horse power. I heard all kinds of dreadful sounds. The general effect was stunning."

Borrow found, as did Anna, that Welsh was the language generally spoken in the town, and he went beyond Anna's view of the dowdiness of the inhabitants by describing them as "savage-looking people" and their houses as being "in general low and mean..." Clearly he, too, was glad to leave the town. Four or five years after Anna's and John's visit (i.e. around 1860), the glory of the great Merthyr Ironworks was beginning to fade, with the industrial rise of the Midlands and the North of England. But during their stay in 1854, the great works at Cyfarthfa, Dowlais, Plymouth and Penydarran were actively producing some 290,000 tons of iron for export. Despite their travels throughout South Wales, where Anna admitted "The scenery here is lovely," one is left with the impression that industrial Merthyr coloured Anna's view of the entire country, leading her to state "I shall be so glad to get out of Wales." At the end of the honeymoon, Anna and John returned home to Bristol – probably sailing into the sunset by Steamer from Cardiff!

Whilst they settled into their married life in No. 6 Bell Vue, Kingsdown, Bristol, another married lady was living her life in Pentwyn, Graigberthlwyd, Treharris, in the Merthyr Valley. This housewife was Mrs. Mary Jenkins, our second "Lady of Letters". In the period 1881 to 1886 Mary Jenkins wrote a number of letters to one of her sons who had left Wales to forge a new life in Australia. The story of the return of these letters to Treharris a hundred years later, in 1980, is a tale of an amazing coincidence and a stroke of pure luck. In 1980 my own elder son, Lyn, was engrossed in a G.C.E. history project. His chosen topic was "The History of Deep Navigation Colliery, Treharris". His grandfather – Glyn Williams of Cilhaul – had spent the whole of his working life in Treharris Pit, some fifty-two years, so in many ways it was an obvious choice of subject. Lyn paid a number of visits to the village and to the pit at this time, including a memorable visit to the underground workings. He was told that a shop in Quakers' Yard sold old sepia postcards of "Top Pit". The shop-keeper (Mrs. Hancock?), after selling him the postcards, soon found out by adroit questioning the reasons for his interest. (Does this sort of thing only happen in South Wales?) The shop-keeper then, in a chance remark, volunteered the information that Australian visitors were currently in the district and had brought with them English translations of the original Welsh letters written by Mrs. Mary Jenkins in the 1880s. Furthermore, Les Evans the Barber (a few doors away from Mrs. Hancock's Newsagent's shop) had access to these letters. A visit followed to Les the Barber, and my son returned to Exmouth with photocopies of the precious letters. Subsequently, Lyn wrote to Geraint and Alice Rees of the Sydney Welsh Society, the translators, and obtained photocopies of the original Mary Jenkins's letters written in Welsh. Geraint Rees wrote that... "The task of translating the letters was one of the most rewarding and satisfying experiences of our lives."

So what do Mary Jenkins's letters tell us of life in Treharris in the last quarter of the 19th century?

First and foremost they are *family* letters and reflect the varied domestic situations of the members of her large family – their work, their lives and their aspirations. They also tell of local industry and its workforce and the general ethos of the growing town. There are stories of births and deaths and of local characters, together with accounts of religious and cultural activities in the area.

In all her letters Mary repeatedly refers to family members by name, though it is not always clear precisely what the actual relationships were. Certainly she had three sons and she writes of a daughter Mary, and of Thomas, Lewis, Elizabeth and Naomi as though they were very special to her. The three sons rejoiced under the names of Shadrach, Meshach and Abednego. Yes, the sons were named after those three Biblical worthies!

Shadrach had emigrated to America, where he was later joined by his wife, Jane. Abednego and his wife remained in Treharris, whilst Meshach and his family had started a new life in Australia. Meshach and his descendants were, of course, responsible for preserving Mary Jenkins's original letters from which so much local history was revealed.

> "Mary and her family are well and comfortable... she has to work very hard... The children are now growing up, and are of great help to her. She is also keeping lodgers, so between everything, she is paying her way excellently... Furthermore she is living a proper and respectable life as befitting to all widows in their widowhood."

Hard work, economic independence and respectability are themes which recur in Mary Jenkins's letters and she obviously admires her daughter Mary for the life she leads in what must have been a fairly common condition of widowhood.

Thomas, Lewis and Abednego...

> "are making the best of it in the pits of Twyngarreg [Treharris]... Abednego is earning about 7/6d a day – but remember, everyone doesn't earn as much as this... [they] are earning good money. Not only that, but they are putting some money aside for the future. This does them far more good than if they spent the lot, as so many do in this neighbourhood.
>
> "These pits are terrible places, there are many accidents happening here and not much attention is given to any man who is injured. Only barely enough to carry the victim home is allowed out of the pit... They are raising some 3,500 tons of coal each week, and there are about 1,500 men working at the pit in all... I am sorry to tell you that the Works of Llancaiach & Powell have stopped completely and everything has been sold, namely the horses and machinery. It is a great loss for the shopkeepers in Nelson. There are many of the Powell & Llancaiach colliers working... [in Treharris pit]... but none like the place very much."

Diligence and thrift obviously were highly rated by Mary Jenkins, but she had no illusions about the coal industry and its demands.

The Deep Navigation Colliery, Treharris, was originally known as Harris's Navigation Pits. (Mary in her letter of 11th July, 1881, reports "Mr. Harris, the Squire of the village is giving £25.0.0. for the object of the... Grand Eisteddfod of Treharris.")

Sinking of the Pit had been started in 1873, the two shafts reaching a record 760 yards in depth. The sinkers lived in "the Huts" – 32 wooden dwellings which were still occupied by Treharris residents until the late 1950s. Most of the Huts were demolished in 1958, much to the disgust of some local people such as sisters Mrs. Sarah Ellen Hollister (75) and Mrs. Elizabeth Jane Glass (72), who were born in the Huts and had lived there all their lives. The last Hut disappeared in 1960. Harris's Navigation Pits started producing coal by 1881 – so were still novel enterprises when Mary's letters were travelling to Australia.

The Ocean Coal Company purchased the Pits in 1897, and by 1916 had installed pit-head baths at Treharris – one of the first baths in the entire coalfield.

Subsequently the pits were nationalised and ended production in the 1990s under the name Deep Navigation Colliery.

Mary was evidently a deeply religious woman and was pleased to report to Meshach "Thomas and his wife are faithful members in the Methodist Chapel in High Street, Nelson, and Abednego's wife is a member in Libanus," and with obvious sadness added "but Abednego is not a member anywhere, and not likely to be one in the near future." She goes on to add, "Mary is a member in the Independent Church in Trelewis. This church has broken away from Libanus, and has joined with Penuel, Nelson. Little did one think that seed which was sown in our house in Pen Groesol would have grown into a Church."

In one of Meshach's replies to his mother he evidently made reference to encountering Spiritualists in Australia. Mary's response to this information (8th January, 1886) was stern and forthright: "I don't know whether it's truth or deceit that they claim. But be assured, it was deceit that was practised by the Spiritualists in this country." Mary goes on to explain this deceit in great detail, ending with...

> "If what the Bible says of the Great Everlasting World is true... the saved souls are delayed from enjoying their Glorious Blessings by

communicating with us on earth. And who gives them the authority to come forth from their prepared places to answer the questions of the inhabitants of this earth ?"

Any veering from the "straight and narrow" attracted Mary's severest strictures. In her early letters she reflects on the moral decline of the local population... "... speaking of ungodliness, this is a place for all sorts of sin, the lowest members of society have gathered here and we have never heard such profanity in this neighbourhood. We can only hope that they will see the errors of their ways very soon."

As explained earlier, industrial activity acted like a magnet, attracting workers from all over Wales and from England, Ireland, Scotland, the Colonies and, later, Spain. There is little doubt that the sinking and the work in pits like Treharris attracted a wide variety of people to the area. Mary doesn't specifically identify any particular groups of miscreants, but later relates the story of a Welshman by the name of Lewis Morgan, to emphasise her viewpoint... "On 22nd November, 1885, Lewis Morgan, Nelson Inn died. Lewis was not sick for very long, but suffered a great deal, and at the peak of his suffering realised that he had much to answer for, and begged forgiveness – so different from his attitude in normal health. His behaviour on his death bed was a lesson to all in the neighbourhood." In the same letter she continues in this vein... "On Saturday morning, 28 November, 1885, Rowland Edmunds [Rowly Phil, Plasterer] was found half dead on the roadside. He was carried into the Angel Inn where he died within a few minutes. It had been cold and stormy the night before, and he, being drunk, had fallen down and nearly froze to death on the spot. Here again is a lesson to all drunkards." Not all reports of deaths in Mary's letters occasioned homilies from her. We are able to gain an insight into some of the prevailing causes of death and the ages of the deceased from her reports to Meshach:

"Shan Shon Hopkins has been buried. She had a fit and died a fortnight later."

"... the old character Mabonwyson has come to the end of his earthly journey. He died after... a long illness in the Pontypridd Workhouse;... he was moved there... by the Parish Officers."

"Timothy Hughes from Nelson died aged 49. Dropsy was his complaint. He was better known as Little Timothy."

"Isaac Jones (Isaac Victoria) died aged 66 years (Inflammation)."

"Emma Fibbs died aged 33 years of consumption."

"William Jones (Billi Edward Shon) died... Inflammation in the stomach. He was 65."

"William, the youngest son of your sister Mary, died with Inflammation of the Bowels. He is seven years old."

"John Jones, better known generally as John Catws has died. He left a widow and six children."

"David Evans, Bastin, was killed when he was crushed between the trucks of the Taff Railway near Basin Station."

"On Wednesday morning before Christmas, 1885, an explosion occurred in the Mardy Pit in the Rhondda Valley where about 81 men lost their lives. They have brought the bodies out, and they are now very busy collecting money to form a fund to aid the widows and orphans."

An "Obituary Column" appeared in all of Mary's letters to her son. It was his link with the past and, no doubt, all of those named meant something to him. To the rest of us, each entry reveals some facet of the social and health conditions of the last quarter of the 19th century... the prevalence of diseases such as dropsy, inflammation and consumption, industrial accidents and disasters, and the role of the "Parish" and of the Workhouse.

On a lighter note Mary included news of marriages... "David Hughes has married a girl named Martha Jones from Deri, the one that was a maid in White Farm near Llechwen. As you see, he has joined the Petticoat Club at last, like so many others."... and births... "John Llewellyn's daughter Ann, gave birth to a daughter. Her name is Edith... Dd. Hughes and his wife now have a beautiful baby boy whose name is Edgar Evan." Another component of Mary's letters reflects the cultural activities of the area...

"The Great Eisteddfod of Treharris (Monday 1st August, 1881) has created quite a stir in the neighbourhood. There has been a United Choir with 200 voices formed here between Treharris, Craigberthlwyd and Quakers' Yard, under the conductorship of Eos Cynon who is working in the pits. The musical judge is Caradog, and the main piece is the Hallelujah Chorus. Prize is £20.0.0. and a gold medal worth £5.0.0. for the conductor."

After the event, in her letter of 28th November, 1881, Mary reports...

"Mountain Ash Choir... won the first prize of £20.0.0. Five choirs competing... the Cymmer Brass Band won the prize of £5 for playing *The March of the Men of Harlech*, *All Through the Night* and *Ash Grove*... Three Brass Bands competing... Old Craigfryn won half the prize of £2 for a descriptive song about Treharris. Also Craigfryn won the prize of £3 at the Great National Eisteddfod in Merthyr for the best novel. The novel, *Rees Trefor*, is serialised in the *Patriot* each week." More news of the local author-celebrity came in Mary's letter of 12th June, 1883... "Craigfryn won £5.0.0. just a few weeks ago in an Eisteddfod in Ynys Mon, North Wales on the novel *Y Ferch o'r Scer* [*The Maid of Sker*]." Interest in literature prompted Mary to send Meshach a copy of a more famous novel... "I was very pleased to hear that you had received the copy of the book *Y Ferch o Cefn Ydfa* [*The Maid of Cefn Ydfa*] and that you had much pleasure in reading it." Mary was obviously closely in touch with her other son, Shadrach, and included news of him and his endeavours in her letters to Meshach in Australia.

Shadrach was one of very many Welshmen and women who emigrated to America in the 19th century. It has been said that there was hardly a family in rural Wales by the mid-century that did not have a relative in America. Sadly, Shadrach met hard times in the New World. Initially there alone until he could earn enough to pay for his wife's passage, Shadrach... "doesn't seem to be doing much good in America up till now. He seems to be very unfortunate in connection with work. He is in good health."

Four months later Mary reports,

"His wife has arrived there safely and both are well and living in a house of their own. The work is not very plentiful there because, for one thing, the death of President Garfield, and the other thing is that only summer work is available in the area... Their address is Frostburgh, Box 138, Alegrany County, Maryland, North America."

On 26th April, 1882, Mary received a letter from Shadrach, but she writes,

"This was not a comforting letter to me at all, as he says that they have a Strike there. Abednego and I sent him a little money... Thomas sent him a pound [£] and I had a letter from him last week [August, 1882],

> and he said that the strike is not over as yet, and no sign of it ending, and that he was going to move from there to another place. They have not been without, as the workers have a Fund to help them when out on strike... I hope he will improve his position... before long."

By June of the following year (1883) Shadrach and his family had moved to Brookwayville, Jefferson County, Pennsylvania, with some improvement reported. "Things are looking more prosperous for him now than before," writes Mary, "and [his] letter was much more hopeful than the previous one I received from him. I am enclosing a photograph of him."

In a postscript to the last of Mary's letters to Meshach, written in January, 1886, evidently a further downturn had occurred in Shadrach's fortunes... since she sadly states, "It is very poor with him all the time."

Whilst Shadrach was facing hard times in North America, other emigrants from Treharris were not deterred. In her letter of November, 1881, there is a report of the departure of a local musician... "Jenkin Jones has emigrated to America. He had a very rough passage, but arrived alive. A Literary meeting was held at Libanus before his departure. The Libanus Choir had won the prize of £2 for singing Jerusalem, under Jenkin's conductorship, and the choir gave it all to Jenkin – Every success to him."

In less than a year there is a further report... "Jenkin Jones is becoming famous as a conductor in America. He has formed a choir there, and has already won many first Prizes – I wish him an easy road.

"Richard Nicholas... and his wife [and]... John, Charles Tarwain, Llanravon's son and his wife emigrated to America... John the son of Rebecca Jones, Felin Caiach, emigrated to America, and Jenkin's wife went with him. They were going out to Jenkin" (Merthyr's most famous musical son, Joseph Parry, almost 30 years' earlier had emigrated with his parents to work in the rolling mills of Danville, Pennsylvania).

We know from other sources that the "Welsh Diaspora" in the 19th century led to settlements in many parts of America and Canada; the great Mormon exodus from Wales, for example, led many to the gathering of the Saints in Utah between 1840 and 1870. The best known emigration was, of course, to Patagonia in 1865, though at much the same time Merthyr's John Hughes and his co-workers were establishing a large industrial settlement in the town of Hughesovka (Yuzovka) in the Donetz basin of Southern Russia at the invitation of the Tsar's government.

Less well known, perhaps, is the fact that many Welsh people set sail for

Australia – some to find fame and fortune there. One successful emigrant was the very distinguished South-Wales-born geologist Sir Edgeworth David, who later became Professor of Geology in the University of Sydney. He is credited with the discovery of some of the important Newcastle-Sydney coalfields. Here exist Aberdare, Neath, Merthyr, Swansea and Cardiff; indeed this major industrial area of the continent has better claim than any other part of the state to the title of "New South Wales". In 1887 another famous son of Merthyr returned to his birth-place from Australia. He was Sir Samuel Griffith, Queen's Counsel, Knight Commander of St. Michael and St. George, Premier of Queensland. (An interesting account of this visit is recorded in *Merthyr Historian*, Volume Five, pages 83-105.)

Meshach Jenkins's career in Australia was not as distinguished. In fact his mother doesn't seem to be at all clear what her son did for a living in Australia. In her letter of 12th June, 1883, she starts enthusiastically... "It is... good to know that you have moved from the bush to a more populated area, and that you are now able to attend a Welsh Church, and I hope that you all, as a family, attend every Sunday." After this familiar exhortation Mary goes on to ask, "I would like you, Meshach, to let me know in your next letter what your profession is in Sydney, and what your wages are. I am sorry to learn that the rent is so high... However, I do hope you will succeed to have enough money to keep together the other necessities of life without much worry." Sadly, we never do discover from Mary's correspondence exactly what career Meshach followed. We know in the last report that he had settled in Sydney and we know from other sources that there was a coal mining and an iron and steel complex there. So, what happened next?

Having learned so much from Mary Jenkins's letters to her son and from Anna Treliving's letter to her sister, we are left with tantalising glimpses of what might have followed in the later years of the 19th century... For example, what were ordinary people's experiences of family relationships and living conditions – economic and cultural? Did Shadrach and his family eventually find their American "Eldorado"? And what of the descendants of Abednego, Lewis, Thomas and Mary? Did they remain in Treharris... and are there members of the family still there today? Also, if later generations of Anna and John Treliving's family ever ventured to South Wales, would they have recognised the features which made such a lasting impression on their forebears?

In the search for answers to these questions, is it too much to hope for more chance remarks and lucky coincidences which might lead us to yet more "Ladies of Letters"? Such chance would indeed be a very fine thing! We live in hope.

*****

* The Census of 1861 revealed the original places of birth of the residents of Merthyr (including Aberdare and Gelligaer), as follows:

Wales 78,036, England 6,543, Ireland 5,256, Scotland 15, Colonies 55 and Foreign 193.

Of the Welsh contingent, as might be expected, the vast majority (48,839) came from Glamorgan, with the remaining 29,197 from Brecknock (8,308), Carmarthen (7,243), Monmouthshire (5,635), Pembrokeshire (4,551) and 3,460 from elsewhere in Wales.

The Irish influx almost matches that of the English, no doubt the potato famines of 1845, 1846 and 1847 could account for this migration of Irish labour into Merthyr. They certainly contributed to the Catholic presence in the town, as did the later Spanish work force.

Acknowledgements

Thanks are recorded to Mrs. June Bateson of Exmouth and to Mr. and Mrs. Geraint Rees of New South Wales, Australia, for making available and kindly lending copies of the letters used in this article.

Bibliography

Merthyr Tydfil: A Valley Community. Merthyr Teachers' Centre Group published jointly with D. Brown & Sons Ltd., Cowbridge, 1981.

Merthyr Historian, Volumes One, Two, Three, The Starling Press, Risca. Five and Seven, WBC Book Manufacturers, Bridgend.

Wild Wales. George Borrow. Collins 1955 Edition.

Welsh Emigration Overseas. Professor E. G. Bowen: Address delivered to Section E (Geography), 2nd September, 1960, at the Cardiff Meeting of the British Association for the Advancement of Science.

The Taff Valley Railway. D. S. M. Barrie. The Oakwood Press – Second Edition Reprinted 1982.

Colliery Settlement in the South Wales Coalfield 1850 to 1926. Philip N. Jones. University of Hull Occasional Papers in Geography No. 14. University of Hull Publications 1969.

Welsh Industrial Workers' Housing 1775-1875. J. B. Lowe. National Museum of Wales, Cardiff, 1977.